Pro Android Augmented Reality

Raghav Sood

Apress®

Pro Android Augmented Reality

ISBN 978-1-4302-3945-1

ISBN 978-1-4302-3946-8 (eBook)

President and Publisher: Paul Manning
Lead Editor: Steve Anglin
Technical Reviewers: Yosun Chang, Chád Darby
Editorial Board: Steve Anglin, Ewan Buckingham, Gary Cornell, Louise Corrigan, Morgan Ertel, Jonathan Gennick, Jonathan Hassell, Robert Hutchinson, Michelle Lowman, James Markham, Matthew Moodie, Jeff Olson, Jeffrey Pepper, Douglas Pundick, Ben Renow-Clarke, Dominic Shakeshaft, Gwenan Spearing, Matt Wade, Tom Welsh
Coordinating Editors: Corbin Collins, Christine Ricketts
Copy Editors: Vanessa Moore; Nancy Sixsmith, ConText Editorial Services
Compositor: Bytheway Publishing Services
Indexer: SPi Global
Artist: SPi Global
Cover Designer: Anna Ishchenko

Distributed to the book trade worldwide by Springer Science+Business Media New York, 233 Spring Street, 6th Floor, New York, NY 10013. Phone 1-800-SPRINGER, fax (201) 348-4505, e-mail orders-ny@springer-sbm.com, or visit www.springeronline.com.

For information on translations, please e-mail rights@apress.com, or visit www.apress.com.

Apress and friends of ED books may be purchased in bulk for academic, corporate, or promotional use. eBook versions and licenses are also available for most titles. For more information, reference our Special Bulk Sales–eBook Licensing web page at www.apress.com/bulk-sales.

Any source code or other supplementary materials referenced by the author in this text is available to readers at www.apress.com. For detailed information about how to locate your book's source code, go to www.apress.com/source-code.

To my family and friends
-Raghav Sood

Contents at a Glance

▓ **About the Author** xi

▓ **About the Technical Reviewers** xii

▓ **Acknowledgments** xiii

▓ **Introduction** xiv

▓ **Chapter 1: Applications of Augmented Reality** 1

▓ **Chapter 2: Basics of Augmented Reality on the Android Platform** 13

▓ **Chapter 3: Adding Overlays** 41

▓ **Chapter 4: Artifical Horizons** 65

▓ **Chapter 5: Common and Uncommon Errors and Problems** 95

▓ **Chapter 6: A Simple Location-Based App Using Augmented Reality** 107

▓ **Chapter 7: A Basic Navigational App Using Augmented Reality** 141

▓ **Chapter 8: A 3D Augmented Reality Model Viewer** 159

▓ **Chapter 9: An Augmented Reality Browser** 221

▓ **Index** 319

Contents

▓ **About the Author** xi

▓ **About the Technical Reviewers** xii

▓ **Acknowledgments** xiii

▓ **Introduction** xiv

▓ **Chapter 1: Applications of Augmented Reality** 1

Augmented Reality vs. Virtual Reality 1

Current Uses 1

    Casual Users 2

    Military and Law Enforcement 4

    Vehicles 4

    Medical 5

    Trial Rooms 6

    Tourism 6

    Architecture 6

    Assembly Lines 7

    Cinema/Performance 7

    Entertainment 7

    Education 8

    Art 8

    Translation 8

    Weather Forecasting 9

    Television 9

    Astronomy 9

    Other 9

Future Uses 10

    Virtual Experiences 10

    Impossible Simulations 10

Holograms 11

Video Conferencing.. 11

Movies 11

Gesture Control 12

Summary... 12

■ Chapter 2: Basics of Augmented Reality on the Android Platform 13

Basics of Augmented Reality on the Android Platform.......................... 13

Creating the App 13

Camera 14

Orientation Sensor 21

Accelerometer... 24

Global Positioning System (GPS) 28

Latitude and Longitude) 29

ProAndroidAR2Activity.java.. 32

AndroidManifest.xml.. 36

main.xml 37

Sample LogCat Output 37

Summary 38

■ Chapter 3: Adding Overlays 41

Adding Overlays 41

Widget Overlays 41

Layout Options.. 43

Updating main.xml with a RelativeLayout 45

TextView Variable Declarations... 49

Updated onCreate 49

Displaying the Sensors' Data... 49

Updated AndroidManifest.xml 52

Testing the App 53

Markers.. 54

Activity.java... 54

CustomObject Overlays 56

CustomRenderer 60

AndroidManifest 62

Summary 63

■ Chapter 4: Artifical Horizons.. 65

A Non-AR Demo App 65

The XML... 66

The Java 67

The Android Manifest..77

Testing the Completed App 78

An AR Demo App 80

Setting Up the Project..81

Updating the XML 82

Updating the Java Files 86

Testing the Completed AR app...92

Summary..93

▓ Chapter 5: Common and Uncommon Errors and Problems 95

Layout Errors 95

UI Alignment Issues 95

ClassCastException 96

Camera Errors..97

Failed to Connect to Camera Service 97

Camera.setParameters() failed...98

Exception in setPreviewDisplay()..99

AndroidManifest Errors...100

Security Exceptions 100

<uses-library> 101

<uses-feature> 101

Errors Related to Maps 102

The Keys 102

Not Extending MapActivity...102

Debugging the App...103

LogCat 103

Black and White Squares When Using the Camera 104

Miscellaneous 105

Not Getting a Location Fix from the GPS 105

Compass Not Working 105

Summary..106

▓ Chapter 6: A Simple Location-Based App Using Augmented Reality... 107

A Simple Location-Based App Using Augmented Reality and the Maps API . 107

Editing the XML..109

Creating Menu Resources 111

Layout Files 112

Getting API Keys 117

Getting the MD5 of Your Keys..118

Java Code **118**

    Main Activity 119

    FlatBack.java 128

    FixLocation.java 132

Running the App **135**

Common errors **138**

Summary **139**

■ **Chapter 7: A Basic Navigational App Using Augmented Reality...** **141**

The New App **141**

    Updated XML files 142

    Updated Java files 145

    Updated AndroidManifest 155

The Completed App **155**

■ **Chapter 8: A 3D Augmented Reality Model Viewer** **159**

Key Features of this App **160**

The Manifest **162**

Java Files **163**

    Main Activity 163

    AssetsFileUtility.java 168

    BaseFileUtil.java 169

    CheckFileManagerActivity.java 170

    Configuration File 175

    Working with Numbers 175

    Group.java 178

    Instructions.java 180

    Working with Light 181

    Creating a Material 183

    MemUtil.java 186

    Model.java 187

    Model3D.java 189

    Viewing the Model 191

    Parsing .mtl files 199

    Parsing the .obj files 203

    ParseException 207

    Rendering 207

    SDCardFileUtil.java 209

    SimpleTokenizer.java 210

    Util.java 211

    3D Vectors 213

XML Files **214**

Strings.xml 214

Layout for the Rows..215

instructions_layout.xml 215

List Header 216

main.xml...216

HTML Help File 217

Completed App...219

Summary 220

Chapter 9: An Augmented Reality Browser...............................221

The XML 222

strings.xml..222

menu.xml..222

The Java Code...223

The Activities and AugmentedView 223

Getting the Data 242

DataSource 242

LocalDataSource...242

NetworkDataSource 243

TwitterDataSource..246

WikipediaDataSource 250

Positioning Classes..252

ScreenPositionUtility 254

The UI Works 255

PaintableObject 255

PaintableBox...258

PaintableBoxedText 260

PaintableCircle..263

PaintableGps...264

PaintableIcon...265

PaintableLine 266

PaintablePoint...267

PaintablePosition 268

PaintableRadarPoints 270

PaintableText...271

Utility Classes 273

Vector 273

Utilities..277

PitchAzimuthCalculator 277

LowPassFilter 278

Matrix 280

Components 285
Radar 285
Marker 289
IconMarker.java 302

Customized Widget 303
VerticalSeekBar.java 304

Controlling the Camera 305
CameraSurface.java 305
CameraCompatibility 309
CameraModel 310

The Global Class... 311
ARData.java 311
AndroidManifest.xml... 316
Running the App 317

Summary... 318
▨ Index 319

About the Author

 **Raghav Sood,** born on April 16, 1997, is a young Android developer. He started seriously working with computers after learning HTML, CSS, and JavaScript while making a website at the age of nine. Over the next three years, Raghav developed several websites and quite a few desktop applications. He has learned several programming languages, including PHP, Java, x86 assembly, PERL, and Python. In February 2011, Raghav received his first Android device, an LG Optimus One running Froyo. The next day, he began work on his first Android app. He is currently the owner of an Android tutorial site, an author on the Android Activist site and the developer of 12 Android apps. Raghav regularly takes part in the android-developers Google Group, trying to help whomever he can. Raghav also enjoys reading, photography and robotics. He currently resides in New Delhi, India. This is his first book.

About the Technical Reviewers

■ **Yosun Chang** has been creating apps for iOS and Android since early 2009, and is currently working on a next generation 3D and augmented reality mobile games startup called nusoy. Prior to that, since 1999 she did web development on the LAMP stack and Flash. She has also spoken at several virtual world, theater, and augmented reality conferences under her artist name of Ina Centaur. She has a graduate level background in physics and philosophy from UC San Diego and UC Berkeley. An avid reader who learned much of her coding chops from technical books like the current volume, she has taken care to read every single word of the chapters she reviewed — and vet the source. Contact her @yosunchang on Twitter.

■ **Chád Darby** is an author, instructor, and speaker in the Java development world. As a recognized authority on Java applications and architectures, he has presented technical sessions at software development conferences worldwide. In his 15 years as a professional software architect, Chád has had the opportunity to work for Blue Cross/Blue Shield, Merck, Boeing, Northrop Grumman, and a handful of startup companies.

Chád is a contributing author to several Java books, including *Professional Java E-Commerce* (Wrox Press), *Beginning Java Networking* (Wrox Press), and *XML and Web Services Unleashed* (Sams Publishing). Chád has Java certifications from Sun Microsystems and IBM. He holds a B.S. in Computer Science from Carnegie Mellon University.

You can read Chád's blog at `www.luv2code.com` and follow him on Twitter @darbyluvs2code.

Acknowledgments

Writing a book is a huge task. It's not the same as writing a blog or a review. It requires a lot of commitment right until the end. The difference in the time zones in which the team and I are located made it a little harder to communicate, but we managed quite well.

I was helped by several people in this project and would like to take the opportunity to thank them here.

First, I would like to thank Steve Anglin for having faith in me when he decided to sign me up for this book. I hope you feel that this faith was well placed. I would also like to thank Corbin Collins, Christine Ricketts, and Kate Blackham for putting up with the delays and giving me a gentle nudge to meet the deadlines, as well as their amazing work on this book.

On the more technical side, I would like to thank my tech reviewers Chád Darby and Yosun Chang for their invaluable input. I would also like to thank Tobias Domhan for writing the excellent AndAR library, the development of which will be continued by both of us from now on.

Finally, I would like to thank my family for their support, particularly for patience while I ignored them while working on this book.

Without all of these people, you would not be reading this book today.

–Raghav Sood

Introduction

Augmented reality is relatively recent development in the field of mobile computing. Despite its young age, it is already one of the fastest growing areas in this industry. Companies are investing lots of money in developing products that use augmented reality, the most notable of which is Google's Project Glass. Most people perceive augmented reality as hard to implement. That's a misconception. Like with any good app, good augmented reality apps will take some amount of effort to write. All you need to do is keep an open mind before diving in.

Who This Book Is For

This book is aimed at people who want to write apps employing augmented reality for the Android platform by Google. The book expects familiarity with the Java language and knowledge of the very basics of Android. However, an effort has been made to ensure that even people without such experience can understand the content and code. Hopefully, by the time you're done with this book, you'll know how to write amazing and rich Android apps that use the power of augmented reality.

How This Book Is Structured

This book is divided into nine chapters. We start with a basic introduction to augmented reality and move up through more and more complex features as we go. In Chapter 5, we take a look at dealing with the common errors that can happen in an augmented reality app. After that, we have four example apps that show use how to make increasingly complex augmented reality applications. A more detailed structure is given here:

- **Chapter 1:** This chapter gives you an idea of what augmented reality really is. It has several examples of how augmented reality has been used throughout the world, along with a short list of potential future applications.
- **Chapter 2:** This chapter guides you through writing a simple augmented reality app that consists of the four main features an augmented reality app usually uses. By the end of this chapter, you will have a skeleton structure that can be extended into any augmented reality application.

- **Chapter 3:** In this chapter, you are introduced to some of augmented reality's most important features: overlays and markers. In the span of two example apps, we cover using standard Android widgets as overlays as well as using the open source AndAR library to add marker recognition to our app.
- **Chapter 4:** The fourth chapter introduces the concept of artificial horizons by using a nonaugmented reality app. Then a second app is written that utilizes artificial horizons in an augmented reality app.
- **Chapter 5:** This chapter talks about the most common errors found while making an augmented reality app and also provides solutions for them. In addition to the errors, it also talks about other problems that don't result in an error, but still manage to stop your app from functioning as intended.
- **Chapter 6:** In this chapter, we write the first of our four example apps. It is an extremely simple AR app that provides basic information about the user's current location as well as plotting it on a map.
- **Chapter 7:** This chapter shows you how to extend the example app from Chapter 6 into a proper app that can be used to allow the user to navigate from his/her current location to one set on the map by the user.
- **Chapter 8:** This chapter shows you how to write an augmented reality model viewer using the AndAR library that allows you to display 3D models on a marker.
- **Chapter 9:** The last chapter of this book demonstrates how to write the most complex app of all: an augmented reality world browser that shows data from Wikipedia and Twitter all around you.

Prerequisites

This book contains some fairly advanced code, and it is assumed that you are familiar with the following:

- Java programming language
- Basic object-oriented concepts
- Android platform (moderate knowledge)
- Eclipse IDE basics

While it is not an absolute requirement to have all these prerequisites, it is highly recommended. You will absolutely need an Android device to test your apps on because many of the features used in the apps are not available on the Android emulator.

Downloading the Code

The code for the examples shown in this book is available on the Apress web site, www.apress.com/9781430239451. A link can be found on the book's information page under the Source Code/Downloads tab. This tab is located underneath the Related Titles section of the page.

You can also get the source code from this book's GitHub repository at http://github.com/RaghavSood/ProAndroidAugmentedReality.

In case you find a bug in our code, please file an issue for it at the GitHub repository, or directly contact the author via the means given below.

Contacting the Author

In case you have any questions, comments, or suggestions, or even find an error in this book, feel free to contact the author at raghavsood@appaholics.in via e-mail or via Twitter at @Appaholics16.

Applications of Augmented Reality

Augmented reality (AR) is a reasonably recent, but still large field. It does not have a very large market share, and most of its current applications are just out of prototyping. This makes AR a very anticipated and untapped niche. There are very few applications that implement AR technology in the Android Market right now. This chapter describes the real-world applications of AR, gives examples (along with images where possible), and discusses whether it is now possible to implement AR in the Android platform.

Augmented Reality vs. Virtual Reality

Augmented reality (AR) and virtual reality (VR) are fields in which the lines of distinction are kind of blurred. To put it another way, you can think of VR as the precursor to AR, with some parts overlapping in both. The main difference between the two technologies is that VR does not use a camera feed. All the things displayed in VR are either animations or prerecorded bits of film.

Current Uses

Despite being a relatively new field, there are enough AR apps available to allow us to make categories out of them. Here we take a look at what has already been implemented in the world of AR.

Casual Users

There are hundreds of apps that use AR that are meant to be used by the average person. They come in many types—for example, games, world browsers, and navigation apps. They are usually using the accelerometer and the GPS to obtain location and the physical state of the device. These apps are meant to be enjoyed and useful. One of the winning apps of the Android Developer Challenge 2 was an AR game: *SpecTrek*. The game uses your GPS to find your location and then prepares ghosts for you to hunt in surrounding areas. The game also has a map on which ghosts are displayed as markers on a Google map. During gameplay, the ghost is added as an overlay over the camera image.

On the other side of things, navigation apps have code to recognize roads and turnings, and mark out the route with arrows. This process is not as easy as it sounds, but is often done today.

In the end, world browsers are probably the most complex of all the casual apps that are widely used. They need several back-end databases and also need a lot of on-the-spot information from several sensors. After all, browsers still have to put everything together and display a set of icons on the screen. Almost every app you see on the market, whether AR or not, looks simple at first sight. But if you delve into the code and back ends, you will realize that most of them are in fact, very very complex and take a long time to create.

The best examples of casual AR apps are *SpecTrek* and *Wikitude*. Together, these apps make use of practically everything you can use to make an AR app on the Android platform. I highly recommend that you install them and become familiar with the features of AR on Android.

Most apps in this category can be implemented on the Android platform. In several cases, they do not even use all the sensors. Some of them can get quite complex. Figure 1-1 and Figure 1-2 show screenshots from *SpecTrek*.

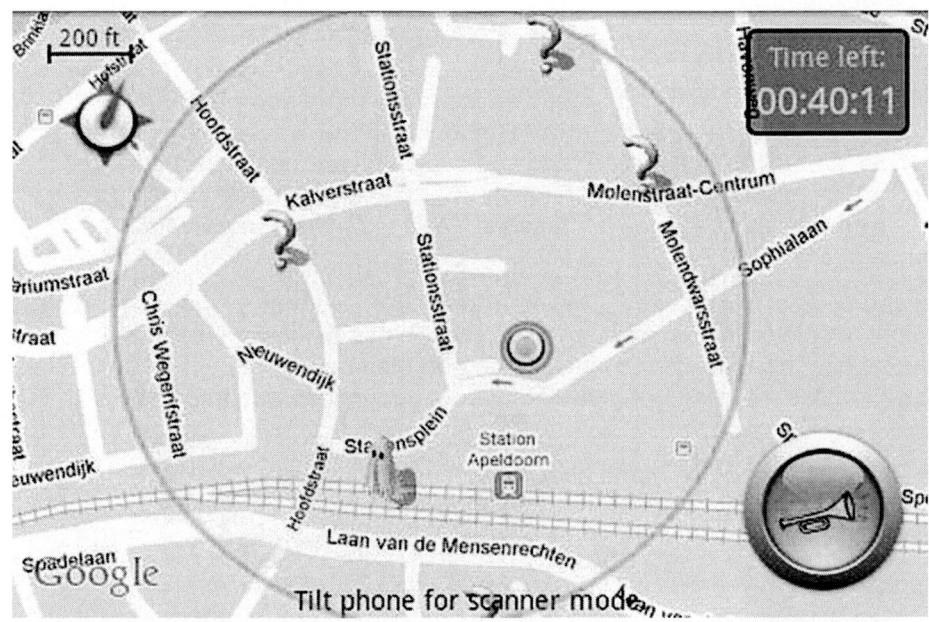

Figure 1-1. *Screenshot of* SpecTrek

Figure 1-2. *Another screenshot of* SpecTrek

Military and Law Enforcement

Uses by military and law enforcement agencies are much more complex and technologically advanced. They range from AR goggles to full simulators designed to help in training. The military and some law enforcement agencies have simulators that make use of AR technology. A wide screen inside a room or a vehicle on which various scenarios is presented, and the trainee must decide the best course of action.

Some advanced Special Forces teams have basic AR goggles that, along with the land in sight, display information such as altitude, angle of viewing, light intensity, and so on. This information is calculated on the spot with mathematical formulas as these goggles do not come equipped with Internet connections.

Specialized night vision goggles come with AR technology as well. These goggles display location and other information, along with trying to fill in gaps that could not be illuminated by the night vision goggles themselves.

Almost all the unmanned vehicles implement AR as well. These vehicles, especially the aerial ones, can be thousands of kilometers away from their operators. These vehicles have one or more cameras mounted on their exterior, which transmit video to their operator. Most of these vehicles come equipped with several sensors as well. The sensor data is sent to the operator along with the video. This data is then processed and augmented over the video. Algorithms on the operator's system process the video and then pick out and mark buildings or objects of interest. All this is displayed as an overlay on the video.

These kinds of apps are quite difficult to implement on Android devices because of two main issues:

- Low processing power (Though with the recent release of the HTC One X and Samsung Galaxy S3, quad core phones released in May 2012, this is not so much of a problem.)

- Lack of more input devices and sensors

Vehicles

As of late, vehicles have started implementing AR technology. The windscreens have been replaced with large, wide, and high-definition displays. Often there are multiple screens in the vehicle, each showing a particular direction. If there is only one screen and multiple cameras, the vehicle will either switch the feed automatically or have the option for the user to do so. The exterior of the vehicle has several cameras, facing multiple directions. The images on the screen are overlayed with useful data such as a small map, compass, direction arrows, alternate routes, weather forecast, and much more. This kind of technology is currently most visible in airplanes and trains at the moment. Smart cars with such technology are being tested out for the market. Submarines and ships are using this technology as well. The recently discontinued Space Shuttles had this kind of AR technology as well.

These apps can be implemented in a sort of hybrid way on the Android platform. Because most Android devices seem to be lacking in features that normal vehicles have, the same kind of features are not achieved. On the other hand, apps can be written that help with navigation by using the GPS to get the location; use direction APIs to get, well, the directions; and use the accelerometer to help with acquiring the speed of the vehicle. The Android device provides the AR power, and the vehicle provides the vehicle part.

Medical

AR-enabled surgeries are becoming more common these days. Surgeries done this way have a smaller error rate because the computer provides valuable inputs on the surgery and uses the information to control robots to perform some or all of the surgery. The computer can often provide alternatives and instructions on what can be done to improve the surgery in real time. The AR stream, along with other data, can also be sent to remote doctors, who can view the information of the patient as if the patient were in front of them.

There are also other medical applications of AR technology. AR machines can be used to monitor a large number of patients and make sure that their vital signs are under observation at all times.

This kind of AR technology has never been implemented on the Android platform because of several reasons:

- It would require an immense amount of information on the device because Internet connections are not yet reliable enough to risk a patient's life.

- The processing power required for some of these medical tasks is currently not available on the devices.

- There is not a very large market for Android devices in surgery and to help with medical tasks.

To top all this off, it is currently very difficult and expensive to design and build such an app. The AI algorithms needed to allow real-time AR work in the medical field are yet to come into existence. Apart from that, you would require a team of very good developers, a team of highly skilled and experienced doctors, and a large amount of money.

Trial Rooms

In several shops, AR is being tried out as a virtual trial room. The user can stand in front of a screen with a camera mounted somewhere. The user will see himself displayed on the screen. The user then uses an input device such as a mouse or keyboard to select any of the available clothing options. The computer will then augment that item onto the user's image and display it on the screen. The user can turn to view himself from all angles.

These apps can be written for the Android platform in principle, but nobody has done it for lack of interest, and probably for lack of any idea as to why someone would want this. Actually apps in the genre have been made, but they are used for entertainment and modifying the facial features of people virtually.

Tourism

Tourism has received some part of the AR magic as well. At several famous spots around the world, organized tours now offer a head-mounted AR system that displays information about the current site and its buildings when you look at it. With AR, tourists can rebuild buildings, cities, landscapes, and terrains as they existed in the past. Tourism AR is also a built-in part of most world browsing applications because they provide markers to famous monuments. Tourism AR is not limited to historical places. It can be used to find parks, restaurants, hotels, and other tourist-related sites and attractions in an unfamiliar city. While not in very widespread use, it has grown exponentially over the past few years.

Features of these apps are already present in world browsers, but have a small back end of information to display. Nobody has yet implemented a complete version of any one city that can provide the required information.

Architecture

There are many camera-equipped machines that can generate a blueprint from an existing structure or display a virtual structure from the blueprints on the proposed site of construction. These speed up architectural work and help to design and check buildings. AR can also simulate natural disaster conditions and show how the building structure will react under that kind of pressure.

Apps in this segment can be written to an extent on Android. The ones that create blueprints out of the view of a room have already been written for the iOS platform and can be written for Android. The ones that display virtual models on a building scale are a little more difficult, but still feasible, as long as the models to be augmented can fit within the size constraints of the Android process and the device's RAM.

Assembly Lines

AR technology helps out a lot on various assembly lines, whether you are assembling cars, planes, mobiles, or anything else. Preprogrammed head goggles can provide step-by-step instructions on how to assemble it.

These apps can be written for Android, as long as the assembly process can incorporate markers at each step that requires instructions to be augmented. The information can be stored on a remote backend in this case.

Cinema/Performance

AR technology has been used to enhance movies and plays by having a static background and a screen with overlays on it to produce images and scenery that would otherwise require expensive and highly detailed sets.

This is a really feasible option. All you need to do is acquire the footage or background information for the performance, place markers at appropriate places, and augment the footage or background when needed.

Entertainment

In several amusement parks around the world, AR technology is being used to make rides that fit within a single room and manage to give you the experience of a whole ride. You will be made to sit in a car or some other vehicle that is mounted on hydraulics. You are surrounded on all sides by massive screens on which the whole scenery is displayed. Depending on whether the scenery is from a live camera or is animated, this could fall under both VR and AR. The vehicle moves in the air as the virtual track progresses. If the track is going down, the vehicle will tilt downward, and you will actually feel as if you are moving down. To provide a more realistic experience, the AR technology is coupled with some fans or water-spraying equipment.

It is possible to implement this on Android, but there are a few limitations. To have a completely immersive experience, you will need a large screen. Some of the tablets might provide sufficient space to have a good experience, but implementing it for phones is a little too optimistic. Additionally, hydraulic mounted vehicles are used in the actual rides to provide the complete experience of movement. To compensate, some innovative thinking will be required on your part.

Education

AR technology has been successfully used in various educational institutes to act as add-ons to the textbook material or as a virtual, 3d textbook in itself. Normally done with head mounts the AR experience allows the students to "relive" events as they are known to have happened, while never leaving their class.

These apps can be implemented on the Android platform, but you need the backing of some course material provider. Apps like these also have the potential to push AR to the forefront because they have a very large potential user base.

Art

AR technology can and has been used to help create paintings, models and other forms of art. It has also helped disabled people realize their creative talent. AR is also used widely to try out a particular design, before actually putting it down in ink or carving it out of stone. Paintings can, for example, be painted virtually to see how they turn out, be refined until the artist is happy with them, and then be put down on the canvas finally.

These kinds of apps are possible as well. They will need to have several fine art-related features and will most likely make little use of the sensors available. The device should ideally have a high-resolution screen, coupled with a high-resolution camera.

Translation

AR-enabled devices are being used to translate text from multiple languages all over the world. These devices feature OCR and either have an entire cross-language dictionary on the device or translate the language over the Internet.

These apps are already in production. You would need to either write or use a ready-made optical character recognition (OCR) library to convert the images from the camera to text. After you have extracted the text from the images, you can either use an on device translation dictionary, which would have to be bundled with the app, or translate it over the Internet and display the results.

Weather Forecasting

On practically every news channel a weather forecaster forecasts the weather on a map of the world behind him. In reality, most of these apps are augmented. The forecaster stands in front of a massive green backdrop. While recording, the green backdrop serves as a marker. After the recording is done, a computer is used to add the map and position it to match the forecaster's actions. If the forecast is being transmitted live to the viewers, the map is added as the forecast is transmitted.

Television

AR can be found in daily life as well. Many game shows, especially the ones with the questions, augment this information over the video of the players. Even in live sports matches, the score and other game-relevant information is augmented over the video and sent to the viewers. The slightly more annoying advertisements are augmented, too.

Many apps that provide live streams of sports matches currently implement this.

Astronomy

There are many apps that are useful to astronomers and good fun for everyone else. These apps can display the location of stars and constellations during the day or on a foggy night and do it in (more or less) real time.

Other

There are many, many more uses of AR that cannot be categorized so easily. They are mostly still in the designing and planning stages, but have the potential to forward AR technology to the forefront of daily gadgets.

Future Uses

As the previous section discussed, AR is quite well known and has enough apps available to make it noteworthy. However, there are some amazing uses for the technology that cannot be implemented right now due to limitations in hardware and algorithms.

Virtual Experiences

In the future, AR technology could be used to create virtual experiences. You could have a head mounted system that could transform your current location into something completely different. For example, you could live through movies by wearing such a system and seeing the movie happen around you. You could convert your house into a medieval castle or into the international space station. Coupled with aural AR and some smell-emitting technology, a whole experience could be made lifelike and feel completely real. In addition to this, wearing a body suit that can emulate the sense of touch will make it absolutely and undeniably real.

This would be quite difficult to implement on Android if and when it turns up because Android is lacking in the required sensors and input methods to implement such a thing. Its visual features could be implemented to an extent, but the sound and feeling ones would be out of reach unless someone creates a bodysuit with a head mounted display and sound on a ported version of Android.

Impossible Simulations

AR technology could do what real hardware cannot, at least as of now. You could have a screen on which you have an ordinary object such as a cube. You could then apply various scenarios and forces to this cube and see how it turns out. You would not be able to do this with real hardware because real hardware usually cannot change shape without being destroyed. You could also test theories using experiments that would otherwise be extremely expensive or completely impossible.

This may be possible to implement on Android by the time other real-world models are developed because the only hard requirement for high-end simulations is the data and a large amount of processing power. At the rate the power of mobile phones is increasing, they could become fast enough to run such apps.

Holograms

AR allows the user to have a live direct or indirect view of the world, which might enable users to have holograms in front of them. These holograms could be interactive or merely descriptive. They could be showing anything.

This could be done even today with a highly modified version of an app that uses markers to display models. Instead of static models, the app could be made to display an animation or recording or live transmission. However this would not provide a true hologram experience as it will be on the device's screen only.

Video Conferencing

AR could allow multiple people to appear in the same conference room if a video feed of a conference room is transmitted to them. The people could use a webcam to "appear" in the seats of the room, along with the others. This could create a collaborative environment, even if the collaborators were thousands of kilometers apart.

This app could be implemented with some advanced placement algorithms and a high-speed Internet connection. You would need the algorithms because it is unlikely that the people taking part in the conference will stay in exactly the same place throughout. You would need to keep positioning them again and again so that they do not overlap with the other people.

Movies

AR could be used to play entire movies. The theatre could be replaced with the background of the movie or the theatre could be replaced with the actors only. In the first way, the actors could be augmented onto the background and in the second method the background could be augmented behind the actors. These could provide for more realistic and fun movies, while keeping the cost of shooting down.

Apps like these are already in production, but not in the quality, popularity, and sophistication to have me drag this out of the future implementations. Although these apps are not that easy to make, they're not very difficult, either.

Gesture Control

AR could be used to implement many gesture controls such as eye dialing. The camera could track the user's eye movement to select the appropriate number key. After the desired key has been selected, the user could blink to press that number and then proceed to select the next key. This could similarly be implemented to control music players, mobile apps, computers, and other forms of technology.

These kinds of apps would require a few things:

- A front camera with a reasonable resolution
- Well written algorithms to detect fine eye movements and to be able to distinguish them from other movements, such as checking a side view mirror

AR has come a long way from its beginnings and has a long way to go. Its basic requirements of a camera, GPS, accelerometer, and compass are fulfilled by almost every Android device on the market. Although apps that use AR technology exist for the Android platform, they are few in number compared with the other kinds of apps. It is a great time to enter the Android platform by making AR apps because the competition is good enough to drive user interest to these apps, but not fierce enough to drive you out of business yet. Considering the relatively few AR apps on the market, there is also a good chance that if you come up with a good AR app it will have no more than 3–5 competing apps, giving you a great advantage. In the next chapter, the basics of AR apps on Android are explained, and a basic app is developed.

Summary

That concludes our look at the current and future uses of AR and their implementation (or likely implementation) on the Android platform. The next chapter looks at the basics of creating an AR app on Android.

Basics of Augmented Reality on the Android Platform

By now, you have a basic idea of what augmented reality (AR) is, what is being done with it around the world, and what you can do with it on an Android device. This chapter will launch you into the world of AR on Android and teach you the basics of it. To aid in your understanding of everything done here (and elsewhere) in this book, we will create apps that demonstrate what is being taught as we move along. This chapter will focus on making a basic app that contains the four main parts of any advanced AR app: the camera, GPS, accelerometer, and compass.

Creating the App

This is a really simple app. It has no overlays and no actual use for any of the data it is receiving from the GPS, compass, camera, and accelerometer. In the next chapter, we will build on this app and add overlays to it.

First, we need to create a new project. In the package name, I am using com.paar.ch2. You can use any name that suits you, but make sure to change any references in the code here to match your package name. The project should be set to support Android 2.1 as the minimum. I am building the project against Android 4.0 (Ice Cream Sandwich), but you can choose your own target.

Camera

The first thing in every AR app is the *camera*, which forms 99 percent of the reality in AR (the other 1 percent consists of the 3 basic sensors). To use the camera in your app, we first need to add the permission request and the uses-feature line to our manifest. We also must tell Android that we want our activity to be landscape and that we will handle certain config changes ourselves. After adding it, the manifest should look something like Listing 2-1:

Listing 2-1. *Updated Manifest Code*

```xml
<?xml version="1.0" encoding="utf-8"?>
<manifest xmlns:android="http://schemas.android.com/apk/res/android"
    package="com.paar.ch2"
    android:versionCode="1"
    android:versionName="1.0" >

    <uses-sdk android:minSdkVersion="7" />

    <application
        android:icon="@drawable/ic_launcher"
        android:label="@string/app_name" >
        <activity
            android:label="@string/app_name"
            android:name=".ProAndroidAR2Activity"
            android:screenOrientation = "landscape"
            android:theme="@android:style/Theme.NoTitleBar.Fullscreen"
            android:configChanges = "keyboardHidden|orientation">
            <intent-filter >
                <action android:name="android.intent.action.MAIN" />

                <category android:name="android.intent.category.LAUNCHER" />
            </intent-filter>
        </activity>
    </application>
<uses-feature android:name="android.hardware.camera" />
<uses-permission android:name="android.permission.CAMERA" />
</manifest>
```

We can also add the permission before the start of the `<application>` element; just make sure that it is part of the manifest and is not invading into any other element.

Now let's get to the actual camera code. The camera requires a `SurfaceView`, on which it will render what it sees. We will create an XML layout with the `SurfaceView` and then use that `SurfaceView` to display the camera preview. Modify your XML file, in this case `main.xml`, to the following:

Listing 2-2. *Modified main.xml*

```xml
<?xml version="1.0" encoding="utf-8"?>
<android.view.SurfaceView
        xmlns:android="http://schemas.android.com/apk/res/android"
        android:id="@+id/cameraPreview"
        android:layout_width="fill_parent"
        android:layout_height="fill_parent" >
</android.view.SurfaceView>
```

Nothing really groundbreaking in that code. Instead of using a normal layout such as LinearLayout or RelativeLayout, we simply add a SurfaceView to the XML file, with its height and width attributes set to allow it to fill the entire available screen. We assign it the ID cameraPreview so we can reference it from our code. The big step now is to use the Android camera service and tell it to tie into our SurfaceView to display the actual preview from the camera.

There are three things that need to be done to get this working:

1. We create a SurfaceView, which is in our XML layout.

2. We will also need a SurfaceHolder, which controls the behavior of our SurfaceView (for example, its size). It will also be notified when changes occur, such as when the preview starts.

3. We need a Camera, obtained from the open() static method on the Camera class.

To string all this together, we simply need to do the following:

4. Get the SurfaceHolder for our SurfaceView via getHolder().

5. Register a SurfaceHolder.Callback so that we are notified when our SurfaceView is ready or changes.

6. Tell the SurfaceView, via the SurfaceHolder, that it has the SURFACE_TYPE_PUSH_BUFFERS type (using setType()). This indicates that something in the system will be updating the SurfaceView and providing the bitmap data to display.

After you've absorbed and understood all this, you can proceed to the actual coding work. First, declare the following variables, and add the imports. The top of your class should look something like this after you're done with it:

Listing 2-3. *Imports and Variable Declarations*

```
package com.paar.ch2;

import android.app.Activity;
import android.hardware.Camera;
import android.os.Bundle;
import android.util.Log;
import android.view.SurfaceHolder;
import android.view.SurfaceView;

public class ProAndroidAR2Activity extends Activity {
        SurfaceView cameraPreview;
        SurfaceHolder previewHolder;
        Camera camera;
        boolean inPreview;
```

Let me elaborate on the imports. The first and third ones are obvious, but the second one is important to note because it is for the camera. Be sure to import Camera from the hardware package, not the graphics package, because that is a different Camera class. The SurfaceView and SurfaceHolder ones are equally important, but there aren't two options to choose from.

On to the variables. cameraPreview is a SurfaceView variable that will hold the reference to the SurfaceView in the XML layout (this will be done in onCreate()). previewHolder is the SurfaceHolder to manage the SurfaceView. camera is the Camera object that will handle all camera stuff. Finally, inPreview is our little Boolean friend that will use his binary logic to tell us if a preview is active, and give us indications so that we can release it properly.

Now we move on to the onCreate() method for our little app:

Listing 2-4. *onCreate()*

```
@Override
    public void onCreate(Bundle savedInstanceState) {
        super.onCreate(savedInstanceState);
        setContentView(R.layout.main);

        inPreview = false;

        cameraPreview = (SurfaceView)findViewById(R.id.cameraPreview);
        previewHolder = cameraPreview.getHolder();
        previewHolder.addCallback(surfaceCallback);
        previewHolder.setType(SurfaceHolder.SURFACE_TYPE_PUSH_BUFFERS);
    }
```

We set our view to our beloved main.xml, set inPreview to false (we are not displaying a preview of the camera right now). After that, we find our

SurfaceView from the XML file and assign it to cameraPreview. Then we run the getHolder() method, add our callback (we'll make this callback in a few minutes; don't worry about the error that will spring up right now), and set the type of previewHolder to SURFACE_TYPE_PUSH_BUFFERS.

Now a Camera object takes a setPreviewDisplay() method that takes a SurfaceHolder and arranges for the camera preview to be displayed on the related SurfaceView. However, the SurfaceView might not be ready immediately after being changed into SURFACE_TYPE_PUSH_BUFFERS mode. Therefore, although the previous setup work could be done in the onCreate() method, we should wait until the SurfaceHolder.Callback has its surfaceCreated() method called before registering the Camera. With this little explanation, we can move back to the coding:

Listing 2-5. *surfaceCallback*

```
SurfaceHolder.Callback surfaceCallback=new SurfaceHolder.Callback() {
        public void surfaceCreated(SurfaceHolder holder) {
                try {
                        camera.setPreviewDisplay(previewHolder);
                }
                catch (Throwable t) {
                    Log.e("ProAndroidAR2Activity", "Exception in
setPreviewDisplay()", t);
                }
        }
```

Now, once the SurfaceView is set up and sized by Android, we need to pass the configuration data to the Camera so it knows how big a preview it should be drawing. As Android has been ported to and installed on hundreds of different hardware devices, there is no way to safely predetermine the size of the preview pane. It would be very simple to wait for our SurfaceHolder.Callback to have its surfaceChanged() method called because this can tell us the size of the SurfaceView. Then we can push that information into a Camera.Parameters object, update the Camera with those parameters, and have the Camera show the preview via startPreview(). Now we can move back to the coding:

Listing 2-6. *sufaceChanged()*

```
public void surfaceChanged(SurfaceHolder holder, int format, int width, int
height) {
        Camera.Parameters parameters=camera.getParameters();
        Camera.Size size=getBestPreviewSize(width, height, parameters);

        if (size!=null) {
                parameters.setPreviewSize(size.width, size.height);
                camera.setParameters(parameters);
```

```
            camera.startPreview();
            inPreview=true;
        }
    }
```

Eventually, you will want your app to release the camera, and reacquire it when needed. This will save resources; and many devices have only one physical camera, which can be used in only one activity at a time. There is more than one way to do this, but we will be using the onPause() and onResume() methods:

Listing 2-7. *onResume() and onPause()*

```
@Override
    public void onResume() {
      super.onResume();

      camera=Camera.open();
    }

    @Override
    public void onPause() {
      if (inPreview) {
        camera.stopPreview();
      }

      camera.release();
      camera=null;
      inPreview=false;

      super.onPause();
    }
```

You could also do it when the activity is destroyed like the following, but we will not be doing that:

Listing 2-8. *surfaceDestroyed()*

```
public void surfaceDestroyed(SurfaceHolder holder) {
                camera.stopPreview();
                camera.release();
                camera=null;
        }
```

Right about now, our little demo app should compile and display a nice little preview of what the camera sees on your screen. We aren't quite finished yet, however, because we still have to add the three sensors.

This brings us to the end of the camera part of our app. Here is the entire code for this class so far, with everything in it. You should update it to look like the following, in case you left out something:

Listing 2-9. *Full Code Listing*

```
package com.paar.ch2;

import android.app.Activity;
import android.hardware.Camera;
import android.os.Bundle;
import android.util.Log;
import android.view.SurfaceHolder;
import android.view.SurfaceView;

public class ProAndroidAR2Activity extends Activity {
        SurfaceView cameraPreview;
        SurfaceHolder previewHolder;
        Camera camera;
        boolean inPreview;
    @Override
    public void onCreate(Bundle savedInstanceState) {
        super.onCreate(savedInstanceState);
        setContentView(R.layout.main);

        inPreview = false;

        cameraPreview = (SurfaceView)findViewById(R.id.cameraPreview);
        previewHolder = cameraPreview.getHolder();
        previewHolder.addCallback(surfaceCallback);
        previewHolder.setType(SurfaceHolder.SURFACE_TYPE_PUSH_BUFFERS);
    }

    @Override
    public void onResume() {
      super.onResume();

      camera=Camera.open();
    }

    @Override
    public void onPause() {
      if (inPreview) {
        camera.stopPreview();
      }

      camera.release();
      camera=null;
      inPreview=false;

      super.onPause();
    }
```

```java
    private Camera.Size getBestPreviewSize(int width, int height,
Camera.Parameters parameters) {
        Camera.Size result=null;

        for (Camera.Size size : parameters.getSupportedPreviewSizes()) {
            if (size.width<=width && size.height<=height) {
                if (result==null) {
                    result=size;
                }
                else {
                    int resultArea=result.width*result.height;
                    int newArea=size.width*size.height;

                    if (newArea>resultArea) {
                        result=size;
                    }
                }
            }
        }

        return(result);
    }

    SurfaceHolder.Callback surfaceCallback=new SurfaceHolder.Callback() {
        public void surfaceCreated(SurfaceHolder holder) {
            try {
                camera.setPreviewDisplay(previewHolder);
            }
            catch (Throwable t) {
                Log.e(TAG, "Exception in setPreviewDisplay()", t);
            }
        }

        public void surfaceChanged(SurfaceHolder holder, int format, int width,
int height) {
            Camera.Parameters parameters=camera.getParameters();
            Camera.Size size=getBestPreviewSize(width, height, parameters);

            if (size!=null) {
                parameters.setPreviewSize(size.width, size.height);
                camera.setParameters(parameters);
                camera.startPreview();
                inPreview=true;
            }
        }

        public void surfaceDestroyed(SurfaceHolder holder) {
            // not used
        }
```

```
        };
}
```

Orientation Sensor

The *orientation sensor* is a combination of the magnetic field sensor and the accelerometer sensor. With the data from these two sensors and a bit of trigonometry, you can get the `pitch`, `roll`, and `heading` (`azimuth`) of the device. If you like trigonometry, you'll be disappointed to know that Android does all the calculations for you, and you can simply pull the values out of a `SensorEvent`.

> **NOTE:** Magnetic field compasses tend to go a bit crazy around metallic objects.
> Guess what large metallic object is likely to be close to your device while testing?
> Your computer! Keep that in mind if your readings aren't what you expected.

Figure 2-1 shows the axes of an orientation sensor.

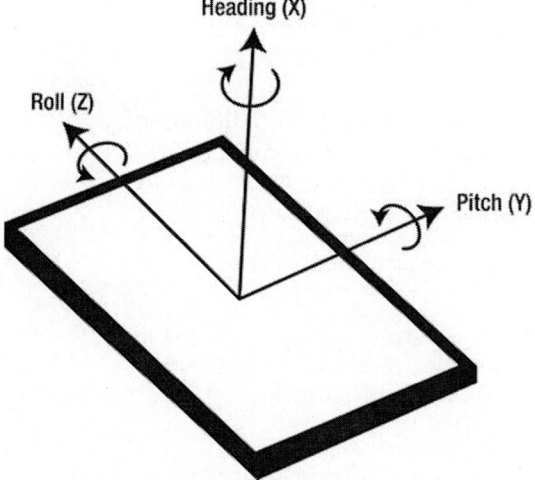

Figure 2-1. *The axes of the device.*

Before we get around to taking these values from Android and using them, let's understand a little more about what they actually are.

- **X-axis or heading:** The X-axis is a bit like a compass. It measures the direction the device is facing, where 0° or 360° is North, 90° is East, 180° is South, and 270° is West.

- **Y-axis or pitch**: This axis measures the tilt of the device. The reading will be 0° if the device is flat, -90° if the top is pointed at the ceiling, and 90° if it is upside down.

- **Z-axis or roll**: This axis measures the sideways tilt of the device. 0° is flat on its back, -90° is facing left, and 90° is the screen facing right.

There are actually two ways to get the preceding data. You can either query the orientation sensor directly, or get the readings of the accelerometer and magnetic field sensors individually and calculate the orientation. The latter is several times slower, but provides for added accuracy. In our app, we will be querying the orientation sensor directly. You can begin by adding the following variables to your class:

Listing 2-10. *New Variable Declarations*

```
final static String TAG = "PAAR";
SensorManager sensorManager;

int orientationSensor;
float headingAngle;
float pitchAngle;
float rollAngle;
```

The TAG string is a constant that we will use as the tag in all our log statements. The sensorManager will be used to get all our sensor data and to manage our sensors. The floats headingAngle, pitchAngle, and rollAngle will be used to store the heading, pitch and the roll of the device, respectively.

After adding the variables given above, add the following lines to your onCreate():

Listing 2-11. *Implementing the SensorManager*

```
sensorManager = (SensorManager) getSystemService(SENSOR_SERVICE);
orientationSensor = Sensor.TYPE_ORIENTATION;
sensorManager.registerListener(sensorEventListener,
    sensorManager.getDefaultSensor(orientationSensor),
    SensorManager.SENSOR_DELAY_NORMAL);
```

SensorManager is a system service, and we get a reference to it in the first line. We then assign to orientationSensor the constant value of Sensor.TYPE_ORIENTATION, which is basically the constant given to the orientation sensor. Finally, we register our SensorEventListener for the default orientation sensor, with the normal delay. SENSOR_DELAY_NORMAL is suitable for UI changes, SENSOR_DELAY_GAME is suitable for use in games, SENSOR_DELAY_UI is suitable for updating the UI thread, and SENSOR_DELAY_FASTEST is the fastest the hardware supports. These settings tell Android approximately how often you want updates from the sensor. Android will not always give it at exactly the intervals specified. It may return values a little slower or faster—generally faster. You should only use the delay that you need because sensors consume a lot of CPU and battery life.

Right about now, there should be a red underline under sensorEventListener. This is because we haven't actually created the listener so far; we will do that now:

Listing 2-12. *sensorEventListener*

```
final SensorEventListener sensorEventListener = new SensorEventListener() {
    public void onSensorChanged(SensorEvent sensorEvent) {
            if (sensorEvent.sensor.getType() == Sensor.TYPE_ORIENTATION)
            {
                    headingAngle = sensorEvent.values[0];
                    pitchAngle = sensorEvent.values[1];
                    rollAngle = sensorEvent.values[2];

                    Log.d(TAG, "Heading: " + String.valueOf(headingAngle));
                    Log.d(TAG, "Pitch: " + String.valueOf(pitchAngle));
                    Log.d(TAG, "Roll: " + String.valueOf(rollAngle));
            }
    }

    public void onAccuracyChanged (Sensor senor, int accuracy) {
            //Not used
    }
};
```

We create and register sensorEventListener as a new SensorEventListener. We then use the onSensorChanged() method to receive updates when the values of the sensors change. Because onSensorChanged() receives updates for all sensors, we use an if statement to filter out everything except the orientation sensor. We then store the values from the sensor in our variables, and print them out to the log. We could also overlay this data on the camera preview, but that is beyond the scope of this chapter. We also have the onAccuracyChanged() method present, which we aren't using for now. It's just there because you must implement it, according to Eclipse.

Now so that our app behaves nicely and doesn't kill off the user's battery, we will register and unregister our sensor in the onResume() and onPause() methods. Update them to the following:

Listing 2-13. *onResume() and onPause()*

```
@Override
public void onResume() {
  super.onResume();
  sensorManager.registerListener(sensorEventListener, sensorManager
.getDefaultSensor(orientationSensor), SensorManager.SENSOR_DELAY_NORMAL);
  camera=Camera.open();
}

@Override
public void onPause() {
  if (inPreview) {
    camera.stopPreview();
  }
  sensorManager.unregisterListener(sensorEventListener);
  camera.release();
  camera=null;
  inPreview=false;

  super.onPause();
}
```

This wraps up the section on the orientation sensor. We'll now take a look at the accelerometer sensor.

Accelerometer

The *accelerometer* measures acceleration along three directional axes: left-right (lateral(X)), forward-backward (longitudinal(Y)) and up-down (vertical(Z)). These values are passed along in the float array of value.

Figure 2-2 shows the axes of the accelerometer.

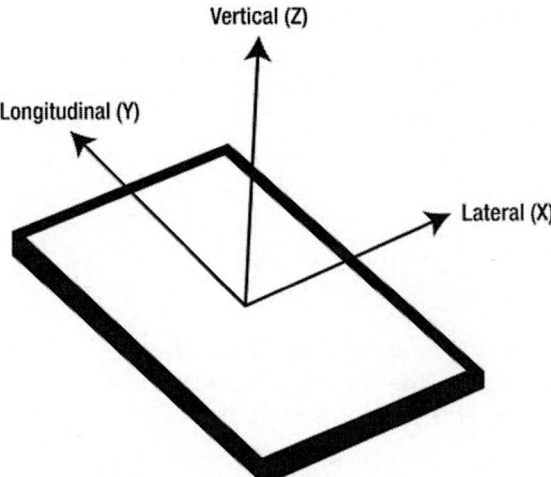

Figure 2-2. *Accelerometer axes*

In our application, we will be receiving the accelerometer values and outputting them through the LogCat. Later on in the book, we will use the accelerometer to determine speed and other things.

Let's take a very quick look at the axes of the accelerometer and exactly what they measure.

- **X-Axis:** On a normal device with a normal accelerometer, the X-axis measures lateral acceleration. That is, left to right; right to left. The reading is positive if you are moving it to your right side, and is negative if you are moving it to your left. For example, a device flat on its back, facing up, and in portrait orientation being moved along a surface to your right will generate a positive reading on the X-axis.

- **Y-Axis:** The Y-axis functions the same way as the X-axis, except it measures the acceleration longitudinally. A positive reading is registered when a device held in the same configuration described in the X-axis is moved in the direction of its top, and a negative reading is registered if moved in the opposite direction.

- **Z-Axis:** This axis measures the acceleration for upward and downward motion, for which positive readings are upward motions, and negative readings are downward motions. When at rest, you will get a reading of approximately -9.8m/s^2 due to gravity. In your calculations, this should be accounted for.

Let's start with the coding work now. We will be using the same SensorManager as before with the accelerometer. We will simply need to add a few variables, get the accelerometer sensor, and add another filtering if statement in the onSensorChanged() method. Let's start with the variables:

Listing 2-14. *Accelerometer Variables*

```
int accelerometerSensor;
float xAxis;
float yAxis;
float zAxis;
```

accelerometerSensor will be used to store the constant for the accelerometer, xAxis will store the value returned by the sensor for the X-axis, yAxis will store the value returned by the sensor for the Y-axis, and zAxis will store the value returned by the sensor for the Z-axis.

After adding the variables, we will need to update our sensor-related code in the onCreate() method as well, so that we can use and listen for the accelerometer later on in the onSensorChanged() method. Modify the sensor code in the onCreate() to the following:

Listing 2-15. *Modified onCreate()*

```
sensorManager = (SensorManager) getSystemService(SENSOR_SERVICE);

        orientationSensor = Sensor.TYPE_ORIENTATION;
        accelerometerSensor = Sensor.TYPE_ACCELEROMETER;

        sensorManager.registerListener(sensorEventListener, sensorManager
.getDefaultSensor(orientationSensor), SensorManager.SENSOR_DELAY_NORMAL);

        sensorManager.registerListener(sensorEventListener, sensorManager
.getDefaultSensor(accelerometerSensor), SensorManager.SENSOR_DELAY_NORMAL);
```

We have simply repeated for the accelerometer what we had already done for the orientation sensor, so you should have no problem understanding what is going on here. Now we must update the sensorEventListener to listen for the accelerometer by changing the code to the following:

Listing 2-16. *Modified sensorEventListener()*

```
final SensorEventListener sensorEventListener = new SensorEventListener() {
    public void onSensorChanged(SensorEvent sensorEvent) {
            if (sensorEvent.sensor.getType() == Sensor.TYPE_ORIENTATION)
            {
                    headingAngle = sensorEvent.values[0];
                    pitchAngle = sensorEvent.values[1];
```

```
            rollAngle = sensorEvent.values[2];

            Log.d(TAG, "Heading: " + String.valueOf(headingAngle));
            Log.d(TAG, "Pitch: " + String.valueOf(pitchAngle));
            Log.d(TAG, "Roll: " + String.valueOf(rollAngle));
        }

    else if (sensorEvent.sensor.getType() == Sensor.TYPE_ACCELEROMETER)
    {
            xAxis = sensorEvent.values[0];
            yAxis = sensorEvent.values[1];
            zAxis = sensorEvent.values[2];

            Log.d(TAG, "X Axis: " + String.valueOf(xAxis));
            Log.d(TAG, "Y Axis: " + String.valueOf(yAxis));
            Log.d(TAG, "Z Axis: " + String.valueOf(zAxis));

    }
}
```

Again, we are repeating what we did for the orientation sensor to listen to the accelerometer sensor changes. We use `if` statements to distinguish between the two sensors, update the appropriate floats with the new values, and print the new values out to the log. Now all that remains is to update the `onResume()` method to register the accelerometer again:

Listing 2-17. *Modified onResume()*

```
@Override
public void onResume() {
  super.onResume();

  sensorManager.registerListener(sensorEventListener, sensorManager
.getDefaultSensor(orientationSensor), SensorManager.SENSOR_DELAY_NORMAL);

  sensorManager.registerListener(sensorEventListener, sensorManager
.getDefaultSensor(accelerometerSensor), SensorManager.SENSOR_DELAY_NORMAL);

  camera=Camera.open();
}
```

We do not need to change anything in `onPause()` as we unregister the entire listener there, all associated sensors included.

With that, we come to the end of our two sensors. Now all that is left to complete our app is to implement the GPS.

Global Positioning System (GPS)

The *global positioning system (GPS)* is a location system that can give an extremely accurate location via satellites. It will be the final part of our amazing little demo app.

First, let's take a brief look at the history of the GPS and how it works.

The GPS is a space-based satellite navigation system. It is managed by the United States and is available for use by anyone with a GPS receiver, although it was originally intended to be military only.

Originally, there were 24 satellites to which a receiver would communicate. The system has been upgraded over the years to have 31 satellites, plus 2 older ones that are currently marked as spares. At any time, a minimum of nine satellites can be viewed from the ground, while the rest are not visible.

To obtain a fix, a receiver must communicate with a minimum of four satellites. The satellites send three pieces of information to the receiver, which are then fed into one of the many algorithms for finding the actual location. The three pieces are the time of broadcast, the orbital location of that particular satellite, and the rough locations of all the other satellites (system health or almanac). The location is calculated using trigonometry. This may make you think that in such a case, three satellites will be enough to obtain a fix, but a timing error in the communications, when multiplied by the speed of light that is used in the algorithms, results in a very big error in the final location.

For our sensor data, we used a `SensorManager`. To use the GPS, however, we will be using a `LocationManager`. Although we used a `SensorEventListener` for the sensors, we will use a `LocationListener` for the GPS. To start off, we will declare the variables that we will be using:

Listing 2-18. *Declaring GPS Variables*

```
LocationManager locationManager;
double latitude;
double longitude;
double altitude;
```

We will only be taking the latitude, longitude and altitude from our `Location` object, but you can also get the bearing, time, and so forth if you want. It all depends on what you want your app to do, and what data you need to do it. Before we get around to actually getting all this data, let's take a look at what latitude and longitude are.

Latitude and Longitude

Latitudes are part of the Earth's grid system; they are imaginary circles that go from the North Pole to the South Pole. The equator is the 0° line, and the only one of the latitudes that is a great circle. All latitudes are parallel to one another. Each latitude is approximately 69 miles, or 111 kilometers, from its immediate previous and next ones. The exact distance varies due to the curvature of the Earth.

Figure 2-3 shows the concept of a sphere.

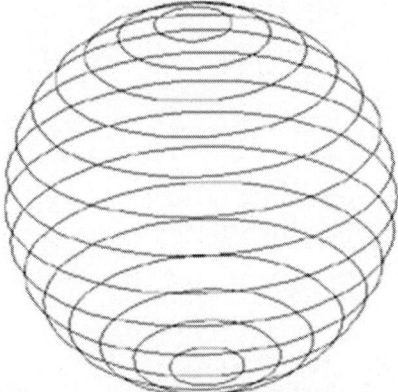

Figure 2-3. *A graphical representation of latitudes*

Longitudes are also imaginary lines of the Earth's grid system. They run from the North Pole to the South Pole, converging at each of the poles. Each longitude is half of a great circle. The 0° longitude is known as the Prime Meridian and passes through Greenwich, England. The distance between two longitudes is greatest at the equator, and is approximately 69 miles, or 111 kilometers, the same as the approximate distance between two latitudes.

Figure 2-4 shows the concept on another sphere.

Figure 2-4. *A graphical representation of longitudes*

With a new understanding of latitudes and longitudes, we can move on to getting the service from the system and asking for location updates in the onCreate() method:

Listing 2-19. *Asking for Location Updates in onCreate()*

```
locationManager = (LocationManager) getSystemService(LOCATION_SERVICE);
locationManager.requestLocationUpdates(LocationManager.GPS_PROVIDER, 2000, 2,
 locationListener);
```

First, we get the location service from Android. After that, we use the requestLocationUpdates() method to request the location updates. The first parameter is the constant of the provider we want to use (in this case, the GPS). We can also use the cell network. The second parameter is the time interval between updates in milliseconds, the third is the minimum distance that the device should move in meters, and the last parameter is the LocationListener that should be notified.

Right now, the locationListener should have a red underline. That is because we haven't yet quite made it. Let's fix that:

Listing 2-20. *locationListener*

```
LocationListener locationListener = new LocationListener() {
    public void onLocationChanged(Location location) {
            latitude = location.getLatitude();
            longitude = location.getLongitude();
            altitude = location.getAltitude();

            Log.d(TAG, "Latitude: " + String.valueOf(latitude));
```

```
            Log.d(TAG, "Longitude: " + String.valueOf(longitude));
            Log.d(TAG, "Altitude: " + String.valueOf(altitude));
    }

        public void onProviderDisabled(String arg0) {
                // TODO Auto-generated method stub

        }

        public void onProviderEnabled(String arg0) {
                // TODO Auto-generated method stub

        }

        public void onStatusChanged(String arg0, int arg1, Bundle arg2) {
                // TODO Auto-generated method stub

        }
};
```

The onLocationChanged() method is invoked every time your minimum time interval takes place or the device moves the minimum distance you specified or more. The Location object received by the method contains a whole host of information: the latitude, longitude, altitude, bearing, and so on. However, in this example we extract and save only the latitude, altitude, and longitude. The Log.d statements simply display the values received.

The GPS is one of the most battery-intensive parts of the Android system and could drain out a fully charged battery in a few hours. This is why we will go through the whole thing of release and acquiring the GPS in the onPause() and onResume() methods:

Listing 2-21. *onResume() and onPause()*

```
@Override
    public void onResume() {
        super.onResume();
        locationManager.requestLocationUpdates(LocationManager.GPS_PROVIDER, 2000,
2, locationListener);
        sensorManager.registerListener(sensorEventListener, sensorManager
.getDefaultSensor(orientationSensor), SensorManager.SENSOR_DELAY_NORMAL);
        sensorManager.registerListener(sensorEventListener, sensorManager
.getDefaultSensor(accelerometerSensor), SensorManager.SENSOR_DELAY_NORMAL);
        camera=Camera.open();
    }

    @Override
    public void onPause() {
      if (inPreview) {
```

```
        camera.stopPreview();
    }
    locationManager.removeUpdates(locationListener);
    sensorManager.unregisterListener(sensorEventListener);
    camera.release();
    camera=null;
    inPreview=false;

    super.onPause();
}
```

This brings us to the end of our demo app. If done right, you should see the camera preview on the screen, coupled with a fast moving LogCat. All the files modified from the default state at project creation are given here now, so that you can make sure that everything is in place.

ProAndroidAR2Activity.java

Listing 2-22. *Full listing for ProAndroidAR2Activity.java*

```
package com.paar.ch2;

import android.app.Activity;
import android.hardware.Camera;
import android.hardware.Sensor;
import android.hardware.SensorEvent;
import android.hardware.SensorEventListener;
import android.hardware.SensorManager;
import android.location.Location;
import android.location.LocationListener;
import android.location.LocationManager;
import android.os.Bundle;
import android.util.Log;
import android.view.SurfaceHolder;
import android.view.SurfaceView;

public class ProAndroidAR2Activity extends Activity{
        SurfaceView cameraPreview;
        SurfaceHolder previewHolder;
        Camera camera;
        boolean inPreview;

        final static String TAG = "PAAR";
        SensorManager sensorManager;

        int orientationSensor;
        float headingAngle;
        float pitchAngle;
```

```java
        float rollAngle;

        int accelerometerSensor;
        float xAxis;
        float yAxis;
        float zAxis;

        LocationManager locationManager;
        double latitude;
        double longitude;
        double altitude;
    @Override
    public void onCreate(Bundle savedInstanceState) {
        super.onCreate(savedInstanceState);
        setContentView(R.layout.main);

        locationManager = (LocationManager) getSystemService(LOCATION_SERVICE);
        locationManager.requestLocationUpdates(LocationManager.GPS_PROVIDER,
2000, 2, locationListener);

        sensorManager = (SensorManager) getSystemService(SENSOR_SERVICE);
        orientationSensor = Sensor.TYPE_ORIENTATION;
        accelerometerSensor = Sensor.TYPE_ACCELEROMETER;
        sensorManager.registerListener(sensorEventListener, sensorManager
.getDefaultSensor(orientationSensor), SensorManager.SENSOR_DELAY_NORMAL);
        sensorManager.registerListener(sensorEventListener, sensorManager
.getDefaultSensor(accelerometerSensor), SensorManager.SENSOR_DELAY_NORMAL);

        inPreview = false;

        cameraPreview = (SurfaceView)findViewById(R.id.cameraPreview);
        previewHolder = cameraPreview.getHolder();
        previewHolder.addCallback(surfaceCallback);
        previewHolder.setType(SurfaceHolder.SURFACE_TYPE_PUSH_BUFFERS);
    }

    LocationListener locationListener = new LocationListener() {
        public void onLocationChanged(Location location) {
                latitude = location.getLatitude();
                longitude = location.getLongitude();
                altitude = location.getAltitude();

                Log.d(TAG, "Latitude: " + String.valueOf(latitude));
                Log.d(TAG, "Longitude: " + String.valueOf(longitude));
                Log.d(TAG, "Altitude: " + String.valueOf(altitude));
        }

                public void onProviderDisabled(String arg0) {
                        // TODO Auto-generated method stub
```

```
            }

            public void onProviderEnabled(String arg0) {
                    // TODO Auto-generated method stub

            }

            public void onStatusChanged(String arg0, int arg1, Bundle arg2)
{
                    // TODO Auto-generated method stub

            }
    };

    final SensorEventListener sensorEventListener = new SensorEventListener() {
        public void onSensorChanged(SensorEvent sensorEvent) {
                if (sensorEvent.sensor.getType() == Sensor.TYPE_ORIENTATION)
                {
                        headingAngle = sensorEvent.values[0];
                        pitchAngle = sensorEvent.values[1];
                        rollAngle = sensorEvent.values[2];

                        Log.d(TAG, "Heading: " + String.valueOf(headingAngle));
                        Log.d(TAG, "Pitch: " + String.valueOf(pitchAngle));
                        Log.d(TAG, "Roll: " + String.valueOf(rollAngle));
                }

                else if (sensorEvent.sensor.getType() ==
Sensor.TYPE_ACCELEROMETER)
                {
                        xAxis = sensorEvent.values[0];
                        yAxis = sensorEvent.values[1];
                        zAxis = sensorEvent.values[2];

                        Log.d(TAG, "X Axis: " + String.valueOf(xAxis));
                        Log.d(TAG, "Y Axis: " + String.valueOf(yAxis));
                        Log.d(TAG, "Z Axis: " + String.valueOf(zAxis));

                }
        }

        public void onAccuracyChanged (Sensor senor, int accuracy) {
                //Not used
        }
    };

    @Override
    public void onResume() {
      super.onResume();
```

```java
    locationManager.requestLocationUpdates(LocationManager.GPS_PROVIDER, 2000,
2, locationListener);
    sensorManager.registerListener(sensorEventListener, sensorManager
.getDefaultSensor(orientationSensor), SensorManager.SENSOR_DELAY_NORMAL);
    sensorManager.registerListener(sensorEventListener, sensorManager
.getDefaultSensor(accelerometerSensor), SensorManager.SENSOR_DELAY_NORMAL);
    camera=Camera.open();
  }

  @Override
  public void onPause() {
    if (inPreview) {
      camera.stopPreview();
    }
    locationManager.removeUpdates(locationListener);
    sensorManager.unregisterListener(sensorEventListener);
    camera.release();
    camera=null;
    inPreview=false;

    super.onPause();
  }

  private Camera.Size getBestPreviewSize(int width, int height,
Camera.Parameters parameters) {
    Camera.Size result=null;

    for (Camera.Size size : parameters.getSupportedPreviewSizes()) {
        if (size.width<=width && size.height<=height) {
            if (result==null) {
                result=size;
            }
            else {
                int resultArea=result.width*result.height;
                int newArea=size.width*size.height;

                if (newArea>resultArea) {
                    result=size;
                }
            }
        }
    }

    return(result);
  }

  SurfaceHolder.Callback surfaceCallback=new SurfaceHolder.Callback() {
    public void surfaceCreated(SurfaceHolder holder) {
        try {
            camera.setPreviewDisplay(previewHolder);
```

```
                    }
                    catch (Throwable t) {
                            Log.e(TAG, "Exception in setPreviewDisplay()", t);
                    }
            }

        public void surfaceChanged(SurfaceHolder holder, int format, int width,
    int height) {
                    Camera.Parameters parameters=camera.getParameters();
                    Camera.Size size=getBestPreviewSize(width, height, parameters);

                    if (size!=null) {
                            parameters.setPreviewSize(size.width, size.height);
                            camera.setParameters(parameters);
                            camera.startPreview();
                            inPreview=true;
                    }
            }

        public void surfaceDestroyed(SurfaceHolder holder) {
                    // not used
            }

        };
}
```

AndroidManifest.xml

Listing 2-23. *Full listing for AndroidManifest.xml*

```xml
<?xml version="1.0" encoding="utf-8"?>
<manifest xmlns:android="http://schemas.android.com/apk/res/android"
    package="com.paar.ch2"
    android:versionCode="1"
    android:versionName="1.0" >

    <uses-sdk android:minSdkVersion="7" />

    <application
        android:icon="@drawable/ic_launcher"
        android:label="@string/app_name" >
        <activity
            android:label="@string/app_name"
            android:name=".ProAndroidAR2Activity"
            android:screenOrientation = "landscape"
            android:theme="@android:style/Theme.NoTitleBar.Fullscreen"
            android:configChanges = "keyboardHidden|orientation">
            <intent-filter >
```

```
                <action android:name="android.intent.action.MAIN" />

                <category android:name="android.intent.category.LAUNCHER" />
            </intent-filter>
        </activity>
    </application>
<uses-feature android:name="android.hardware.camera" />
<uses-permission android:name="android.permission.CAMERA" />
<uses-permission android:name="android.permission.ACCESS_FINE_LOCATION" />
</manifest>
```

main.xml

Listing 2-24. *Full listing for main.xml*

```xml
<?xml version="1.0" encoding="utf-8"?>
<android.view.SurfaceView
        xmlns:android="http://schemas.android.com/apk/res/android"
        android:id="@+id/cameraPreview"
        android:layout_width="fill_parent"
        android:layout_height="fill_parent" >
</android.view.SurfaceView>
```

Sample LogCat Output

After you have written the app out, run it from Eclipse using the Run As button on top. If you are running it on an emulator, you will get nothing because the sensors are not emulated. On a device, you should see a camera preview on the screen, coupled with a fast-moving LogCat that looks something like Figure 2-5.

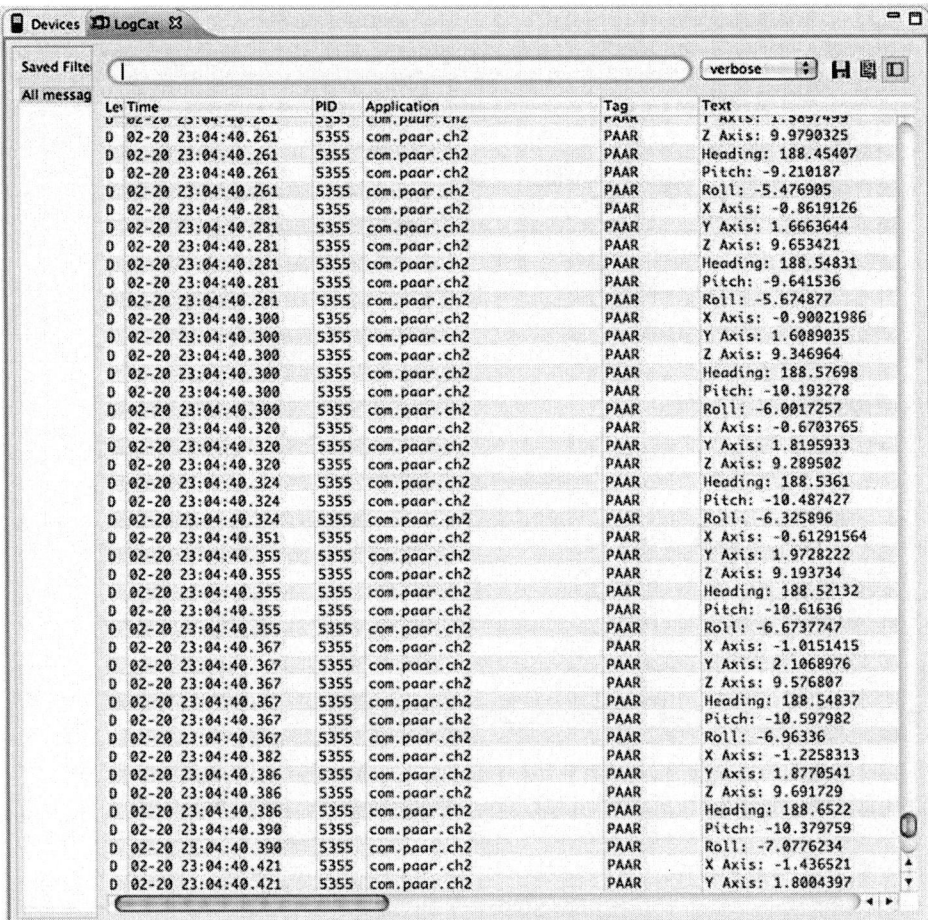

Figure 2-5. *Screenshot of the LogCat while the app is running.*

If you have a clear view of the sky, the LogCat will also include three lines that tell you the latitude, longitude, and altitude.

Summary

In this chapter, you learned how to use the camera, how to read the values from the accelerometer and orientation sensor, and how to get the user's location using GPS.

You also learned to utilize the four base components of any full-featured AR app. You will not always use all four of these things in your app. In fact, it is very rare to have an app with such a requirement.

This chapter should give you a basic understanding of AR, and the project from this app is essentially the skeleton of a proper AR app.

The next chapter discusses overlays and how they give the user a real augmented experience.

Adding Overlays

As mentioned before, augmented reality (AR) is the overlaying of data that is related to the direct or indirect camera preview being displayed. In the majority of AR apps, the camera preview is first scanned for markers. In the translator kind of apps, the preview is scanned for text. And in some gaming apps, no scanning is done; instead, characters, buttons, text, and so on are overlaid on the preview.

All the source code from this chapter can be downloaded from this book's page at http://www.apress.com or the GitHub repository.

In Chapter 2, we made a basic app that displayed the device camera's preview, retrieved the location via GPS, got the accelerometer readings, and retrieved the orientation sensor readings. We will keep building on this app in this chapter and also add overlays to it. We will be adding normal Android widget overlays and implementing marker recognition. Let's start with the simplest: widget overlays.

Widget Overlays

The Android platform provides a bunch of standard widgets such as TextViews, Buttons, and Checkboxes. These are included by default in the Android OS and can be used by any application. They are probably the easiest things you can overlay on your camera preview.

To get started, create a new Android project. The one used in this example is called Pro Android AR 3 Widget Overlay, builds against Android 4, has its minSdkVersion set to 7 (Android 2.1), and has the package name com.paar.ch3widgetoverlay. (You can change all that to whatever suits your needs, but be sure to also update the example code given here.) Figure 3-1 shows the project setup screen.

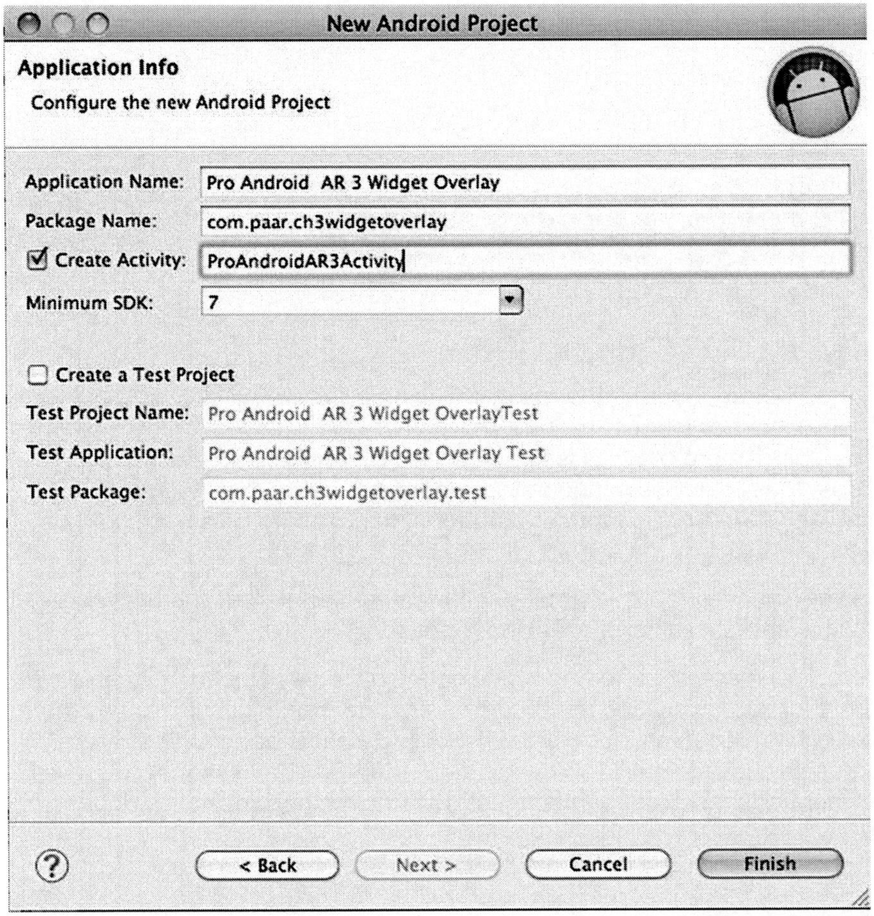

Figure 3-1. *The application details*

Start by duplicating everything we did in the last chapter. You can type it all out by hand, or copy and paste. That's your call. Be sure to update the package name and so on in the code so that it works in the new project.

After everything from the previous chapter's code is duplicated, we will need to modify the XML file defining our layout to allow for widget overlays. Earlier, the entire layout was a single SurfaceView, which displayed the camera preview. Because of this, we cannot currently add other widgets to the layout. Therefore, we will change our XML file to have a RelativeLayout, and have the SurfaceView and all other widgets inside that RelativeLayout. We are using a RelativeLayout because it allows us to easily overlap the widgets on the SurfaceView. In this example, we will be adding various TextViews to display the sensor data. So before we get to the layout editing, we need to add some string resources to the project's strings.xml:

Listing 3-1. *String Resources*

```
<string name="xAxis">X Axis:</string>
<string name="yAxis">Y Axis:</string>
<string name="zAxis">Z Axis:</string>
<string name="heading">Heading:</string>
<string name="pitch">Pitch:</string>
<string name="roll">Roll:</string>
<string name="altitude">Altitude:</string>
<string name="longitude">Longitude:</string>
<string name="latitude">Latitude:</string>
<string name="empty"></string>
```

These strings will provide the labels for some of the TextViews. Half of them, to be exact. The other half will be updated with the data from the sensors. After this, you should update your main.xml file so that it has a RelativeLayout. Let's take a quick look at what a RelativeLayout is and how it compares to other layouts before we move onto the actual code.

Layout Options

In Android, there are many different root layouts available. These layouts define the user interface of any app. All layouts are usually defined in XML files located in /res/layout. However, layouts and their elements can be dynamically created at runtime through Java code. This is done only if the app needs to add widgets on the fly. Layouts can be declared in XML and then be modified later through the Java code, as we will frequently do in our apps. This is done by acquiring a reference to a part of the layout, for example a TextView, and calling various methods of that class to alter it. We can do this because each layout element (including the layout) has a corresponding Java class in the Android framework, which defines the methods that modify it. There are currently four different layout options:

- Frame layout

- Table layout

- Linear layout

- Relative layout

When Android was first released, there was a fifth layout option called Absolute layout. This layout allowed you to specify the position of an element using exact x and y coordinates. This layout is now deprecated because it is difficult to use across different screen sizes.

Frame Layout

The Frame layout is the simplest type of layout. It is essentially a large blank space on which you can put a single child object, which will be pinned to the top-left corner of the screen. Any other objects added after the first one will be drawn directly on top of it.

Table Layout

A Table layout positions its children into rows and columns. TableLayout containers do not display border lines for their rows, columns, or cells. The table will have as many columns as the row with the most cells. A table can leave cells empty, but cells can't span columns as they can in HTML. TableRow objects are the child views of a TableLayout (each TableRow defines a single row in the table). Each row has zero or more cells, each of which is defined by any kind of other view. So the cells of a row can be composed of a variety of View objects such as ImageView or TextView. A cell can also be a ViewGroup object (for example, you can nest another TableLayout as a cell).

Linear Layout

A Linear layout aligns all children in a single direction—vertically or horizontally, depending on how you define the orientation attribute. All children are stacked one after the other, so a vertical list has only one child per row, no matter how wide they are; and a horizontal list is only one row high (the height of the tallest child, plus padding). A LinearLayout respects margins between children and the gravity (right, center, or left alignment) of each child.

Relative Layout

Finally, the Relative layout lets child views specify their position relative to the parent view or to each other (specified by ID). So you can align two elements by the right border, make one below another, center it in the screen, center it left, and so on. Elements are rendered in the order given, so if the first element is centered in the screen, other elements aligning themselves to that element will be aligned relative to the screen center. Also, because of this ordering, if using XML to specify this layout, the element that you will reference (in order to position other view objects) must be listed in the XML file before you refer to it from the other views via its reference ID.

A Relative layout is the only layout that allows us to overlap views in the way that our application needs it. Due to its need to reference other parts of the layout to place a view on the screen, you must ensure that all `RelativeLayouts` in this book are copied out exactly into your code; otherwise, your entire layout will look very jumbled up, with views going everywhere except where you put them.

Updating main.xml with a RelativeLayout

Inside the `RelativeLayout` is one `SurfaceView` and 18 `TextViews`. The ordering and IDs of the widgets are important because it is a `RelativeLayout`. Here is the layout file:

Listing 3-2. *RelativeLayout*

```xml
<RelativeLayout
    xmlns:android="http://schemas.android.com/apk/res/android"
        android:id="@+id/relativeLayout1"
        android:layout_width="fill_parent"
        android:layout_height="fill_parent" >
        <SurfaceView
                android:id="@+id/cameraPreview"
                android:layout_width="fill_parent"
                android:layout_height="fill_parent" />

        <TextView
            android:id="@+id/xAxisLabel"
            android:layout_width="wrap_content"
            android:layout_height="wrap_content"
            android:layout_alignParentLeft="true"
            android:layout_alignParentTop="true"
            android:layout_marginLeft="18dp"
            android:layout_marginTop="15dp"
            android:text="@string/xAxis" />

        <TextView
            android:id="@+id/yAxisLabel"
            android:layout_width="wrap_content"
            android:layout_height="wrap_content"
            android:layout_alignLeft="@+id/xAxisLabel"
```

```
        android:layout_below="@+id/xAxisLabel"
        android:text="@string/yAxis" />

    <TextView
        android:id="@+id/zAxisLabel"
        android:layout_width="wrap_content"
        android:layout_height="wrap_content"
        android:layout_alignLeft="@+id/yAxisLabel"
        android:layout_below="@+id/yAxisLabel"
        android:text="@string/zAxis" />

    <TextView
        android:id="@+id/headingLabel"
        android:layout_width="wrap_content"
        android:layout_height="wrap_content"
        android:layout_alignLeft="@+id/zAxisLabel"
        android:layout_below="@+id/zAxisLabel"
        android:layout_marginTop="19dp"
        android:text="@string/heading" />

    <TextView
        android:id="@+id/pitchLabel"
        android:layout_width="wrap_content"
        android:layout_height="wrap_content"
        android:layout_alignLeft="@+id/headingLabel"
        android:layout_below="@+id/headingLabel"
        android:text="@string/pitch" />

    <TextView
        android:id="@+id/rollLabel"
        android:layout_width="wrap_content"
        android:layout_height="wrap_content"
        android:layout_alignLeft="@+id/pitchLabel"
        android:layout_below="@+id/pitchLabel"
        android:text="@string/roll" />

    <TextView
        android:id="@+id/latitudeLabel"
        android:layout_width="wrap_content"
        android:layout_height="wrap_content"
        android:layout_alignLeft="@+id/rollLabel"
        android:layout_below="@+id/rollLabel"
        android:layout_marginTop="34dp"
        android:text="@string/latitude" />

    <TextView
        android:id="@+id/longitudeLabel"
        android:layout_width="wrap_content"
        android:layout_height="wrap_content"
        android:layout_alignLeft="@+id/latitudeLabel"
```

```
        android:layout_below="@+id/latitudeLabel"
        android:text="@string/longitude" />

<TextView
    android:id="@+id/altitudeLabel"
    android:layout_width="wrap_content"
    android:layout_height="wrap_content"
    android:layout_alignLeft="@+id/longitudeLabel"
    android:layout_below="@+id/longitudeLabel"
    android:text="@string/altitude" />

<TextView
    android:id="@+id/xAxisValue"
    android:layout_width="wrap_content"
    android:layout_height="wrap_content"
    android:layout_alignBottom="@+id/xAxisLabel"
    android:layout_marginLeft="56dp"
    android:layout_toRightOf="@+id/longitudeLabel"
    android:text="@string/empty" />

<TextView
    android:id="@+id/yAxisValue"
    android:layout_width="wrap_content"
    android:layout_height="wrap_content"
    android:layout_alignBaseline="@+id/yAxisLabel"
    android:layout_alignBottom="@+id/yAxisLabel"
    android:layout_alignLeft="@+id/xAxisValue"
    android:text="@string/empty" />

<TextView
    android:id="@+id/zAxisValue"
    android:layout_width="wrap_content"
    android:layout_height="wrap_content"
    android:layout_above="@+id/headingLabel"
    android:layout_alignLeft="@+id/yAxisValue"
    android:text="@string/empty" />

<TextView
    android:id="@+id/headingValue"
    android:layout_width="wrap_content"
    android:layout_height="wrap_content"
    android:layout_alignBaseline="@+id/headingLabel"
    android:layout_alignBottom="@+id/headingLabel"
    android:layout_alignLeft="@+id/zAxisValue"
    android:text="@string/empty" />

<TextView
    android:id="@+id/pitchValue"
    android:layout_width="wrap_content"
    android:layout_height="wrap_content"
```

```
            android:layout_alignBaseline="@+id/pitchLabel"
            android:layout_alignBottom="@+id/pitchLabel"
            android:layout_alignLeft="@+id/headingValue"
            android:text="@string/empty" />

        <TextView
            android:id="@+id/rollValue"
            android:layout_width="wrap_content"
            android:layout_height="wrap_content"
            android:layout_above="@+id/latitudeLabel"
            android:layout_alignLeft="@+id/pitchValue"
            android:text="@string/empty" />

        <TextView
            android:id="@+id/latitudeValue"
            android:layout_width="wrap_content"
            android:layout_height="wrap_content"
            android:layout_alignBottom="@+id/latitudeLabel"
            android:layout_alignLeft="@+id/rollValue"
            android:text="@string/empty" />

        <TextView
            android:id="@+id/longitudeValue"
            android:layout_width="wrap_content"
            android:layout_height="wrap_content"
            android:layout_alignBaseline="@+id/longitudeLabel"
            android:layout_alignBottom="@+id/longitudeLabel"
            android:layout_alignLeft="@+id/latitudeValue"
            android:text="@string/empty" />

        <TextView
            android:id="@+id/altitudeValue"
            android:layout_width="wrap_content"
            android:layout_height="wrap_content"
            android:layout_alignBaseline="@+id/altitudeLabel"
            android:layout_alignBottom="@+id/altitudeLabel"
            android:layout_alignLeft="@+id/longitudeValue"
            android:text="@string/empty" />
```

```
</RelativeLayout>
```

You can get an idea of what each TextView is for by looking at the IDs. Make sure that you get the layout code exactly right; otherwise, your entire layout will look like it's been pushed through a blender (the kitchen kind, not the I-can-make-cool-graphics-with-this-software kind). We will reference only TextViews that have "Value" in their IDs from the code, as the others are only labels. Those TextViews will be used to display the various sensor values that our app will be receiving.

TextView Variable Declarations

After the layout is in the project, we can start referencing all those TextViews from the code and updating them with the appropriate data. To be able to reference the TextViews from the code, we need to have some variables to store those references. Add the following nine variables to the top of the class (the names are self-explanatory):

Listing 3-3. *Variable Declarations*

```
TextView xAxisValue;
TextView yAxisValue;
TextView zAxisValue;
TextView headingValue;
TextView pitchValue;
TextView rollValue;
TextView altitudeValue;
TextView latitudeValue;
TextView longitudeValue;
```

Updated onCreate

After that, add the following code to the onCreate() method so that each TextView object holds a reference to the corresponding TextView in our XML.

Listing 3-4. *Supplying References to the XML TextViews*

```
xAxisValue = (TextView) findViewById(R.id.xAxisValue);
yAxisValue = (TextView) findViewById(R.id.yAxisValue);
zAxisValue = (TextView) findViewById(R.id.zAxisValue);
headingValue = (TextView) findViewById(R.id.headingValue);
pitchValue = (TextView) findViewById(R.id.pitchValue);
rollValue = (TextView) findViewById(R.id.rollValue);
altitudeValue = (TextView) findViewById(R.id.altitudeValue);
longitudeValue = (TextView) findViewById(R.id.longitudeValue);
latitudeValue = (TextView) findViewById(R.id.latitudeValue);
```

Displaying the Sensors' Data

Now that we have a reference to all the TextViews that we will be updating with our data, we should do just that. To have the ones for the accelerometer and orientation sensors updated with the correct data, modify the SensorEventListener to the following:

Listing 3-5. *Modified SensorEventListener*

```
final SensorEventListener sensorEventListener = new SensorEventListener() {
    public void onSensorChanged(SensorEvent sensorEvent) {
            if (sensorEvent.sensor.getType() == Sensor.TYPE_ORIENTATION)
            {
                    headingAngle = sensorEvent.values[0];
                    pitchAngle = sensorEvent.values[1];
                    rollAngle = sensorEvent.values[2];

                    Log.d(TAG, "Heading: " + String.valueOf(headingAngle));
                    Log.d(TAG, "Pitch: " + String.valueOf(pitchAngle));
                    Log.d(TAG, "Roll: " + String.valueOf(rollAngle));

                    headingValue.setText(String.valueOf(headingAngle));
                    pitchValue.setText(String.valueOf(pitchAngle));
                    rollValue.setText(String.valueOf(rollAngle));
            }

            else if (sensorEvent.sensor.getType() == Sensor.TYPE_ACCELEROMETER)
            {
                    xAxis = sensorEvent.values[0];
                    yAxis = sensorEvent.values[1];
                    zAxis = sensorEvent.values[2];

                    Log.d(TAG, "X Axis: " + String.valueOf(xAxis));
                    Log.d(TAG, "Y Axis: " + String.valueOf(yAxis));
                    Log.d(TAG, "Z Axis: " + String.valueOf(zAxis));

                    xAxisValue.setText(String.valueOf(xAxis));
                    yAxisValue.setText(String.valueOf(yAxis));
                    zAxisValue.setText(String.valueOf(zAxis));
            }
    }

    public void onAccuracyChanged (Sensor senor, int accuracy) {
            //Not used
    }
};
```

Now the sensor data is written both to the log and the TextViews. Because the sensor delay is set to SENSOR_DELAY_NORMAL, the TextViews will update at a moderate sort of rate. If the delay had been set to SENSOR_DELAY_GAME, we would have had the TextViews updating faster than the eye can follow. That would be very taxing on the CPU. Even now, on some of the slower devices, the app might seem to lag.

> **NOTE:** You can get around the lag by shifting the code for updating the TextViews into a TimerTask or Handler.

Now that the data is coming through from the orientation and accelerometer sensors, we should do the same for the GPS. This is more or less a repeat of what we did to the SensorEventListener, except that it is done to the LocationListener:

Listing 3-6. *Modified LocationListener*

```
LocationListener locationListener = new LocationListener() {
    public void onLocationChanged(Location location) {
            latitude = location.getLatitude();
            longitude = location.getLongitude();
            altitude = location.getAltitude();

            Log.d(TAG, "Latitude: " + String.valueOf(latitude));
            Log.d(TAG, "Longitude: " + String.valueOf(longitude));
            Log.d(TAG, "Altitude: " + String.valueOf(altitude));

            latitudeValue.setText(String.valueOf(latitude));
            longitudeValue.setText(String.valueOf(longitude));
            altitudeValue.setText(String.valueOf(altitude));
    }

        public void onProviderDisabled(String arg0) {
                // TODO Auto-generated method stub

        }

        public void onProviderEnabled(String arg0) {
                // TODO Auto-generated method stub

        }

        public void onStatusChanged(String arg0, int arg1, Bundle arg2) {
                // TODO Auto-generated method stub

        }
};
```

Once more, the data is written out to both the log and the TextViews. If you debug the app now, you should see one camera preview and 18 TextViews on the screen, of which 6 should be changing quickly, while 3 change, but more slowly. Because the GPS needs an unbroken view of the sky to work and might take a while to get a fix on your location, the fields related to the GPS can take some time to be updated.

Updated AndroidManifest.xml

Finally, you need to change the AndroidManifest.xml for this project:

Listing 3-7. *Modified AndroidManifest.xml*

```xml
<?xml version="1.0" encoding="utf-8"?>
<manifest xmlns:android="http://schemas.android.com/apk/res/android"
    package="com.paar.ch3widgetoverlay"
    android:versionCode="1"
    android:versionName="1.0" >

    <uses-sdk android:minSdkVersion="7" />

    <application
        android:icon="@drawable/ic_launcher"
        android:label="@string/app_name" >
        <activity
            android:label="@string/app_name"
            android:name=".ProAndroidAR3Activity"
            android:screenOrientation = "landscape"
            android:theme="@android:style/Theme.NoTitleBar.Fullscreen"
            android:configChanges = "keyboardHidden|orientation">
            <intent-filter >
                <action android:name="android.intent.action.MAIN" />

                <category android:name="android.intent.category.LAUNCHER" />
            </intent-filter>
        </activity>
    </application>
<uses-feature android:name="android.hardware.camera" />
<uses-permission android:name="android.permission.CAMERA" />
<uses-permission android:name="android.permission.ACCESS_FINE_LOCATION" />
</manifest>
```

These are the basics of overlaying the standard Android widgets on your camera preview. Make sure that the widget is in place and that all your IDs line up. After that, using the widgets in your app is exactly the same as in any other app. You will call the same methods, use the same functions, and do the same things. This hold true for all the widgets present in the Android framework.

Testing the App

With that, we come to the end of overlaying standard Android widgets onto your camera preview. Figures 3-2 and 3-3 show how the app should look upon completion.

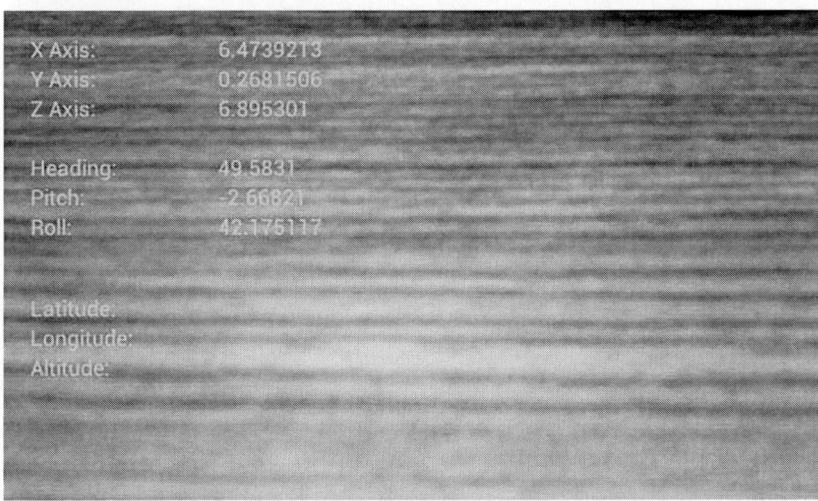

Figure 3-2. *Screenshot of the app with no GPS fix*

Figure 3-3. *Screenshot of the app with a GPS fix*

Next, we will take a look at adding marker recognition to our app.

Markers

Markers are visual cues used by AR apps to know where to put overlays. You select any easily identifiable image (like a black question mark on a white background). One copy of the image is saved in your app, while another is printed out and put somewhere in the real world (or painted if you have a very steady hand). Marker recognition is an ongoing part of research in the field of artificial intelligence.

We will be using an open source Android library called AndAR to help us with the marker recognition. The details of the AndAR project can be found at http://code.google.com/p/andar.

Create a new project. The one on my end has the package name com.paar.ch3marker. The default activity is called Activity.java.

The application will have four markers that it will recognize. For each of the markers, we will supply a .patt file that AndAR can use to recognize the markers. These files describe how the markers look in a way that AndAR can understand.

You can also create and supply your own markers, if you don't like the ones provided or are feeling bored and adventurous. There are a few limitations, though:

- The marker must be square in shape.
- The borders must contrast well.
- The border must be a solid color.

The markers can be black and white or color. Figure 3-4 shows an example of a marker.

Figure 3-4. *Sample Android marker*

You can create your own markers using the online flash tool available at http://flash.tarotaro.org/blog/2009/07/12/mgo2/.

Activity.java

Let's start by editing Activity.java, which is a relatively small class.

Listing 3-8. *Modified Activity.java*

```java
public class Activity extends AndARActivity {

        private ARObject someObject;
        private ARToolkit artoolkit;
        @Override
        public void onCreate(Bundle savedInstanceState) {

                super.onCreate(savedInstanceState);
                CustomRenderer renderer = new CustomRenderer();
                setNonARRenderer(renderer);
                try {
                        artoolkit = getArtoolkit();


                        someObject = new CustomObject1
                        ("test", "marker_at16.patt", 80.0, new double[]{0,0});
                        artoolkit.registerARObject(someObject);

                        someObject = new CustomObject2
                        ("test", "marker_peace16.patt", 80.0, new
double[]{0,0});

                        artoolkit.registerARObject(someObject);

                        someObject = new CustomObject3
                        ("test", "marker_rupee16.patt", 80.0, new
double[]{0,0});

                        artoolkit.registerARObject(someObject);

                        someObject = new CustomObject4
                        ("test", "marker_hand16.patt", 80.0, new double[]{0,0});
                        artoolkit.registerARObject(someObject);

                } catch (AndARException ex){
                        System.out.println("");
                }
                startPreview();
        }

        public void uncaughtException(Thread thread, Throwable ex) {
                Log.e("AndAR EXCEPTION", ex.getMessage());
                finish();
        }
}
```

In the onCreate() method, we first get the savedInstanceState. After that, we create a reference to the CustomRenderer class, which we will create a few pages down the line. We then set the non-AR renderer. Now comes the main part of the class. We register all four of the markers with AndAR and their related objects. CustomObject1-4 are classes that define what is to be augmented over each marker. Finally, the uncaughtException() method is used to cleanly exit the app if a fatal exception happens.

CustomObject Overlays

The custom objects are basically 3D boxes in 4 different colors. They rotate and so on depending on the view of the marker. Figure 3-5 shows one of the cubes being displayed.

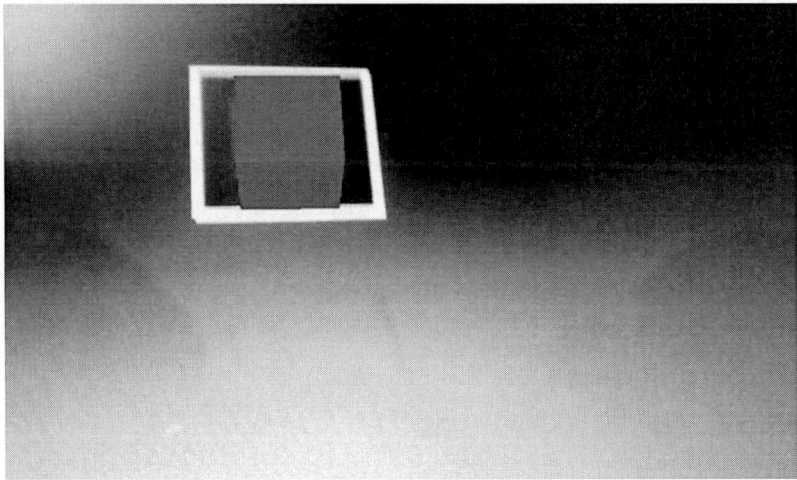

Figure 3-5. *One of the four custom object overlays*

First up is CustomObject1.java.

Listing 3-9. *CustomObject1*

```java
public class CustomObject1 extends ARObject {

        public CustomObject1(String name, String patternName,
                    double markerWidth, double[] markerCenter) {
            super(name, patternName, markerWidth, markerCenter);
            float   mat_ambientf[]    = {0f, 1.0f, 0f, 1.0f};
            float   mat_flashf[]      = {0f, 1.0f, 0f, 1.0f};
            float   mat_diffusef[]    = {0f, 1.0f, 0f, 1.0f};
            float   mat_flash_shinyf[] = {50.0f};

            mat_ambient = GraphicsUtil.makeFloatBuffer(mat_ambientf);
```

```java
                mat_flash = GraphicsUtil.makeFloatBuffer(mat_flashf);
                mat_flash_shiny =
GraphicsUtil.makeFloatBuffer(mat_flash_shinyf);
                mat_diffuse = GraphicsUtil.makeFloatBuffer(mat_diffusef);

        }
        public CustomObject1(String name, String patternName,
                        double markerWidth, double[] markerCenter, float[]
customColor) {
                super(name, patternName, markerWidth, markerCenter);
                float   mat_flash_shinyf[] = {50.0f};

                mat_ambient = GraphicsUtil.makeFloatBuffer(customColor);
                mat_flash = GraphicsUtil.makeFloatBuffer(customColor);
                mat_flash_shiny =
GraphicsUtil.makeFloatBuffer(mat_flash_shinyf);
                mat_diffuse = GraphicsUtil.makeFloatBuffer(customColor);

        }

        private SimpleBox box = new SimpleBox();
        private FloatBuffer mat_flash;
        private FloatBuffer mat_ambient;
        private FloatBuffer mat_flash_shiny;
        private FloatBuffer mat_diffuse;


        @Override
        public final void draw(GL10 gl) {
                super.draw(gl);

                gl.glMaterialfv(GL10.GL_FRONT_AND_BACK,
GL10.GL_SPECULAR,mat_flash);
                gl.glMaterialfv(GL10.GL_FRONT_AND_BACK, GL10.GL_SHININESS,
mat_flash_shiny);
                gl.glMaterialfv(GL10.GL_FRONT_AND_BACK, GL10.GL_DIFFUSE,
mat_diffuse);
                gl.glMaterialfv(GL10.GL_FRONT_AND_BACK, GL10.GL_AMBIENT,
mat_ambient);

            gl.glColor4f(0, 1.0f, 0, 1.0f);
            gl.glTranslatef( 0.0f, 0.0f, 12.5f );

            box.draw(gl);
        }
        @Override
        public void init(GL10 gl) {

        }
}
```

We start by setting the various lightings for the box and creating FloatBuffers out of them in the constructors. We then get a simple box directly from AndAR, so that we are spared the trouble of making it. In the draw() method, we draw everything. In this case, everything done in the draw() method will be done directly on the marker.

The other three CustomObject classes are exactly the same as CustomObject1, except we change the colors a bit. Following are the changes you need to make for CustomObject2.

Listing 3-10. *CustomObject2*

```
        public CustomObject2(String name, String patternName,
                    double markerWidth, double[] markerCenter) {
            super(name, patternName, markerWidth, markerCenter);
            float    mat_ambientf[]    = {1.0f, 0f, 0f, 1.0f};
            float    mat_flashf[]      = {1.0f, 0f, 0f, 1.0f};
            float    mat_diffusef[]    = {1.0f, 0f, 0f, 1.0f};
            float    mat_flash_shinyf[] = {50.0f};

            mat_ambient = GraphicsUtil.makeFloatBuffer(mat_ambientf);
            mat_flash = GraphicsUtil.makeFloatBuffer(mat_flashf);
            mat_flash_shiny =
GraphicsUtil.makeFloatBuffer(mat_flash_shinyf);
            mat_diffuse = GraphicsUtil.makeFloatBuffer(mat_diffusef);

        }

//Same code everywhere else, except the draw() method

        @Override
        public final void draw(GL10 gl) {
            super.draw(gl);

            gl.glMaterialfv(GL10.GL_FRONT_AND_BACK,
GL10.GL_SPECULAR,mat_flash);
            gl.glMaterialfv(GL10.GL_FRONT_AND_BACK, GL10.GL_SHININESS,
mat_flash_shiny);
            gl.glMaterialfv(GL10.GL_FRONT_AND_BACK, GL10.GL_DIFFUSE,
mat_diffuse);
            gl.glMaterialfv(GL10.GL_FRONT_AND_BACK, GL10.GL_AMBIENT,
mat_ambient);

        gl.glColor4f(1.0f, 0, 0, 1.0f);
            gl.glTranslatef( 0.0f, 0.0f, 12.5f );

            box.draw(gl);
        }
```

Following are the changes for CustomObject3.

Listing 3-11. *CustomObject3*

```
public CustomObject3(String name, String patternName,
                double markerWidth, double[] markerCenter) {
        super(name, patternName, markerWidth, markerCenter);
        float    mat_ambientf[]    = {0f, 0f, 1.0f, 1.0f};
        float    mat_flashf[]      = {0f, 0f, 1.0f, 1.0f};
        float    mat_diffusef[]    = {0f, 0f, 1.0f, 1.0f};
        float    mat_flash_shinyf[] = {50.0f};

        mat_ambient = GraphicsUtil.makeFloatBuffer(mat_ambientf);
        mat_flash = GraphicsUtil.makeFloatBuffer(mat_flashf);
        mat_flash_shiny =
GraphicsUtil.makeFloatBuffer(mat_flash_shinyf);
        mat_diffuse = GraphicsUtil.makeFloatBuffer(mat_diffusef);

    }

//Same code everywhere else, except the draw() method

    @Override
    public final void draw(GL10 gl) {
        super.draw(gl);

        gl.glMaterialfv(GL10.GL_FRONT_AND_BACK,
GL10.GL_SPECULAR,mat_flash);
        gl.glMaterialfv(GL10.GL_FRONT_AND_BACK, GL10.GL_SHININESS,
mat_flash_shiny);
        gl.glMaterialfv(GL10.GL_FRONT_AND_BACK, GL10.GL_DIFFUSE,
mat_diffuse);
        gl.glMaterialfv(GL10.GL_FRONT_AND_BACK, GL10.GL_AMBIENT,
mat_ambient);

    gl.glColor4f(0f, 0, 1.0, 1.0f);
    gl.glTranslatef( 0.0f, 0.0f, 12.5f );

        box.draw(gl);
    }
```

And finally, the changes for CustomObject4 follow.

Listing 3-12. *CustomObject4*

```
public CustomObject4(String name, String patternName,
              double markerWidth, double[] markerCenter) {
      super(name, patternName, markerWidth, markerCenter);
      float    mat_ambientf[]    = {1.0f, 0f, 1.0f, 1.0f};
      float    mat_flashf[]      = {1.0f, 0f, 1.0f, 1.0f};
      float    mat_diffusef[]    = {1.0f, 0f, 1.0f, 1.0f};
      float    mat_flash_shinyf[] = {50.0f};

      mat_ambient = GraphicsUtil.makeFloatBuffer(mat_ambientf);
      mat_flash = GraphicsUtil.makeFloatBuffer(mat_flashf);
      mat_flash_shiny =
GraphicsUtil.makeFloatBuffer(mat_flash_shinyf);
      mat_diffuse = GraphicsUtil.makeFloatBuffer(mat_diffusef);

}

//Same code everywhere else, except the draw() method

      @Override
      public final void draw(GL10 gl) {
            super.draw(gl);

            gl.glMaterialfv(GL10.GL_FRONT_AND_BACK,
GL10.GL_SPECULAR,mat_flash);
                  gl.glMaterialfv(GL10.GL_FRONT_AND_BACK, GL10.GL_SHININESS,
mat_flash_shiny);
                  gl.glMaterialfv(GL10.GL_FRONT_AND_BACK, GL10.GL_DIFFUSE,
mat_diffuse);
                  gl.glMaterialfv(GL10.GL_FRONT_AND_BACK, GL10.GL_AMBIENT,
mat_ambient);

      gl.glColor4f(1.0f, 0, 1.0, 1.0f);
      gl.glTranslatef( 0.0f, 0.0f, 12.5f );

      box.draw(gl);
}
```

CustomRenderer

Now we have only CustomRenderer.java to deal with. This class allows us to do any non-AR stuff as well as set up the OpenGL environment.

Listing 3-13. *CustomRenderer*

```
public class CustomRenderer implements OpenGLRenderer {
```

```java
        private float[] ambientlight1 = {.3f, .3f, .3f, 1f};
        private float[] diffuselight1 = {.7f, .7f, .7f, 1f};
        private float[] specularlight1 = {0.6f, 0.6f, 0.6f, 1f};
        private float[] lightposition1 = {20.0f,-40.0f,100.0f,1f};

        private FloatBuffer lightPositionBuffer1 =
GraphicsUtil.makeFloatBuffer(lightposition1);
        private FloatBuffer specularLightBuffer1 =
GraphicsUtil.makeFloatBuffer(specularlight1);
        private FloatBuffer diffuseLightBuffer1 =
GraphicsUtil.makeFloatBuffer(diffuselight1);
        private FloatBuffer ambientLightBuffer1 =
GraphicsUtil.makeFloatBuffer(ambientlight1);


        public final void draw(GL10 gl) {
        }


        public final void setupEnv(GL10 gl) {
                gl.glEnable(GL10.GL_LIGHTING);
                gl.glLightfv(GL10.GL_LIGHT1, GL10.GL_AMBIENT,
ambientLightBuffer1);
                gl.glLightfv(GL10.GL_LIGHT1, GL10.GL_DIFFUSE,
diffuseLightBuffer1);
                gl.glLightfv(GL10.GL_LIGHT1, GL10.GL_SPECULAR,
specularLightBuffer1);
                gl.glLightfv(GL10.GL_LIGHT1, GL10.GL_POSITION,
lightPositionBuffer1);
                gl.glEnable(GL10.GL_LIGHT1);
                gl.glDisableClientState(GL10.GL_TEXTURE_COORD_ARRAY);
                gl.glDisable(GL10.GL_TEXTURE_2D);
                initGL(gl);
        }

        public final void initGL(GL10 gl) {
                gl.glDisable(GL10.GL_COLOR_MATERIAL);
                gl.glEnable(GL10.GL_CULL_FACE);
                gl.glShadeModel(GL10.GL_SMOOTH);
                gl.glDisable(GL10.GL_COLOR_MATERIAL);
                gl.glEnable(GL10.GL_LIGHTING);
                gl.glEnable(GL10.GL_CULL_FACE);
                gl.glEnable(GL10.GL_DEPTH_TEST);
                gl.glEnable(GL10.GL_NORMALIZE);
        }
}
```

In the variable declarations, we specify the different types of lighting and create
FloatBuffers from them. The setupEnv() is called before we display any of the

boxes. It sets up the lighting and other OpenGL-specific stuff. The `initGL()` method is called once when the Surface is created.

AndroidManifest

Finally, the `AndroidManifest.xml` needs to be updated.

Listing 3-14. *Updated AndroidManifest.xml*

```xml
<?xml version="1.0" encoding="utf-8"?>
<manifest xmlns:android="http://schemas.android.com/apk/res/android"
    package="com.paar.ch3marker"
    android:versionCode="1"
    android:versionName="1.0" >

    <uses-sdk android:minSdkVersion="7" />

    <application
        android:icon="@drawable/ic_launcher"
        android:label="@string/app_name" >
        <activity
            android:label="@string/app_name"
            android:name=".Activity"
            android:clearTaskOnLaunch="true"
            android:screenOrientation="landscape"
            android:noHistory="true">
            <intent-filter >
                <action android:name="android.intent.action.MAIN" />

                <category android:name="android.intent.category.LAUNCHER" />
            </intent-filter>
        </activity>
    </application>
    <uses-permission android:name="android.permission.CAMERA"/>
    <uses-permission android:name="android.permission.WRITE_EXTERNAL_STORAGE"/>
    <uses-feature android:name="android.hardware.camera" />
    <uses-feature android:name="android.hardware.camera.autofocus" />
</manifest>
```

This brings us to the end of the coding for this app. If you have not downloaded the source code for this chapter yet, please do so and take the .patt files and put them in your projects /assets directory. Along with the source, you will find a folder called "Markers," which contains the markers used in this app and further on in the book. You can print them for your use.

Summary

In this chapter, we learned how to overlay standard Android widgets in our app and how to use markers to make our augmented reality apps more interactive. about the chapter also discussed AndAR, an opensource AR toolkit available for Android that allows us to implement a lot of AR features painlessly and quickly.

The next chapter discusses Artificial Horizon, a feature of AR that is central to any military or navigational app.

Artificial Horizons

An *artificial horizon* is defined by the *Oxford English Dictionary* as "a gyroscopic instrument or a fluid surface, typically one of mercury, used to provide the pilot of an aircraft with a horizontal reference plane for navigational measurement when the natural horizon is obscured." Artificial horizons have been used for navigational purposes long before augmented reality (AR) came into existence, and navigation still remains their primary use. They came into prominence when heads up displays came into mass use in planes, especially with military aircraft.

Artificial horizons are basically a horizontal reference line for navigators to use if the natural horizon is obscured. For all of us people who are obsessed with using AR in our apps, this is an important feature to be familiar with. It can be very useful when making navigational apps and even games.

It may be difficult to grasp the concept of a horizon that actually doesn't exist, but must be used to make all sorts of calculations that could affect the user in several ways. To get around this problem, we'll make a small sample app that doesn't implement AR, but shows you what an artificial horizon is and how it is implemented. After that, we'll make an AR app to use artificial horizons.

A Non-AR Demo App

In this app, we will have a compass with an artificial horizon indicator inside it. I will only be providing an explanation for the artificial horizon code, as the rest of it is not part of the book's subject.

The XML

Let's get the little XML files out of the way first. We will need a /res/layout/main.xml, a /res/values/strings.xml and a /res/values/colors.xml.

Let's start with the main.xml file:

Listing 4-1. *main.xml*

```
<?xml version="1.0" encoding="utf-8"?>
<LinearLayout xmlns:android="http://schemas.android.com/apk/res/android"
  android:orientation="vertical"
  android:layout_width="fill_parent"
  android:layout_height="fill_parent">
  <com.paar.ch4nonardemo.HorizonView
    android:id="@+id/horizonView"
    android:layout_width="fill_parent"
    android:layout_height="fill_parent"
  />
</LinearLayout>
```

Nothing special here. We simply set the view of our Activity to a custom view, which we'll get around to making in a few minutes.

Let's take a look at strings.xml now:

Listing 4-2. *strings.xml*

```
<?xml version="1.0" encoding="utf-8"?>
<resources>
  <string name="app_name">Pro Android AR 4 Non AR Demo</string>
  <string name="cardinal_north">N</string>
  <string name="cardinal_east">E</string>
  <string name="cardinal_south">S</string>
  <string name="cardinal_west">W</string>
</resources>
```

This file declared the string resources for four cardinals: N corresponds to North, E to East, S to South, and W to West.

Let's move on to the colours.xml:

Listing 4-3. *colours.xml*

```
<?xml version="1.0" encoding="utf-8"?>
<resources>
  <color name="text_color">#FFFF</color>
  <color name="background_color">#F000</color>
  <color name="marker_color">#FFFF</color>
```

```xml
<color name="shadow_color">#7AAA</color>

<color name="outer_border">#FF444444</color>
<color name="inner_border_one">#FF323232</color>
<color name="inner_border_two">#FF414141</color>
<color name="inner_border">#FFFFFFFF</color>

<color name="horizon_sky_from">#FFA52A2A</color>
<color name="horizon_sky_to">#FFFFC125</color>
<color name="horizon_ground_from">#FF5F9EA0</color>
<color name="horizon_ground_to">#FF00008B</color>
</resources>
```

All of the colors are specified in either ARGB or AARRGGBB. They are used to add a bit of visual appeal to our little demo app. There is a slight difference in the "to" and "from" colors so that we can have a gradient in our final demo. The sky colors are shades of blue, and the ground colors are shades of orange.

The Java

Now we will create that custom view we mentioned in the main.xml.

Creating the View

Create a Java file called HorizonView.java in your main package (com.paar.ch4nonardemo on my end). Add the following global variables to it:

Listing 4-4. *HorizonView.java Global Variables*

```java
public class HorizonView extends View {
  private enum CompassDirection { N, NNE, NE, ENE,
                                  E, ESE, SE, SSE,
                                  S, SSW, SW, WSW,
                                  W, WNW, NW, NNW }

  int[] borderGradientColors;
  float[] borderGradientPositions;

  int[] glassGradientColors;
  float[] glassGradientPositions;

  int skyHorizonColorFrom;
  int skyHorizonColorTo;
  int groundHorizonColorFrom;
  int groundHorizonColorTo;
```

```
private Paint markerPaint;
private Paint textPaint;
private Paint circlePaint;
private int textHeight;

private float bearing;
float pitch = 0;
float roll = 0;
```

The names of the variables are reasonably good descriptions of their task. CompassDirections provides the strings we will use to create our 16-point compass. The ones with *Gradient*, *Color*, and *Paint* in their names are used in drawing the View, as is textHeight.

Getting and Setting the Bearing, Pitch, and Roll

Now add the following methods to the class:

Listing 4-5. *Bearing, Pitch, and Roll Methods*

```
public void setBearing(float _bearing) {
  bearing = _bearing;
}
public float getBearing() {
  return bearing;
}

public float getPitch() {
  return pitch;
}
public void setPitch(float pitch) {
  this.pitch = pitch;
}

public float getRoll() {
  return roll;
}
public void setRoll(float roll) {
  this.roll = roll;
}
```

These methods let us get and set the bearing, pitch and roll, which is later normalized and used to draw our view.

Calling and Initializing the Compass

Next, add the following three constructors to the class:

Listing 4-6. *HorizonView Constructors*

```
public HorizonView(Context context) {
  super(context);
  initCompassView();
}

public HorizonView(Context context, AttributeSet attrs) {
  super(context, attrs);
  initCompassView();
}

public HorizonView(Context context,
                   AttributeSet ats,
                   int defaultStyle) {
  super(context, ats, defaultStyle);
  initCompassView();
}
```

All three of the constructors end up calling initCompassView(), which does the main work in this class.

Speaking of initCompassView(), here's its code:

Listing 4-7. *initCompassView()*

```
protected void initCompassView() {
  setFocusable(true);
  Resources r = this.getResources();

  circlePaint = new Paint(Paint.ANTI_ALIAS_FLAG);
  circlePaint.setColor(R.color.background_color);
  circlePaint.setStrokeWidth(1);
  circlePaint.setStyle(Paint.Style.STROKE);

  textPaint = new Paint(Paint.ANTI_ALIAS_FLAG);
  textPaint.setColor(r.getColor(R.color.text_color));
  textPaint.setFakeBoldText(true);
  textPaint.setSubpixelText(true);
  textPaint.setTextAlign(Align.LEFT);

  textHeight = (int)textPaint.measureText("yY");

  markerPaint = new Paint(Paint.ANTI_ALIAS_FLAG);
  markerPaint.setColor(r.getColor(R.color.marker_color));
  markerPaint.setAlpha(200);
  markerPaint.setStrokeWidth(1);
  markerPaint.setStyle(Paint.Style.STROKE);
  markerPaint.setShadowLayer(2, 1, 1, r.getColor(R.color.shadow_color));
```

```
borderGradientColors = new int[4];
borderGradientPositions = new float[4];

borderGradientColors[3] = r.getColor(R.color.outer_border);
borderGradientColors[2] = r.getColor(R.color.inner_border_one);
borderGradientColors[1] = r.getColor(R.color.inner_border_two);
borderGradientColors[0] = r.getColor(R.color.inner_border);
borderGradientPositions[3] = 0.0f;
borderGradientPositions[2] = 1-0.03f;
borderGradientPositions[1] = 1-0.06f;
borderGradientPositions[0] = 1.0f;

glassGradientColors = new int[5];
glassGradientPositions = new float[5];

int glassColor = 245;
glassGradientColors[4] = Color.argb(65, glassColor,
                                    glassColor, glassColor);
glassGradientColors[3] = Color.argb(100, glassColor,
                                    glassColor, glassColor);
glassGradientColors[2] = Color.argb(50, glassColor,
                                    glassColor, glassColor);
glassGradientColors[1] = Color.argb(0, glassColor,
                                    glassColor, glassColor);
glassGradientColors[0] = Color.argb(0, glassColor,
                                    glassColor, glassColor);
glassGradientPositions[4] = 1-0.0f;
glassGradientPositions[3] = 1-0.06f;
glassGradientPositions[2] = 1-0.10f;
glassGradientPositions[1] = 1-0.20f;
glassGradientPositions[0] = 1-1.0f;

skyHorizonColorFrom = r.getColor(R.color.horizon_sky_from);
skyHorizonColorTo = r.getColor(R.color.horizon_sky_to);

groundHorizonColorFrom = r.getColor(R.color.horizon_ground_from);
groundHorizonColorTo = r.getColor(R.color.horizon_ground_to);
}
```

In this method, we work with our colors to form proper gradients. We also assign values to some of the variables we declared in the beginning.

Calculating the Size of the Compass

Now add the following two methods to the class:

Listing 4-8. *onMeasure() and Measure()*

```
@Override
protected void onMeasure(int widthMeasureSpec, int heightMeasureSpec) {

    int measuredWidth = measure(widthMeasureSpec);
    int measuredHeight = measure(heightMeasureSpec);

    int d = Math.min(measuredWidth, measuredHeight);

    setMeasuredDimension(d, d);
}

private int measure(int measureSpec) {
    int result = 0;

    int specMode = MeasureSpec.getMode(measureSpec);
    int specSize = MeasureSpec.getSize(measureSpec);

    if (specMode == MeasureSpec.UNSPECIFIED) {
        result = 200;
    } else {
        result = specSize;
    }
    return result;
}
```

These two methods allow us to measure the screen and let us decide how big we want our compass to be.

Drawing the Compass

Now finally add the onDraw() method to the class:

Listing 4-9. *onDraw()*

```
    @Override
    protected void onDraw(Canvas canvas) {
        float ringWidth = textHeight + 4;
        int height = getMeasuredHeight();
        int width =getMeasuredWidth();

        int px = width/2;
        int py = height/2;
        Point center = new Point(px, py);

        int radius = Math.min(px, py)-2;
```

```
        RectF boundingBox = new RectF(center.x - radius,
                                      center.y - radius,
                                      center.x + radius,
                                      center.y + radius);

        RectF innerBoundingBox = new RectF(center.x - radius + ringWidth,
                                           center.y - radius + ringWidth,
                                           center.x + radius - ringWidth,
                                           center.y + radius - ringWidth);

        float innerRadius = innerBoundingBox.height()/2;
        RadialGradient borderGradient = new RadialGradient(px, py, radius,
    borderGradientColors, borderGradientPositions, TileMode.CLAMP);

        Paint pgb = new Paint();
        pgb.setShader(borderGradient);

        Path outerRingPath = new Path();
        outerRingPath.addOval(boundingBox, Direction.CW);

        canvas.drawPath(outerRingPath, pgb);
        LinearGradient skyShader = new LinearGradient(center.x,
    innerBoundingBox.top, center.x, innerBoundingBox.bottom,
     skyHorizonColorFrom, skyHorizonColorTo, TileMode.CLAMP);

        Paint skyPaint = new Paint();
        skyPaint.setShader(skyShader);

        LinearGradient groundShader = new LinearGradient(center.x,
    innerBoundingBox.top, center.x, innerBoundingBox.bottom,
     groundHorizonColorFrom, groundHorizonColorTo, TileMode.CLAMP);

        Paint groundPaint = new Paint();
        groundPaint.setShader(groundShader);
        float tiltDegree = pitch;
        while (tiltDegree > 90 || tiltDegree < -90) {
          if (tiltDegree > 90) tiltDegree = -90 + (tiltDegree - 90);
            if (tiltDegree < -90) tiltDegree = 90 - (tiltDegree + 90);
        }

        float rollDegree = roll;
        while (rollDegree > 180 || rollDegree < -180) {
          if (rollDegree > 180) rollDegree = -180 + (rollDegree - 180);
            if (rollDegree < -180) rollDegree = 180 - (rollDegree + 180);
        }
        Path skyPath = new Path();
        skyPath.addArc(innerBoundingBox, -tiltDegree, (180 + (2 * tiltDegree)));
        canvas.rotate(-rollDegree, px, py);
        canvas.drawOval(innerBoundingBox, groundPaint);
        canvas.drawPath(skyPath, skyPaint);
```

```java
canvas.drawPath(skyPath, markerPaint);
int markWidth = radius / 3;
int startX = center.x - markWidth;
int endX = center.x + markWidth;

double h = innerRadius*Math.cos(Math.toRadians(90-tiltDegree));
double justTiltY = center.y - h;

float pxPerDegree = (innerBoundingBox.height()/2)/45f;
for (int i = 90; i >= -90; i -= 10) {
  double ypos = justTiltY + i*pxPerDegree;

  if ((ypos < (innerBoundingBox.top + textHeight)) ||
      (ypos > innerBoundingBox.bottom - textHeight))
    continue;

  canvas.drawLine(startX, (float)ypos,
                  endX, (float)ypos,
                  markerPaint);
  int displayPos = (int)(tiltDegree - i);
  String displayString = String.valueOf(displayPos);
  float stringSizeWidth = textPaint.measureText(displayString);
  canvas.drawText(displayString,
                  (int)(center.x-stringSizeWidth/2),
                  (int)(ypos)+1,
                  textPaint);
}
markerPaint.setStrokeWidth(2);
canvas.drawLine(center.x - radius / 2,
                (float)justTiltY,
                center.x + radius / 2,
                (float)justTiltY,
                markerPaint);
markerPaint.setStrokeWidth(1);

Path rollArrow = new Path();
rollArrow.moveTo(center.x - 3, (int)innerBoundingBox.top + 14);
rollArrow.lineTo(center.x, (int)innerBoundingBox.top + 10);
rollArrow.moveTo(center.x + 3, innerBoundingBox.top + 14);
rollArrow.lineTo(center.x, innerBoundingBox.top + 10);
canvas.drawPath(rollArrow, markerPaint);
String rollText = String.valueOf(rollDegree);
double rollTextWidth = textPaint.measureText(rollText);
canvas.drawText(rollText,
                (float)(center.x - rollTextWidth / 2),
                innerBoundingBox.top + textHeight + 2,
                textPaint);
canvas.restore();
```

```
canvas.save();
canvas.rotate(180, center.x, center.y);
for (int i = -180; i < 180; i += 10) {
  if (i % 30 == 0) {
    String rollString = String.valueOf(i*-1);
    float rollStringWidth = textPaint.measureText(rollString);
    PointF rollStringCenter = new PointF(center.x-rollStringWidth /2,
                                innerBoundingBox.top+1+textHeight);
    canvas.drawText(rollString,
                    rollStringCenter.x, rollStringCenter.y,
                    textPaint);
  }
  else {
    canvas.drawLine(center.x, (int)innerBoundingBox.top,
                    center.x, (int)innerBoundingBox.top + 5,
                    markerPaint);
  }

  canvas.rotate(10, center.x, center.y);
}
canvas.restore();
canvas.save();
canvas.rotate(-1*(bearing), px, py);

double increment = 22.5;

for (double i = 0; i < 360; i += increment) {
  CompassDirection cd = CompassDirection.values()
                        [(int)(i /  22.5)];
  String headString = cd.toString();

  float headStringWidth = textPaint.measureText(headString);
  PointF headStringCenter = new PointF(center.x - headStringWidth / 2,
                                boundingBox.top + 1 + textHeight);

  if (i % increment == 0)
    canvas.drawText(headString,
                    headStringCenter.x, headStringCenter.y,
                    textPaint);
  else
    canvas.drawLine(center.x, (int)boundingBox.top,
                    center.x, (int)boundingBox.top + 3,
                    markerPaint);

  canvas.rotate((int)increment, center.x, center.y);
}
canvas.restore();
RadialGradient glassShader = new RadialGradient(px, py, (int)innerRadius,
glassGradientColors, glassGradientPositions, TileMode.CLAMP);
Paint glassPaint = new Paint();
```

```
    glassPaint.setShader(glassShader);

    canvas.drawOval(innerBoundingBox, glassPaint);
    canvas.drawOval(boundingBox, circlePaint);

    circlePaint.setStrokeWidth(2);
    canvas.drawOval(innerBoundingBox, circlePaint);

    canvas.restore();
  }
}
```

The onDraw() method draws the outer circles, clamps the pitch and roll values, colors the circles, takes care of adding the compass directions to the circle, rotates it when required, and draws the actual artificial horizon lines and moves them around.

In a nutshell, we create a circle with N, NE, and so on markers at 30-degree intervals. Inside the compass, we have an altimeter-like view that gives the position of the horizon relative to the way the phone is held.

Updating the Activity

We need to update this entire display from our main activity. For that to happen, we need to update AHActivity.java:

Listing 4-10. *AHActivity.java*

```
public class AHActivity extends Activity {
        float[] aValues = new float[3];
        float[] mValues = new float[3];
        HorizonView horizonView;
        SensorManager sensorManager;

        @Override
        public void onCreate(Bundle icicle) {
          super.onCreate(icicle);
          setContentView(R.layout.main);

          horizonView = (HorizonView)this.findViewById(R.id.horizonView);
          sensorManager =
(SensorManager)getSystemService(Context.SENSOR_SERVICE);
          updateOrientation(new float[] {0, 0, 0});
        }

    private void updateOrientation(float[] values) {
      if (horizonView!= null) {
      horizonView.setBearing(values[0]);
```

```java
        horizonView.setPitch(values[1]);
          horizonView.setRoll(-values[2]);
          horizonView.invalidate();
        }
      }

    private float[] calculateOrientation() {
      float[] values = new float[3];
      float[] R = new float[9];
      float[] outR = new float[9];

      SensorManager.getRotationMatrix(R, null, aValues, mValues);
      SensorManager.remapCoordinateSystem(R,
                                    SensorManager.AXIS_X,
                                    SensorManager.AXIS_Z,
                                    outR);

      SensorManager.getOrientation(outR, values);

      values[0] = (float) Math.toDegrees(values[0]);
      values[1] = (float) Math.toDegrees(values[1]);
      values[2] = (float) Math.toDegrees(values[2]);

      return values;
    }

    private final SensorEventListener sensorEventListener = new
SensorEventListener() {
      public void onSensorChanged(SensorEvent event) {
        if (event.sensor.getType() == Sensor.TYPE_ACCELEROMETER)
          aValues = event.values;
        if (event.sensor.getType() == Sensor.TYPE_MAGNETIC_FIELD)
          mValues = event.values;

        updateOrientation(calculateOrientation());
      }

      public void onAccuracyChanged(Sensor sensor, int accuracy) {}
      };

      @Override
      protected void onResume() {
        super.onResume();

        Sensor accelerometer =
sensorManager.getDefaultSensor(Sensor.TYPE_ACCELEROMETER);
        Sensor magField =
sensorManager.getDefaultSensor(Sensor.TYPE_MAGNETIC_FIELD);
```

```
        sensorManager.registerListener(sensorEventListener,
                                       accelerometer,
                                       SensorManager.SENSOR_DELAY_FASTEST);
        sensorManager.registerListener(sensorEventListener,
                                       magField,
                                       SensorManager.SENSOR_DELAY_FASTEST);
    }

    @Override
    protected void onStop() {
      sensorManager.unregisterListener(sensorEventListener);
      super.onStop();
    }
}
```

This is where that actual work happens. In the onCreate() method, we set the view to main.xml, get a reference to the horizonView, register a SensorEventListener and update the orientation to an ideal situation. The updateOrientation() method is responsible for passing new values to our view so that it can change appropriately. calculateOrientation() uses some of the provided methods from the SDK to accurately calculate the orientation from the raw values provided by the sensors. These methods provided by Android take care of a lot of complex math for us. You should be able to understand the SensorEventListener, onResume(), and onStop() easily enough. They do the same job they did in the previous chapters.

The Android Manifest

Finally, you should update your AndroidManifest to the following:

Listing 4-11. *AndroidManifest.xml*

```
<?xml version="1.0" encoding="utf-8"?>
<manifest xmlns:android="http://schemas.android.com/apk/res/android"
    package="com.paar.ch4nonardemo"
    android:versionCode="1"
    android:versionName="1.0" >

    <uses-sdk android:minSdkVersion="7" />

    <application
        android:icon="@drawable/ic_launcher"
        android:label="@string/app_name" >
        <activity
            android:label="@string/app_name"
            android:name=".AHActivity"
            android:screenOrientation="portrait"
```

```
        android:theme="@android:style/Theme.NoTitleBar.Fullscreen" >
        <intent-filter >
            <action android:name="android.intent.action.MAIN" />

            <category android:name="android.intent.category.LAUNCHER" />
        </intent-filter>
    </activity>
</application>

</manifest>
```

Testing the Completed App

If you run the app now, you will get a very good idea of what an artificial horizon truly is. Figures 4-1 and 4-2 give you an idea about what the finished app looks like.

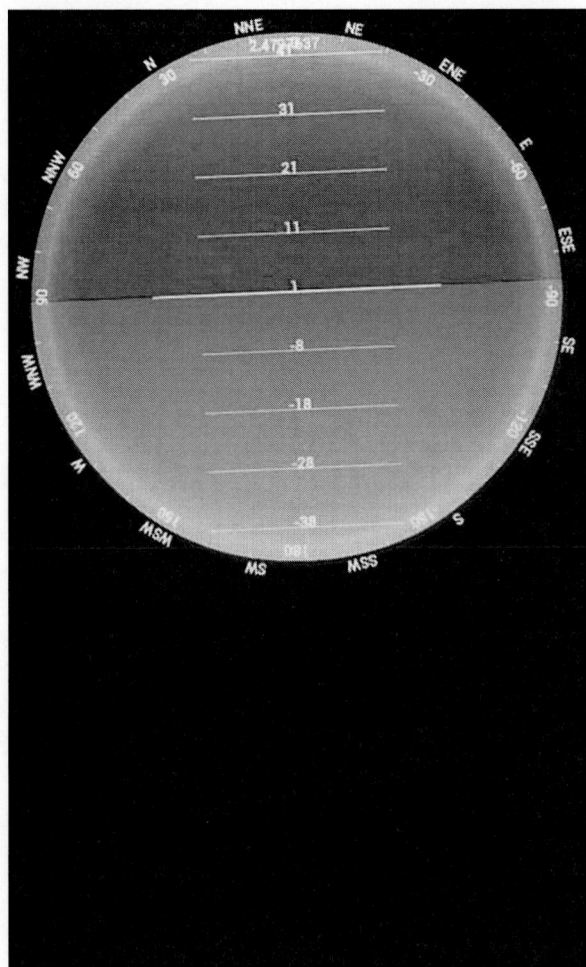

Figure 4-1. *The app when device is upright*

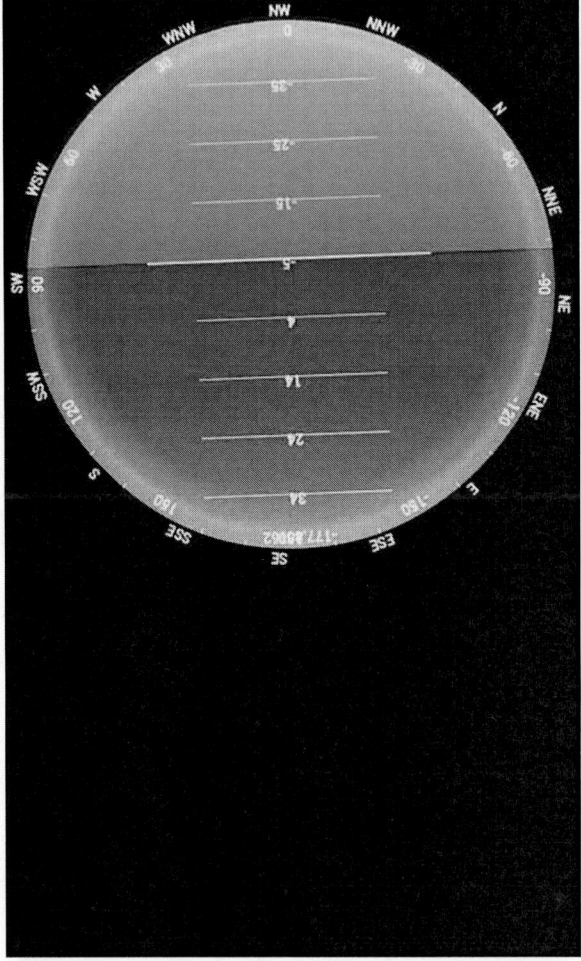

Figure 4-2. *The app when the device is upside down*

An AR Demo App

After going through and running the previous example, you should understand the concept of artificial horizons pretty well now. We will now be designing an app that does the following:

■ Displays the live camera preview

- Displays a semitransparent version of `HorizonView` over the camera preview, colored like the movie versions in the aircrafts

- Tells you what your altitude will be in 5 minutes, assuming you continue at the current inclination

There are a few things to keep in mind before we start on the coding. Seeing as it is almost impossible for the user to hold the device perfectly still, the inclination will keep changing, which will cause the altitude in 5 minutes to change as well. To get around this, we will add a button that allows the user to update the altitude whenever they want.

> **NOTE:** On some devices, this app moves the artificial horizon in a clockwise and anticlockwise direction, instead of moving it up and down as in the non-AR demo. All the values are correct, except the display has a problem that can be fixed by running the app in portrait mode.

Setting Up the Project

To begin, create a new project. The one used as the example has the package name com.paar.ch4ardemo, and targets Android 2.1. As usual, you can change the name to whatever you like; just make sure to update any references in the example code as well. The screenshot in Figure 4-3 shows the project details.

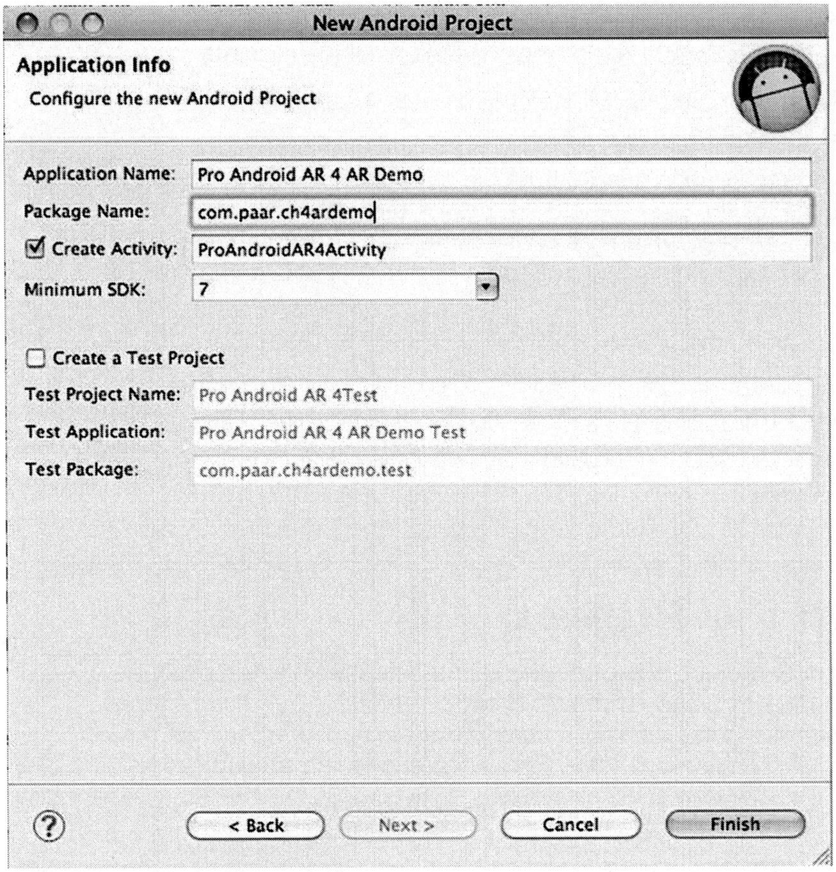

Figure 4-3. *The application details*

After you have created the new project, copy everything from the nonaugmented reality demo into this one. We will be building upon the previous project. Make sure to update the package name in the files where needed.

Updating the XML

To begin, we need to update the XML for our app. Our app currently has only four XML files: AndroidManifest.xml, main.xml, colours.xml, and strings.xml. We will just edit the ones copied over from the previous example instead of building new ones from scratch. The updated and new lines are in bold.

Updating AndroidManifest.xml to Access the GPS

Let's begin with `AndroidManifest.xml`. Because our updated app will require the altitude of the user, we will need to use the GPS to get it. The GPS requires the `ACCESS_FINE_LOCATION` permission to be declared in the manifest. In addition to the new permission, we must update that package name and change the orientation of the `Activity` to landscape.

Listing 4-12. *Updated AndroidManifest.xml*

```xml
<?xml version="1.0" encoding="utf-8"?>
<manifest xmlns:android="http://schemas.android.com/apk/res/android"
    package="com.paar.ch4ardemo"
    android:versionCode="1"
    android:versionName="1.0" >

    <uses-sdk android:minSdkVersion="7" />

    <application
        android:icon="@drawable/ic_launcher"
        android:label="@string/app_name" >
        <activity
            android:label="@string/app_name"
            android:name=".AHActivity"
            android:screenOrientation="landscape"
android:theme="@android:style/Theme.NoTitleBar.Fullscreen"
            android:configChanges = "keyboardHidden|orientation">
            <intent-filter >
                <action android:name="android.intent.action.MAIN" />

                <category android:name="android.intent.category.LAUNCHER" />
            </intent-filter>
        </activity>
    </application>
    <uses-feature android:name="android.hardware.camera" />
    <uses-permission android:name="android.permission.CAMERA" />
    <uses-permission android:name="android.permission.ACCESS_FINE_LOCATION" />
</manifest>
```

Updating strings.xml to Display the Altitude

Next, let's take a look at `strings.xml`. We will be adding two new strings that will serve as the labels for the `Button` and `TextView`. We do not add a string for the other TextView because it will be updated at runtime when the user clicks the button. Add the following two strings anywhere in your strings.xml file.

Listing 4-13. *Updated strings.xml*

```
<string name="altitudeButtonLabel">Update Altitude</string>
  <string name="altitudeLabel">Altitude in \n 5 minutes</string>
```

That little \n in the second string tells Android to print out the remainder of the string on a new line. We do this because on the smaller screen devices, the string might overlap with the button.

Updating colours.xml to Provide a Two-Color Display

Now let's update colours.xml. This time, we need only two colors, out of which only one is a visible color. In the previous example, we set a different color for the ground, sky, and so on. Doing so here will result in the dial of the meter covering our camera preview. However, using the ARGB color codes, we can make everything except the text transparent. Completely replace the contents of your colours.xml file with the following code.

Listing 4-14. *Updated colours.xml*

```
<?xml version="1.0" encoding="utf-8"?>
<resources>
  <color name="text_color">#F0F0</color>
  <color name="transparent_color">#0000</color>
</resources>
```

Updating main.xml to a RelativeLayout

Now we come to our final XML file—and the one with the maximum changes: main.xml. Previously, main.xml had only a LinearLayout with a HorizonView inside it. However, to allow for our AR overlaps, we will be replacing the LinearLayout with a RelativeLayout, and adding two TextViews and a Button, in addition to the HorizonView. Update the main.xml to the following code.

Listing 4-15. *Updated main.xml*

```
<?xml version="1.0" encoding="utf-8"?>
<RelativeLayout xmlns:android="http://schemas.android.com/apk/res/android"
  android:orientation="vertical"
  android:layout_width="fill_parent"
  android:layout_height="fill_parent">
```

```xml
<SurfaceView
        android:id="@+id/cameraPreview"
        android:layout_width="fill_parent"
        android:layout_height="fill_parent" />
<com.paar.ch4ardemo.HorizonView
    android:id="@+id/horizonView"
    android:layout_width="fill_parent"
    android:layout_height="fill_parent"
/>
<TextView
    android:id="@+id/altitudeLabel"
    android:layout_width="wrap_content"
    android:layout_height="wrap_content"
    android:layout_centerVertical="true"
    android:layout_toRightOf="@id/horizonView"
    android:text="@string/altitudeLabel"
    android:textColor="#00FF00">
</TextView>
<TextView
    android:id="@+id/altitudeValue"
    android:layout_width="wrap_content"
    android:layout_height="wrap_content"
    android:layout_centerVertical="true"
    android:layout_below="@id/altitudeLabel"
    android:layout_toRightOf="@id/horizonView"
    android:textColor="#00FF00">
</TextView>
<Button
    android:id="@+id/altitudeUpdateButton"
    android:layout_width="wrap_content"
    android:layout_height="wrap_content"
    android:text="@string/altitudeButtonLabel"
    android:layout_centerVertical="true"
    android:layout_alignParentRight="true">
</Button>
</RelativeLayout>
```

In this case, there are only five lines that were not modified. As usual, being a RelativeLayout, any mistake in the ids or position is fatal.

This takes care of the XML part of our app. Now we must move onto the Java files.

Updating the Java Files

The Java files have considerably more changes than the XML files, and some of the changes might not make sense at first. We'll take each change, one block of code at a time.

Updating HorizonView.java to make the compass transparent

Let's begin with HorizonView.java. We are modifying our code to make the dial transparent and work in landscape mode. Let's start by modifying initCompassView(). The only change we are making is replacing the old colors with the updated ones. The lines that have been modified are in bold.

Listing 4-16. *Updated initCompassView()*

```
protected void initCompassView() {
    setFocusable(true);
    Resources r = this.getResources();

    circlePaint = new Paint(Paint.ANTI_ALIAS_FLAG);
    circlePaint.setColor(R.color.transparent_color);
    circlePaint.setStrokeWidth(1);
    circlePaint.setStyle(Paint.Style.STROKE);

    textPaint = new Paint(Paint.ANTI_ALIAS_FLAG);
    textPaint.setColor(r.getColor(R.color.text_color));
    textPaint.setFakeBoldText(true);
    textPaint.setSubpixelText(true);
    textPaint.setTextAlign(Align.LEFT);

    textHeight = (int)textPaint.measureText("yY");

    markerPaint = new Paint(Paint.ANTI_ALIAS_FLAG);
    markerPaint.setColor(r.getColor(R.color.transparent_color));
    markerPaint.setAlpha(200);
    markerPaint.setStrokeWidth(1);
    markerPaint.setStyle(Paint.Style.STROKE);
    markerPaint.setShadowLayer(2, 1, 1, r.getColor(R.color.transparent_color));

    borderGradientColors = new int[4];
    borderGradientPositions = new float[4];

    borderGradientColors[3] = r.getColor(R.color.transparent_color);
    borderGradientColors[2] = r.getColor(R.color.transparent_color);
    borderGradientColors[1] = r.getColor(R.color.transparent_color);
```

```
borderGradientColors[0] = r.getColor(R.color.transparent_color);
borderGradientPositions[3] = 0.0f;
borderGradientPositions[2] = 1-0.03f;
borderGradientPositions[1] = 1-0.06f;
borderGradientPositions[0] = 1.0f;

glassGradientColors = new int[5];
glassGradientPositions = new float[5];

int glassColor = 245;
glassGradientColors[4] = Color.argb(65, glassColor,
                                    glassColor, glassColor);
glassGradientColors[3] = Color.argb(100, glassColor,
                                    glassColor, glassColor);
glassGradientColors[2] = Color.argb(50, glassColor,
                                    glassColor, glassColor);
glassGradientColors[1] = Color.argb(0, glassColor,
                                        glassColor, glassColor);
glassGradientColors[0] = Color.argb(0, glassColor,
                                        glassColor, glassColor);
glassGradientPositions[4] = 1-0.0f;
glassGradientPositions[3] = 1-0.06f;
glassGradientPositions[2] = 1-0.10f;
glassGradientPositions[1] = 1-0.20f;
glassGradientPositions[0] = 1-1.0f;

skyHorizonColorFrom = r.getColor(R.color.transparent_color);
skyHorizonColorTo = r.getColor(R.color.transparent_color);

groundHorizonColorFrom = r.getColor(R.color.transparent_color);
groundHorizonColorTo = r.getColor(R.color.transparent_color);
}
```

Next, we need to update the onDraw() method to work with the landscape orientation. Because a good amount of the first part is unchanged, the entire method isn't given here. We are updating code right after the clamping of the pitch and roll takes place.

Listing 4-17. *Updated onDraw()*

```
//Cut Here
Path skyPath = new Path();
    skyPath.addArc(innerBoundingBox, -rollDegree, (180 + (2 * rollDegree)));
    canvas.rotate(-tiltDegree, px, py);
    canvas.drawOval(innerBoundingBox, groundPaint);
    canvas.drawPath(skyPath, skyPaint);
    canvas.drawPath(skyPath, markerPaint);
    int markWidth = radius / 3;
    int startX = center.x - markWidth;
    int endX = center.x + markWidth;
```

```
    Log.d("PAARV ", "Roll " + String.valueOf(rollDegree));
    Log.d("PAARV ", "Pitch " + String.valueOf(tiltDegree));


double h = innerRadius*Math.cos(Math.toRadians(90-tiltDegree));
double justTiltX = center.x - h;

float pxPerDegree = (innerBoundingBox.height()/2)/45f;
for (int i = 90; i >= -90; i -= 10) {
    double ypos = justTiltX + i*pxPerDegree;

    if ((ypos < (innerBoundingBox.top + textHeight)) ||
        (ypos > innerBoundingBox.bottom - textHeight))
      continue;

    canvas.drawLine(startX, (float)ypos,
                    endX, (float)ypos,
                    markerPaint);
    int displayPos = (int)(tiltDegree - i);
    String displayString = String.valueOf(displayPos);
    float stringSizeWidth = textPaint.measureText(displayString);
    canvas.drawText(displayString,
                    (int)(center.x-stringSizeWidth/2),
                    (int)(ypos)+1,
                    textPaint);
}
markerPaint.setStrokeWidth(2);
canvas.drawLine(center.x - radius / 2,
                (float)justTiltX,
                center.x + radius / 2,
                (float)justTiltX,
                markerPaint);
markerPaint.setStrokeWidth(1);
//Cut Here
```

These changes make our app look nice and transparent.

Updating the Activity to Access GPS, and Find and Display the Altitude

Now, we must move onto our final file, AHActivity.java. In this file, we will be adding GPS code, TextView and Button references, slightly modifying our Sensor code, and finally putting in a small algorithm to calculate our altitude after 5 minutes. We will be using trigonometry to find the change in altitude, so if yours is a little rusty, you might want to brush up on it quickly.

To begin, add the following variables to the top of your class.

Listing 4-18. *New Variable Declarations*

```
LocationManager locationManager;

Button updateAltitudeButton;
TextView altitudeValue;

double currentAltitude;
double pitch;
double newAltitude;
double changeInAltitude;
double thetaSin;
```

locationManager will, well, be our location manager. updateAltitudeButton and altitudeValue will hold references to their XML counterparts so that we can listen for clicks and update them. currentAltitude, newAltitude, and changeInAltitude will all be used to store values during the operation of our algorithm. The pitch variable will be storing the pitch, and thetaSin will be storing the sine of the pitch angle.

We will now update our onCreate() method to get the location service from Android, set the location listener, and set the OnClickListener for the button. Update it to the following code.

Listing 4-19. *Updated onCreate()*

```
  @Override
  public void onCreate(Bundle icicle) {
    super.onCreate(icicle);
    setContentView(R.layout.main);

inPreview = false;

cameraPreview = (SurfaceView)findViewById(R.id.cameraPreview);
previewHolder = cameraPreview.getHolder();
previewHolder.addCallback(surfaceCallback);
previewHolder.setType(SurfaceHolder.SURFACE_TYPE_PUSH_BUFFERS);

altitudeValue = (TextView) findViewById(R.id.altitudeValue);

updateAltitudeButton = (Button) findViewById(R.id.altitudeUpdateButton);
updateAltitudeButton.setOnClickListener(new OnClickListener() {

        public void onClick(View arg0) {
                updateAltitude();
        }
```

```
});

locationManager = (LocationManager) getSystemService(LOCATION_SERVICE);
locationManager.requestLocationUpdates(LocationManager.GPS_PROVIDER, 2000, 2,↵
 locationListener);

    horizonView = (HorizonView)this.findViewById(R.id.horizonView);
    sensorManager = (SensorManager)getSystemService(Context.SENSOR_SERVICE);
    updateOrientation(new float[] {0, 0, 0});
  }
```

Right about now, Eclipse should be telling you that the updateAltitude()
method and the locationListener don't exist. We'll fix that by creating them.
Add the following LocationListener to any part of your class, outside of a
method. If you're wondering why we have three unused methods, it's because a
LocationListener must implement all four of the methods, even if they aren't
used. Removing them will throw an error when compiling.

Listing 4-20. *LocationListener*

```
LocationListener locationListener = new LocationListener() {
      public void onLocationChanged(Location location) {
            currentAltitude = location.getAltitude();
      }

      public void onProviderDisabled(String arg0) {
            //Not Used
      }

      public void onProviderEnabled(String arg0) {
            //Not Used
      }

      public void onStatusChanged(String arg0, int arg1, Bundle arg2) {
            //Not Used
      }
  };
```

Before we move on to the updateAltitude() method, we will quickly add a line
to the calculateOrientation() method so that the pitch variable isn't empty.
Add the following right before the return statement.

Listing 4-21. *Ensuring the Pitch Variable isn't Empty in calculateOrientation()*

```
pitch = values[1];
```

Calculating the Altitude

Now that our pitch has a value, let's move to the updateAltitude() method. This method implements an algorithm to find the altitude of a person after 5 minutes, taking the current pitch as the angle at which they're moving up. We take the walking speed as 4.5 feet/second, which is the average speed of an adult. Using the speed and time, we can find out the distance traveled in 5 minutes. Then using trigonometry, we can find out the change in altitude from the distance traveled and the angle of inclination. We then add the change in altitude to the old altitude to get our updated altitude and show it in a TextView. If either the pitch or the current altitude is zero, the app asks the user to try again. See Figure 4-4 for a graphical explanation of the concept.

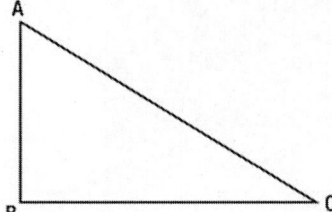

AC = distance moved (Speed*time)
AB = change in altitude
Angle C = Angle of inclination (pitch)
△ABC = right angled triangle
sin(c) = AB/AC
Hence, AB = AC*sin(c)

Figure 4-4. *A graphical representation of the algorithm*

Here's the code for updateAltitude():

Listing 4-22. *Calculating and Displaying the Altitude*

```
public void updateAltitude() {
        int time = 300;
        float speed = 4.5f;

        double distanceMoved = (speed*time)*0.3048;
        if(pitch != 0 && currentAltitude != 0)
        {
                thetaSin = Math.sin(pitch);
                changeInAltitude = thetaSin * distanceMoved;
                newAltitude = currentAltitude + changeInAltitude;
                altitudeValue.setText(String.valueOf(newAltitude));
        }
        else
```

```
        {
                altitudeValue.setText("Try Again");
        }
}
```

And with that, we have finished the AR version of our example app.

Testing the Completed AR app

Take a look at the screenshots in Figures 4-5 and 4-6 to see how the app functions.

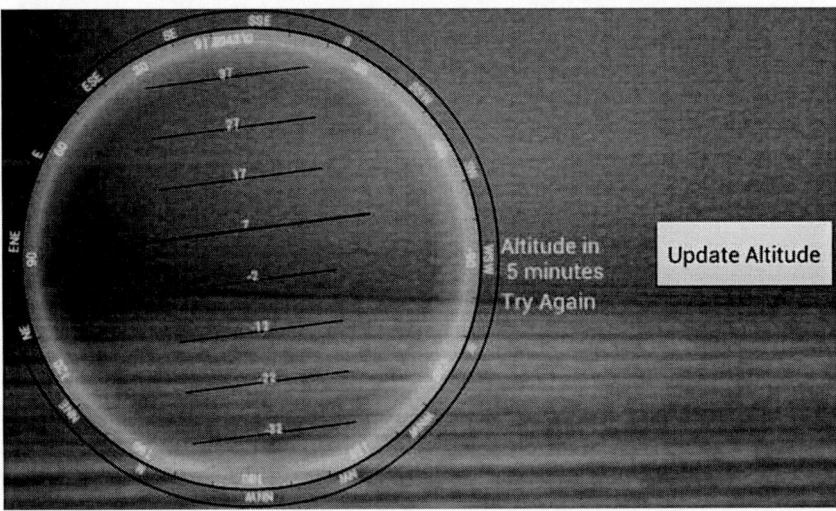

Figure 4-5. *The app running, with a try again message being displayed to the user*

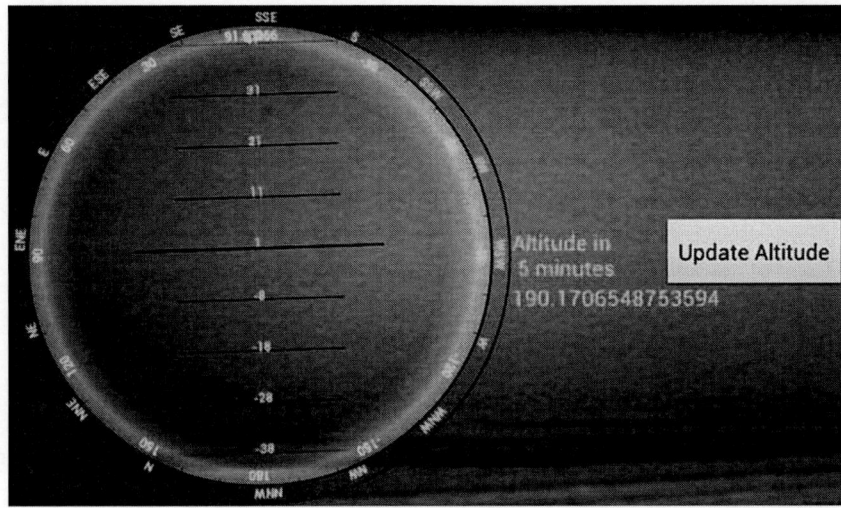

Figure 4-6. *The user is shown the altitude as well this time*

Summary

This chapter explored the concept of artificial horizons and how to create apps utilizing them. We devised an algorithm to find the change in altitude and implemented it in an example app. The apps given here are only an example of what you can do with artificial horizons. They are widely used in the military, especially the Air Force; and in cities, where the natural horizon is distorted due to height or is blocked by buildings.

Common and Uncommon Errors and Problems

This chapter deals with the errors and problems you are likely to encounter while writing the example apps from this book or any other augmented reality (AR) app. We'll take a look at errors related to layouts, the camera, the manifest, and maps. We also have a section for the ones that don't fit into any of these categories.

Layout Errors

First we'll take a look at the errors that occur in layouts. There are many such errors, but we'll be looking only at those that are prone to turning up in AR apps.

UI Alignment Issues

The majority of AR apps use a RelativeLayout in the base layout file. The RelativeLayout then has all the widgets, surface views, and custom views as its children. It is the preferred layout because it easily allows us to overlay UI elements one on top of the other.

One of the most common problems faced when using a RelativeLayout is that the layout doesn't end up looking as expected. Elements end up all over the place instead of staying in the order you put them. The most common reason for this is for an ID to be missing or some layout rule not having been defined. For example, if you miss out on an android:layout_* in your definition of a TextView, for example, the TextView has no set layout options because it doesn't know where to go on the screen, so the layout ends up looking jumbled up. In addition, any other widgets that use the aforementioned TextView in their alignment will also end up going to random places on the screen.

The solution is very simple. You simply need to check all your alignment values, and fix any typos, or add any that are missing. An easy way to do this is by using either the inbuilt graphical editor in Eclipse, or the open source program DroidDraw, available from http://code.google.com/p/droiddraw/. In both cases, moving an element around in the graphical layout will alter its corresponding XML code. It allows you to easily check and correct the layout.

ClassCastException

Another problem often seen when working with layouts is getting a ClassCastException when trying to reference a particular widget from the Java code. Let's say we have a TextView declared as follows:

Listing 5-1. *An Example TextView*

```
<TextView
    android:id="@+id/textView1"
    android:layout_width="wrap_content"
    android:layout_height="wrap_content"
    android:layout_alignParentLeft="true"
    android:layout_alignParentTop="true"
    android:text="@string/hello" />
```

Having defined it in the XML, we reference it from within the Java code as follows:

Listing 5-2. *Referencing a TextView*

```
TextView textView = (TextView) findViewById(R.id.textView1);
```

When compiling, we sometimes get a ClassCastException on the preceding code. This error is commonly received after large changes in our XML files. When we reference to the TextView, we use the method findViewById() from the View class to get the View corresponding to the ID passed as the argument. We then cast the View that is returned by findViewById() to a TextView. All the R.*.* parts of your app are stored in the R.java file that is generated when the app is compiled. Sometimes this file does not update properly, and findViewById() returns a View that is not the one we are looking for (for example, a Button instead of a TextView). Then when we try to cast the incorrect View to a TextView, we get a ClassCastException because you cannot cast those two to one another.

The fix for this one is simple. You simply clean the project by going to **Project ➤ Clean** in Eclipse or run ant clean from the command line.

Another reason for this error is that you are actually referencing an incorrect View, like a Button instead of a TextView. To fix this one, you'll need to double-check your Java code, and make sure you got the IDs right.

Camera Errors

The camera is an integral part of any AR app. It adds most of the reality to it, if you think about it. The camera is also the part where a slightly shaky implementation will work fine on some devices, but fail completely on others. We will look at the most common Java errors and deal with the single manifest error in the section on the AndroidManifest.

Failed to Connect to Camera Service

Perhaps the most common error found when using the Camera on Android is the Failed to Connect to Camera Service. This error occurs when you try to access the camera when it is already being used by an application (your own or otherwise) or has been disabled entirely by one or more device administrators. Device administrators are apps that can change things such as minimum password length and camera usage in devices running Froyo and above. You can check to see whether an administrator has disabled the camera by using DeviceManagerPolicy.getCameraDisabled() in android.app.admin. You can pass the name of an admin while checking or pass null to check across all admins.

There isn't much you can do if another application is using the camera, but you can make sure that your application isn't the one causing the problems by properly releasing the Camera object. The main code for this is generally in onPause() and surfaceDestroyed(). You can use either or both of them in your app. Throughout this book, we have done the releasing in onPause(). The code for both is given as follows:

Listing 5-3. *Releasing the Camera*

```
@Override
public void surfaceDestroyed(SurfaceHolder holder) {
```

```
        if (mCam != null) {
            mCam.stopPreview();
            mCam.setPreviewCallback(null);
            mCam.release();
            mCam = null;
        }
    }

    @Override
    public void onPause() {
        super.onPause();
        if (mCam != null) {
            mCam.stopPreview();
            mCam.setPreviewCallback(null);
            mCam.release();
            mCam = null;
        }
    }
```

In the previous code, mCam is the camera object. There can be additional code in either of these methods, depending on what your app does.

Camera.setParameters() failed

One of the most common errors is the failure of setParameters(). There are several reasons for this, but in most cases it happens because an incorrect width or height is provided for the preview.

The fix for this is quite easy. You need to make sure that the preview size you are passing to Android is supported. To allow this, we have used a getBestPreviewSize() method in all our example apps throughout this book. The method is shown in Listing 5-4:

Listing 5-4. *Calculating the Optimal Preview Size*

```
private Camera.Size getBestPreviewSize(int width, int height, Camera.Parameters
parameters) {
    Camera.Size result=null;

    for (Camera.Size size : parameters.getSupportedPreviewSizes()) {
        if (size.width<=width && size.height<=height) {
            if (result==null) {
                result=size;
            }
            else {
                int resultArea=result.width*result.height;
                int newArea=size.width*size.height;
```

```
        if (newArea>resultArea) {
            result=size;
        }
      }
    }
  }
  return(result);
}
```

To use it, do the following:

Listing 5-5. *Calling the Calculator of the Optimal Preview Size*

```
public void surfaceChanged(SurfaceHolder holder, int format, int width, int
height) {
    Camera.Parameters parameters=camera.getParameters();
    Camera.Size size=getBestPreviewSize(width, height, parameters);

    if (size!=null) {
    parameters.setPreviewSize(size.width, size.height);
    camera.setParameters(parameters);
    camera.startPreview();
    inPreview=true;
    }
}
```

`surfaceChanged()` is part of the `SurfaceHolder.Callback` part of our app.

Exception in setPreviewDisplay()

Another common problem with the camera is getting an exception when calling `setPreviewDisplay()`. This method is used to tell the Camera which SurfaceView to use for the live preview or has null passed to remove the preview surface. This method throws an IOException if an unsuitable surface is passed to it.

The fix is to make sure the SurfaceView being passed is suitable for the camera. A suitable SurfaceView can be created as follows:

Listing 5-6. *Creating a Camera-Appropriate SurfaceView*

```
SurfaceView previewHolder;
previewHolder = cameraPreview.getHolder();
previewHolder.addCallback(surfaceCallback);
previewHolder.setType(SurfaceHolder.SURFACE_TYPE_PUSH_BUFFERS);
```

We change the type of the SurfaceView to SURFACE_TYPE_PUSH_BUFFERS because it tells Android that it will be receiving a Bitmap from somewhere else. Because the SurfaceView might not be immediately ready after having its type changed, you should do the rest of the initialization in the surfaceCallback.

AndroidManifest Errors

A major source of errors in any Android project is the AndroidManifest.xml. Developers often forget to update it, or put certain elements in the wrong part.

Security Exceptions

It is highly possible that you will get some security exceptions while working on an app. If you take a look at the LogCat, you will see something like this:

```
04-09 22:44:36.957: E/AndroidRuntime(13347): java.lang.RuntimeException: Unable
to start activity
ComponentInfo{com.paar.ch2/com.paar.ch2.ProAndroidAR2Activity}:
java.lang.SecurityException: Provider gps requires ACCESS_FINE_LOCATION
permission
```

In this case, the exception is being thrown because I have not declared the android.permission.ACCESS_FINE_LOCATION in my manifest and am trying to use the GPS, which requires the permission.

You might also get the same error even if you have declared the permission, but it is not in the correct part of the manifest. A common problem is when developers put it inside the <application> or <activity> elements, when it should be in the root <manifest> element. Additionally, there have been reports from developers that sometimes the problem occurs even if it is in the correct part, and can be solved by moving it from after the <application> element to before it.

Table 5-1 lists common permissions in AR apps and what they allow you to do.

Table 5-1. *Common Permissions in AR Apps*

Permission Name	Description
android.permission.ACCESS_COARSE_LOCATION	Allows you to access the location via the WiFi or cellular network

Permission Name	Description
android.permission.ACCESS_FINE_LOCATION	Allows you to access the GPS. On most devices, requesting this automatically gives you the ACCESS_COARSE_LOCATION permission, even if it isn't declared in your manifest.
android.permission.CAMERA	Allows you to access the camera and related features, such as the flash.
android.permission.INTERNET	Allows you to access the Internet. Required to load map tiles.
android.permission.WRITE_EXTERNAL_STORAGE	Allows you to write data to the external storage volume on the device, SD card, and so on.

A missing CAMERA permission might also cause a Failed to Connect to Camera Service error on some devices.

<uses-library>

The `<uses-library>` element is put in the `<application>` element of the Android Manifest. By default, the standard android widgets and so on are included in every project. However, some libraries, like the Google Maps library need to be explicitly included via the `<uses-library>` part of the manifest. The Maps library is the one most commonly used in AR apps. You might include it as follows inside the `<application>` element:

Listing 5-7. *Adding the Google Maps Library to Your Application's Manifest*

```
<uses-library android:name="com.google.android.maps" />
```

To include this library, you must be targeting the Google APIs. In all our example apps with maps, we target the Google APIs for Android 2.1.

<uses-feature>

Although strictly speaking a missing `<uses-feature>` is not an actual error, it is best to put it in your app because it is used by various distribution channels to see whether your app will work on a particular device. The two most common ones in augmented reality apps are these:

```
android.hardware.camera
android.hardware.camera.autofocus
```

Errors Related to Maps

Maps are an important part of many AR applications. There are a couple of very common errors that are made when using them, however. We'll take a look at both of them.

The Keys

The Google Maps API, which is used to provide the maps in this book, requires each app to get an API key for the debug certificate (the one that Eclipse signs your app with while debugging) and another one for your release certificate (the one you use to sign your .apk before publishing it). Often developers forget to change the keys when switching from debugging to production or forget to put a key at all. In these cases, your map works fine, except that the map tiles do not load, and you get a white background with a grid on it and some overlays if you have them.

It is a good practice to keep both keys as comments in your XML files, so that you do not repeatedly have to generate them online. List 5-8 shows an example:

Listing 5-8. *A Sample MapView with Both Keys*

```
<com.google.android.maps.MapView
    android:id="@+id/mapView"
    android:layout_width="fill_parent"
    android:layout_height="fill_parent"
    android:clickable="true"
    android:apiKey="OnU9aMfHubxd2LIZ_dht3zDDRBb2IG6T3NrnvUA" />
<!-- Debug Key: OnU9aMfHubxd2LIZ_dht3zDDRBb2IG6T3NrnvUA-->
<!-- Production Key: OnU9aMfHubxfPn5-rCLQ9uBWEixm3HLSovWC3hg -->
```

Not Extending MapActivity

To use the Google Maps API in your app, the activity that is to display the map must extend com.google.android.maps.MapActivity instead of the usual Activity. If you do not do this, you will get an error that will look something like this:

```
04-03 14:40:33.670: E/AndroidRuntime(414): Caused by:
java.lang.IllegalArgumentException: MapViews can only be created inside
instances of MapActivity.
```

To fix this, simply change the class declaration as follows:

Normal Activity

```
public class example extends Activity {
```

Activity with Maps

```
public class example extends MapActivity {
```

To use the MapActivity, you must import it, have the appropriate <uses-library> declared in the Manifest, and build for a Google API version of the SDK.

Debugging the App

This section deals with debugging the app. It will explain what you have to do in order to solve problems in your app.

LogCat

Let's start by looking at the LogCat. In the top-right corner of your Eclipse there will be two tabs: Java and Debug. Click the Debug tab. In all probability you will see two columns there. One will have Console and Tasks tabs; the other will have just one tab reading LogCat. If the LogCat tab is not visible, go to **Window ➤ Show View ➤ LogCat**. Now start your debug run. After plugging in the device via USB, you should see something like Figure 5-1 in the LogCat, provided USB Debugging is enabled.

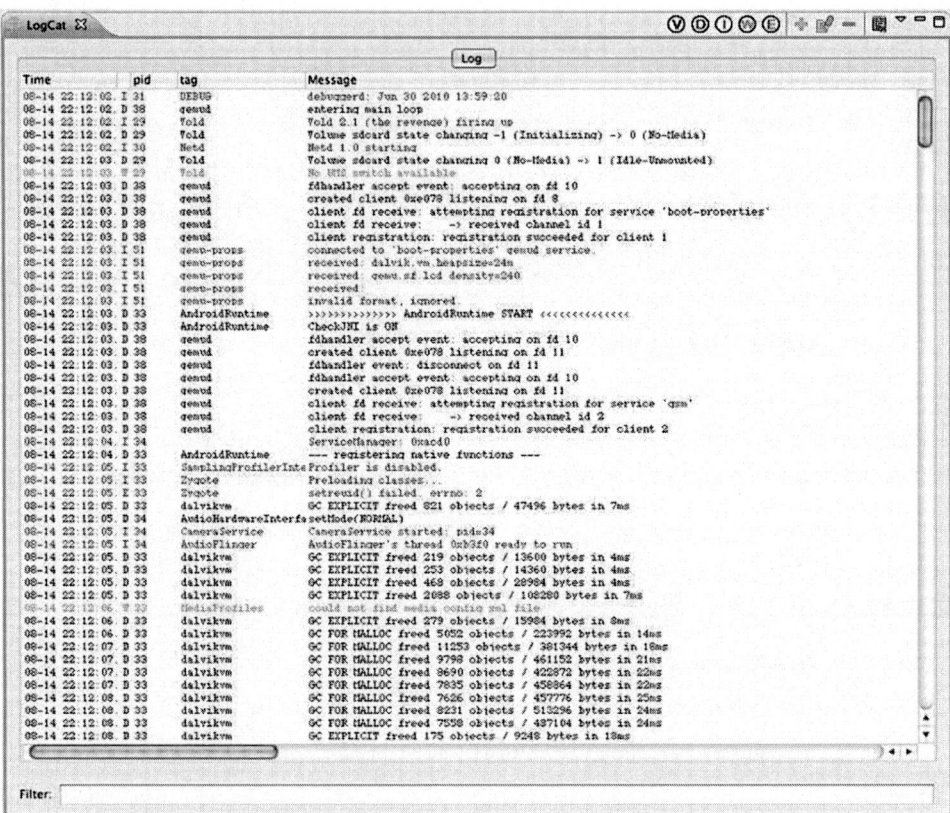

Figure 5-1. *An example logcat output*

Exceptions and errors will be red blocks in the LogCat and roughly 10–25 lines long, depending on the exact problem. At about the halfway point, there will be a line that states "Cause by:…". In this line and after this you'll find the exact line numbers in your app's files that caused the error.

Black and White Squares When Using the Camera

There is only one way to get such a problem: by running an app using the camera in the emulator. The emulator does not support the camera or any other sensor, except the GPS via Mock Locations. When you try to create a camera preview in the emulator, you will see a grid of black and white squares, arranged like a chessboard. However, all overlays should appear as intended.

Miscellaneous

There are some errors that really don't fall into any of the previous categories. We will discuss them in this miscellaneous section.

Not Getting a Location Fix from the GPS

While testing or using your apps, there will be times when your code is perfect, but you still fail to get a GPS fix in your app. This can be due to any of the following reasons:

- **You are indoors:** The GPS requires a clear view of the sky to get a location fix. Try standing near an open door or window, or going outside.

- **You are outside, but still don't have a fix:** This sometimes happens in stormy or cloudy weather. Your only option is to wait for the weather to clear up a bit before trying again.

- **No GPS fix outside in clear weather:** This one usually happens if you forget to turn the GPS on in your device to begin with. Some devices automatically turn it on if an app tries to use it when it is off, but most require the user to do so. Another easy check is to open another app that uses GPS. You can try with Google Maps because it is preinstalled on almost every Android device. If even that cannot get a fix, the problem is probably not in your app.

Compass Not Working

A lot of augmented reality apps use the compass that is present in most Android devices these days. The compass helps in navigational apps, apps designed for stargazing and so on.

Often the compass will give an incorrect reading. This can be due to one of the following reasons:

- **The compass is close to a metallic/magnetic object or a strong electrical current:** These can create a strong localized magnetic field and confuse the hardware into giving an incorrect reading. Try moving to a clear open area.

▓ **The compass is not calibrated:** Sometimes the hardware compass is not calibrated to the magnetic fields in an area. In most devices, vigorously flipping and shaking the device, or waving it in a figure eight (8) pattern, resets the compass.

If your compass does not give a correct reading even after trying the solutions given previously, you should probably have it sent to a service center for a checkup because it is likely that your hardware is faulty.

Summary

This chapter discusses the common errors you might face while writing AR apps and how to solve them. Depending on the kind of app you're writing, you will no doubt face many other logical standard Java and other Android errors that are not really related to the AR part of the app. Discussing every conceivable error you could face would fill an entire book on its own, so we discuss only the AR-related errors here.

In the next chapter, we will be creating our first example app.

A Simple Location-Based App Using Augmented Reality and the Maps API

This chapter outlines how to make a very simple real world augmented reality (AR) application. By the end of this chapter, you will have a fully functional example app.

The app will have the following basic features:

- The app will start and display a live camera preview on the screen.

- The camera preview will be overlayed with the sensor and location data, as in the Chapter 3 widget overlay example app.

▪ When the phone is held parallel to the ground, the app will switch over to display a map. We will add a margin of ±7 because it is unlikely that the user will be able to hold the device perfectly parallel to the ground. The user's current location will be marked on the app. The map will have the option to switch among satellite view, street view, and both. The map will be provided using the Google maps application programming interface (API).

▪ When the device is moved into an orientation that is not parallel to the ground, the app will switch back to a camera view.

This app can act as a standalone application or be extended to provide an augmented reality navigation system, which we will do in the next chapter.

To start, create a new Android project. The project should target the Google APIs (API level 7, as we are targeting 2.1 and above) so that we can use the map functionality of Android. The project used throughout this chapter has the package name com.paar.ch06, with the project name Pro Android AR 6: A Simple App Using AR. You can use any other package and project name you want, as long as you remember to change any references in the example code to match your changes.

After creating the project, add another class to your project by right-clicking the package name in the left bar of eclipse and selecting Class from the New menu (see Figure 6-1):

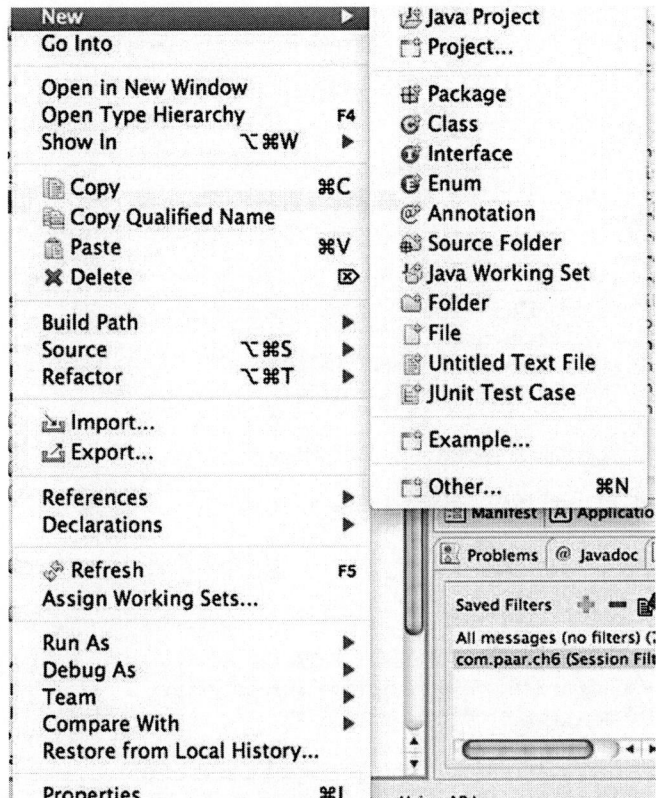

Figure 6-1. *The menu to create a new class.*

Name this class FlatBack. It will hold the MapView and related location APIs. Then create another class called FixLocation. You'll learn more about this class later in the chapter.

Editing the XML

After the necessary classes are created, we can start the coding work. First of all, edit AndroidManifest.xml to declare the new activity and ask for the necessary features, libraries, and permissions. Update the AndroidManifest.xml as follows:

Listing 6-1. *Updated AndroidManifest.xml*

```
<?xml version="1.0" encoding="utf-8"?>
<manifest xmlns:android="http://schemas.android.com/apk/res/android"
```

```
package="com.paar.ch6"
android:versionCode="1"
android:versionName="1.0" >

<uses-sdk android:minSdkVersion="7" />

<application
    android:icon="@drawable/ic_launcher"
    android:label="@string/app_name" >
    <activity
        android:label="@string/app_name"
        android:name=".ASimpleAppUsingARActivity"
        android:screenOrientation = "landscape"
        android:theme="@android:style/Theme.NoTitleBar.Fullscreen"
        android:configChanges = "keyboardHidden|orientation">
        <intent-filter >
            <action android:name="android.intent.action.MAIN" />

            <category android:name="android.intent.category.LAUNCHER" />
        </intent-filter>
    </activity>
    <activity
        android:name=".FlatBack"
        android:screenOrientation="landscape"
        android:theme="@android:style/Theme.NoTitleBar.Fullscreen"
        android:configChanges="keyboardHidden|orientation"></activity>
    <uses-library android:name="com.google.android.maps" />
</application>
<uses-feature android:name="android.hardware.camera" />
<uses-permission android:name="android.permission.CAMERA" />
<uses-permission android:name="android.permission.ACCESS_FINE_LOCATION" />
<uses-permission android:name="android.permission.INTERNET"/>
</manifest>
```

Make sure that the FlatBack Activity is declared exactly as previously, that the `<uses-library>` tag is inside the `<application>` tag, and that all the permissions and feature requests are outside the `<application>` tag and inside the `<manifest>` tag. This is pretty much everything that needs to be done in the AndroidManifest for now.

We will need to add some strings now, which will be used in the overlays and in the Help dialog box for the app. Modify your strings.xml to the following:

Listing 6-2. *Updated strings.xml*

```
<?xml version="1.0" encoding="utf-8"?>
<resources>
        <string name="hello">Hello World, ASimpleAppUsingARActivity!</string>
        <string name="app_name">A Simple App Using AR</string>
```

```
        <string name="xAxis">X Axis:</string>
        <string name="yAxis">Y Axis:</string>
        <string name="zAxis">Z Axis:</string>
        <string name="heading">Heading:</string>
        <string name="pitch">Pitch:</string>
        <string name="roll">Roll:</string>
        <string name="altitude">Altitude:</string>
        <string name="longitude">Longitude:</string>
        <string name="latitude">Latitude:</string>
        <string name="empty"></string>
        <string name="help">This is the example app from Chapter 6 of Pro
Android Augmented Reality. This app outlines some of the basic features of
Augmented Reality and how to implement them in real world applications.</string>
        <string name="helpLabel">Help</string>

</resources>
```

Creating Menu Resources

You will create two menu resources: one for the camera preview `Activity`, and one for the `MapActivity`. To do this, create a new subfolder in the `/res` directory of your project called menu. Create two XML files in that directory titled `main_menu` and `map_toggle`, respectively. In `main_menu`, add the following:

Listing 6-3. *main_menu.xml*

```
<?xml version="1.0" encoding="utf-8"?>
<menu xmlns:android="http://schemas.android.com/apk/res/android" >
    <item
        android:id="@+id/help"
        android:title="Help"></item>
</menu>
```

This is basically the help option in the main `Activity`. Now in `map_toggle`, we will be having three options so add the following to it:

Listing 6-4. *map_toggle.xml*

```
<?xml version="1.0" encoding="utf-8"?>
<menu
  xmlns:android="http://schemas.android.com/apk/res/android">
    <item
        android:id="@+id/map"
        android:title="Map View"></item>
    <item
        android:id="@+id/sat"
        android:title="Satellite View"></item>
```

```
<item
    android:id="@+id/both"
    android:title="Map + Satellite View"></item>
</menu>
```

The first option allows users to set the kind of map displayed to the street view, as you see on a roadmap. The second option allows them to use satellite images on the map. The third option overlays a roadmap onto satellite images of that place. Of course, both these files only define parts of the user interface, and the actual work will be done in the Java files.

Layout Files

There are three layout files in this project. One is for the main camera preview and related overlays, one is for the Help dialog box, and one is for the map.

Camera Preview

The camera preview `Activity` layout file is the normal `main.xml`, with a few changes to its standard contents:

Listing 6-5. *The Camera Preview Layout File*

```
<RelativeLayout
    xmlns:android="http://schemas.android.com/apk/res/android"
        android:id="@+id/relativeLayout1"
        android:layout_width="fill_parent"
        android:layout_height="fill_parent" >
        <SurfaceView
                android:id="@+id/cameraPreview"
                android:layout_width="fill_parent"
                android:layout_height="fill_parent" />

        <TextView
            android:id="@+id/xAxisLabel"
            android:layout_width="wrap_content"
            android:layout_height="wrap_content"
            android:layout_alignParentLeft="true"
            android:layout_alignParentTop="true"
            android:layout_marginLeft="18dp"
            android:layout_marginTop="15dp"
            android:text="@string/xAxis" />

        <TextView
            android:id="@+id/yAxisLabel"
            android:layout_width="wrap_content"
            android:layout_height="wrap_content"
```

```
        android:layout_alignLeft="@+id/xAxisLabel"
        android:layout_below="@+id/xAxisLabel"
        android:text="@string/yAxis" />

    <TextView
        android:id="@+id/zAxisLabel"
        android:layout_width="wrap_content"
        android:layout_height="wrap_content"
        android:layout_alignLeft="@+id/yAxisLabel"
        android:layout_below="@+id/yAxisLabel"
        android:text="@string/zAxis" />

    <TextView
        android:id="@+id/headingLabel"
        android:layout_width="wrap_content"
        android:layout_height="wrap_content"
        android:layout_alignLeft="@+id/zAxisLabel"
        android:layout_below="@+id/zAxisLabel"
        android:layout_marginTop="19dp"
        android:text="@string/heading" />

    <TextView
        android:id="@+id/pitchLabel"
        android:layout_width="wrap_content"
        android:layout_height="wrap_content"
        android:layout_alignLeft="@+id/headingLabel"
        android:layout_below="@+id/headingLabel"
        android:text="@string/pitch" />

    <TextView
        android:id="@+id/rollLabel"
        android:layout_width="wrap_content"
        android:layout_height="wrap_content"
        android:layout_alignLeft="@+id/pitchLabel"
        android:layout_below="@+id/pitchLabel"
        android:text="@string/roll" />

    <TextView
        android:id="@+id/latitudeLabel"
        android:layout_width="wrap_content"
        android:layout_height="wrap_content"
        android:layout_alignLeft="@+id/rollLabel"
        android:layout_below="@+id/rollLabel"
        android:layout_marginTop="34dp"
        android:text="@string/latitude" />

    <TextView
        android:id="@+id/longitudeLabel"
```

```
        android:layout_width="wrap_content"
        android:layout_height="wrap_content"
        android:layout_alignLeft="@+id/latitudeLabel"
        android:layout_below="@+id/latitudeLabel"
        android:text="@string/longitude" />

    <TextView
        android:id="@+id/altitudeLabel"
        android:layout_width="wrap_content"
        android:layout_height="wrap_content"
        android:layout_alignLeft="@+id/longitudeLabel"
        android:layout_below="@+id/longitudeLabel"
        android:text="@string/altitude" />

    <TextView
        android:id="@+id/xAxisValue"
        android:layout_width="wrap_content"
        android:layout_height="wrap_content"
        android:layout_alignBottom="@+id/xAxisLabel"
        android:layout_marginLeft="56dp"
        android:layout_toRightOf="@+id/longitudeLabel"
        android:text="@string/empty" />

    <TextView
        android:id="@+id/yAxisValue"
        android:layout_width="wrap_content"
        android:layout_height="wrap_content"
        android:layout_alignBaseline="@+id/yAxisLabel"
        android:layout_alignBottom="@+id/yAxisLabel"
        android:layout_alignLeft="@+id/xAxisValue"
        android:text="@string/empty" />

    <TextView
        android:id="@+id/zAxisValue"
        android:layout_width="wrap_content"
        android:layout_height="wrap_content"
        android:layout_above="@+id/headingLabel"
        android:layout_alignLeft="@+id/yAxisValue"
        android:text="@string/empty" />

    <TextView
        android:id="@+id/headingValue"
        android:layout_width="wrap_content"
        android:layout_height="wrap_content"
        android:layout_alignBaseline="@+id/headingLabel"
        android:layout_alignBottom="@+id/headingLabel"
        android:layout_alignLeft="@+id/zAxisValue"
        android:text="@string/empty" />
```

```
<TextView
    android:id="@+id/pitchValue"
    android:layout_width="wrap_content"
    android:layout_height="wrap_content"
    android:layout_alignBaseline="@+id/pitchLabel"
    android:layout_alignBottom="@+id/pitchLabel"
    android:layout_alignLeft="@+id/headingValue"
    android:text="@string/empty" />

<TextView
    android:id="@+id/rollValue"
    android:layout_width="wrap_content"
    android:layout_height="wrap_content"
    android:layout_above="@+id/latitudeLabel"
    android:layout_alignLeft="@+id/pitchValue"
    android:text="@string/empty" />

<TextView
    android:id="@+id/latitudeValue"
    android:layout_width="wrap_content"
    android:layout_height="wrap_content"
    android:layout_alignBottom="@+id/latitudeLabel"
    android:layout_alignLeft="@+id/rollValue"
    android:text="@string/empty" />

<TextView
    android:id="@+id/longitudeValue"
    android:layout_width="wrap_content"
    android:layout_height="wrap_content"
    android:layout_alignBaseline="@+id/longitudeLabel"
    android:layout_alignBottom="@+id/longitudeLabel"
    android:layout_alignLeft="@+id/latitudeValue"
    android:text="@string/empty" />

<TextView
    android:id="@+id/altitudeValue"
    android:layout_width="wrap_content"
    android:layout_height="wrap_content"
    android:layout_alignBaseline="@+id/altitudeLabel"
    android:layout_alignBottom="@+id/altitudeLabel"
    android:layout_alignLeft="@+id/longitudeValue"
    android:text="@string/empty" />

<Button
    android:id="@+id/helpButton"
    android:layout_width="wrap_content"
    android:layout_height="wrap_content"
    android:layout_alignLeft="@+id/altitudeLabel"
    android:layout_below="@+id/altitudeValue"
    android:layout_marginTop="15dp"
```

```
                        android:text="@string/helpLabel" />

</RelativeLayout>
```

Once more, you will need to make sure that all the IDs are in order and you haven't made any typos anywhere because it will affect the entire layout. The only major difference from the layout in the first part of Chapter 3 is the addition of a Help button that will launch the Help dialog box. The Help menu option will do the same thing, but it is good to have a more easily visible option available.

Help Dialog Box

Now create another XML file in the /res/layout directory called help.xml. This will contain the layout design for the Help dialog box, which has a scrollable TextView to display the actual help text and a button to close the dialog box. Add the following to the help.xml file:

Listing 6-6. *The Help Dialog Box Layout File*

```
<?xml version="1.0" encoding="utf-8"?>
<RelativeLayout
 xmlns:android="http://schemas.android.com/apk/res/android"
 android:layout_width="wrap_content"
 android:layout_height="wrap_content">

<ScrollView
    android:id="@+id/ScrollView01"
    android:layout_width="wrap_content"
    android:layout_height="200px">

<TextView
    android:text="@+id/TextView01"
    android:id="@+id/TextView01"
    android:layout_width="wrap_content"
    android:layout_height="wrap_content" />

</ScrollView>

<Button
    android:id="@+id/Button01"
    android:layout_below="@id/ScrollView01"
    android:layout_width="wrap_content"
    android:layout_height="wrap_content"
    android:layout_centerHorizontal="true"
    android:text="Okay" />

</RelativeLayout>
```

As you can see, it is a relatively simple `RelativeLayout` that is used in the dialog box layout. There is a `ScrollView` with a `TextView` inside it to hold the Help dialog box content and a `Button` to close the dialog box has been placed right at the bottom of the file.

Map Layout

Now we need to create the final layout file: the map layout. Create a `map.xml` in your `/res/layout` folder and add the following to it:

Listing 6-7. *The Map Layout File*

```xml
<?xml version="1.0" encoding="utf-8"?>
<LinearLayout xmlns:android="http://schemas.android.com/apk/res/android"
    android:layout_width="fill_parent"
    android:layout_height="fill_parent"
    android:orientation="vertical" >
<com.google.android.maps.MapView
    android:id="@+id/mapView"
    android:layout_width="fill_parent"
    android:layout_height="fill_parent"
    android:clickable="true"
    android:apiKey="<your_key_here>" />
</LinearLayout>
```

Getting API Keys

You will get an error if your project is not set to build against a Google APIs target. The other important thing here is the API key. This is assigned to you by Google on a certificate basis. It is generated from your certificate's MD5 hash, which you must submit in an online form. Android uses digital certificates to validate the install files for applications. If the signing certificates are a mismatch across the installed and new version, Android will throw a security exception and not let you update the install. The map API key is unique to each certificate. Therefore, if you plan to publish your application, you have to generate two API keys: one for your debug certificate (the one Eclipse signs your app with during the development and testing process) and one for your release certificate (the one you'll sign your app with before uploading it to an online market such as the Android Market). The steps are different for getting the MD5 of any key on different operating systems.

Getting the MD5 of Your Keys

For the debug key:

The debug key is normally in the following locations:

- Mac/Linux: ~/.android/debug.keystore

- Windows Vista/7: C:\Users\<user>\.android\debug.keystore

- Windows XP: C:\Documents and Settings\<user>\.android\debug.keystore

You will need to run the following command to get the MD5 out. The command uses the Keytool utility:

```
keytool -list -alias androiddebugkey -keystore <path_to_debug_keystore>.keystore
-storepass android -keypass android
```

For the signing key:

The signing key has no fixed location on the system. It is saved wherever you saved it or moved it during or after its creation. Run the following command to get its MD5, replacing alias_name with the alias on the key and my-release-key with the location to your key:

```
keytool -list -alias alias_name -keystore my-release-key.keystore
```

After you have extracted whatever keys' MD5 you wanted, navigate to http://code.google.com/android/maps-api-signup.html using your favorite web browser. Enter the MD5 and complete anything else you are asked to do. After submitting the form, you will be presented with the API key you need for your app to work.

Java Code

Now the XML setup is ready to go. All that is needed is the marker image and the actual code. Let's start with the marker image. It is called ic_maps_current_position_indicator.png and can be found in the drawable-mdpi and drawable-hdpi folders of this project's source. Make sure to copy each folder's image to its counterpart in your project and not switch them over by mistake.

Main Activity

With the image out of the way, we can get down to the code. We will start with the main Activity.

Imports and Variable Declarations

First, we'll take a look at the imports and class declaration and variable declarations:

Listing 6-8. *Main Activity Imports and Declarations*

```
package com.paar.ch6;

import android.app.Activity;
import android.app.Dialog;
import android.content.Intent;
import android.hardware.Camera;
import android.hardware.Sensor;
import android.hardware.SensorEvent;
import android.hardware.SensorEventListener;
import android.hardware.SensorManager;
import android.location.Location;
import android.location.LocationListener;
import android.location.LocationManager;
import android.os.Bundle;
import android.util.Log;
import android.view.Menu;
import android.view.MenuInflater;
import android.view.MenuItem;
import android.view.SurfaceHolder;
import android.view.SurfaceView;
import android.view.View;
import android.view.View.OnClickListener;
import android.widget.Button;
import android.widget.TextView;

public class ASimpleAppUsingARActivity extends Activity {
        SurfaceView cameraPreview;
        SurfaceHolder previewHolder;
        Camera camera;
        boolean inPreview;

        final static String TAG = "PAAR";
        SensorManager sensorManager;

        int orientationSensor;
        float headingAngle;
```

```
float pitchAngle;
float rollAngle;

int accelerometerSensor;
float xAxis;
float yAxis;
float zAxis;

LocationManager locationManager;
double latitude;
double longitude;
double altitude;

TextView xAxisValue;
TextView yAxisValue;
TextView zAxisValue;
TextView headingValue;
TextView pitchValue;
TextView rollValue;
TextView altitudeValue;
TextView latitudeValue;
TextView longitudeValue;

Button button;
```

The import statements and class declaration are standard Java, and the variables have been named to describe their function. Let's move on to the different methods in the class now.

onCreate() Method

The first method of the app, onCreate(), does a lot of things. It sets the main.xml file as the Activity view. It then gets the location and sensor system services. It registers listeners for the accelerometer and orientation sensors and the global positioning system (GPS). It then does part of the camera initialization (the rest of it is done later on). Finally, it gets references to nine of the TextViews so that they can be updated later on in the app and gets a reference to the Help button and sets its onClickListener. The code for this method is as follows:

Listing 6-9. *Main Activity's onCreate()*

```
@Override
public void onCreate(Bundle savedInstanceState) {
    super.onCreate(savedInstanceState);
    setContentView(R.layout.main);

    locationManager = (LocationManager) getSystemService(LOCATION_SERVICE);
```

```
    locationManager.requestLocationUpdates(LocationManager.GPS_PROVIDER, 2000,
2, locationListener);

    sensorManager = (SensorManager) getSystemService(SENSOR_SERVICE);
    orientationSensor = Sensor.TYPE_ORIENTATION;
    accelerometerSensor = Sensor.TYPE_ACCELEROMETER;
    sensorManager.registerListener(sensorEventListener, sensorManager
.getDefaultSensor(orientationSensor), SensorManager.SENSOR_DELAY_NORMAL);
    sensorManager.registerListener(sensorEventListener, sensorManager
.getDefaultSensor(accelerometerSensor), SensorManager.SENSOR_DELAY_NORMAL);

    inPreview = false;

    cameraPreview = (SurfaceView)findViewById(R.id.cameraPreview);
    previewHolder = cameraPreview.getHolder();
    previewHolder.addCallback(surfaceCallback);
    previewHolder.setType(SurfaceHolder.SURFACE_TYPE_PUSH_BUFFERS);

    xAxisValue = (TextView) findViewById(R.id.xAxisValue);
    yAxisValue = (TextView) findViewById(R.id.yAxisValue);
    zAxisValue = (TextView) findViewById(R.id.zAxisValue);
    headingValue = (TextView) findViewById(R.id.headingValue);
    pitchValue = (TextView) findViewById(R.id.pitchValue);
    rollValue = (TextView) findViewById(R.id.rollValue);
    altitudeValue = (TextView) findViewById(R.id.altitudeValue);
    longitudeValue = (TextView) findViewById(R.id.longitudeValue);
    latitudeValue = (TextView) findViewById(R.id.latitudeValue);
    button = (Button) findViewById(R.id.helpButton);
    button.setOnClickListener(new OnClickListener() {
            public void onClick(View v) {
        showHelp();
    }
    });
}
```

LocationListener

Next in the code is the LocationListener, which listens for location updates from the location services (the GPS, in this case). Upon receiving an update from the GPS, it updates the local variables with new information, prints out the new information to the LogCat, and updates three of the TextViews with the new information. It also contains autogenerated method stubs for methods that aren't used in the app.

Listing 6-10. *LocationListener*

```
LocationListener locationListener = new LocationListener() {
    public void onLocationChanged(Location location) {
            latitude = location.getLatitude();
            longitude = location.getLongitude();
            altitude = location.getAltitude();

            Log.d(TAG, "Latitude: " + String.valueOf(latitude));
            Log.d(TAG, "Longitude: " + String.valueOf(longitude));
            Log.d(TAG, "Altitude: " + String.valueOf(altitude));

            latitudeValue.setText(String.valueOf(latitude));
            longitudeValue.setText(String.valueOf(longitude));
            altitudeValue.setText(String.valueOf(altitude));
    }

        public void onProviderDisabled(String arg0) {
                // TODO Auto-generated method stub

        }

        public void onProviderEnabled(String arg0) {
                // TODO Auto-generated method stub

        }

        public void onStatusChanged(String arg0, int arg1, Bundle arg2) {
                // TODO Auto-generated method stub

        }
};
```

Launching the Map

Up next for explanation is the launchFlatBack() method. This method is called by the SensorEventListener whenever the condition for the phone being more or less parallel to the ground is met. This method then launches the map.

Listing 6-11. *launchFlatBack()*

```
public void launchFlatBack() {
    Intent flatBackIntent = new Intent(this, FlatBack.class);
    startActivity(flatBackIntent);
}
```

Options Menu

The Options menu is created and used by overriding the onCreateOptionsMenu()
and onOptionsItemSelected() methods. The first one creates it from the menu
resource (main_menu.xml), and the second one listens for click events on the
menu. If the Help item has been clicked, it calls the appropriate method that will
show the Help dialog box.

Listing 6-12. *onCreateOptionsMenu() and onOptionsItemSelected()*

```
@Override
public boolean onCreateOptionsMenu(Menu menu) {
    MenuInflater inflater = getMenuInflater();
    inflater.inflate(R.menu.main_menu, menu);
    return true;
}

public boolean onOptionsItemSelected(MenuItem item) {
    // Handle item selection
    switch (item.getItemId()) {
    case R.id.help:
            showHelp();
    default:
        return super.onOptionsItemSelected(item);
    }
}
```

Showing the Help Dialog box

showHelp() is the appropriate method mentioned previously. It is called when
the Help menu item is clicked.

Listing 6-13. *showHelp()*

```
public void showHelp() {
        final Dialog dialog = new Dialog(this);
        dialog.setContentView(R.layout.help);
        dialog.setTitle("Help");
        dialog.setCancelable(true);
        //there are a lot of settings, for dialog, check them all out!

        //set up text
        TextView text = (TextView) dialog.findViewById(R.id.TextView01);
        text.setText(R.string.help);
```

```
//set up button
Button button = (Button) dialog.findViewById(R.id.Button01);
button.setOnClickListener(new OnClickListener() {
public void onClick(View v) {
        dialog.cancel();
    }
});
//now that the dialog is set up, it's time to show it
dialog.show();
}
```

Listening to the Sensors

Now we come to the SensorEventListener. There is an if statement that differentiates between the orientation sensor and accelerometer. Both of the sensor's updates are printing out to the LogCat and the appropriate TextViews. In addition, an if statement inside the orientation sensor part of the code decides whether the device is more or less parallel to the ground. There is a leeway of 14 degrees because it is unlikely that anyone will be able to hold the device perfectly parallel to the ground.

Listing 6-14. *SensorEventListener*

```
final SensorEventListener sensorEventListener = new SensorEventListener() {
    public void onSensorChanged(SensorEvent sensorEvent) {
            if (sensorEvent.sensor.getType() == Sensor.TYPE_ORIENTATION)
            {
                    headingAngle = sensorEvent.values[0];
                    pitchAngle = sensorEvent.values[1];
                    rollAngle = sensorEvent.values[2];

                    Log.d(TAG, "Heading: " + String.valueOf(headingAngle));
                    Log.d(TAG, "Pitch: " + String.valueOf(pitchAngle));
                    Log.d(TAG, "Roll: " + String.valueOf(rollAngle));

                    headingValue.setText(String.valueOf(headingAngle));
                    pitchValue.setText(String.valueOf(pitchAngle));
                    rollValue.setText(String.valueOf(rollAngle));

                    if (pitchAngle < 7 && pitchAngle > -7 && rollAngle < 7 &&
rollAngle > -7)
                    {
                            launchFlatBack();
                    }
            }
```

```
            else if (sensorEvent.sensor.getType() == Sensor.TYPE_ACCELEROMETER)
            {
                    xAxis = sensorEvent.values[0];
                    yAxis = sensorEvent.values[1];
                    zAxis = sensorEvent.values[2];

                    Log.d(TAG, "X Axis: " + String.valueOf(xAxis));
                    Log.d(TAG, "Y Axis: " + String.valueOf(yAxis));
                    Log.d(TAG, "Z Axis: " + String.valueOf(zAxis));

                    xAxisValue.setText(String.valueOf(xAxis));
                    yAxisValue.setText(String.valueOf(yAxis));
                    zAxisValue.setText(String.valueOf(zAxis));
            }
    }

    public void onAccuracyChanged (Sensor senor, int accuracy) {
            //Not used
    }
};
```

onResume(), onPause(), and onDestroy() methods

We override the onResume(), onPause(), and onDestroy() methods so that we can release and reacquire the SensorEventListener, LocationListener, and Camera. We release them when the app is paused (the user switches to another app) or destroyed (Android terminates the process) to save the user's battery and use up fewer system resources. Also, only one app can use the Camera at a time, so by releasing it we make it available to the other applications.

Listing 6-15. *onResume(), onPause() and onDestroy()*

```
@Override
public void onResume() {
  super.onResume();
  locationManager.requestLocationUpdates(LocationManager.GPS_PROVIDER, 2000, 2,
locationListener);
  sensorManager.registerListener(sensorEventListener, sensorManager
.getDefaultSensor(orientationSensor), SensorManager.SENSOR_DELAY_NORMAL);
  sensorManager.registerListener(sensorEventListener, sensorManager
.getDefaultSensor(accelerometerSensor), SensorManager.SENSOR_DELAY_NORMAL);
  //Camera camera;
}

@Override
public void onPause() {
  if (inPreview) {
    camera.stopPreview();
```

```
    }
    locationManager.removeUpdates(locationListener);
    sensorManager.unregisterListener(sensorEventListener);
    if (camera != null)
    {
        camera.release();
        camera=null;
    }
    inPreview=false;

    super.onPause();
}

@Override
public void onDestroy() {
    camera.release();
    camera=null;
}
```

Managing the SurfaceView and Camera

These last four methods deal with managing the SurfaceView, its SurfaceHolder, and the Camera.

- ▨ The getBestPreviewSize() method gets a list of available preview sizes and chooses the best one.

- ▨ The surfaceCallback is called when the SurfaceView is ready. The camera is set up and opened there.

- ▨ The surfaceChanged() method is called if any changes are made by Android to the SurfaceView (after an orientation change, for example).

- ▨ The surfaceDestroyed() method is called when the SurfaceView is, well, destroyed.

Listing 6-16. *getBestPreviewSize(), surfaceCallback(), surfaceChanged() and surfaceDestroyed()*

```
    private Camera.Size getBestPreviewSize(int width, int height,
Camera.Parameters parameters) {
        Camera.Size result=null;

        for (Camera.Size size : parameters.getSupportedPreviewSizes()) {
                if (size.width<=width && size.height<=height) {
                        if (result==null) {
                                result=size;
                        }
```

```
                    else {
                            int resultArea=result.width*result.height;
                            int newArea=size.width*size.height;

                            if (newArea>resultArea) {
                                    result=size;
                            }
                    }
            }
        }

    return(result);
}

SurfaceHolder.Callback surfaceCallback=new SurfaceHolder.Callback() {
    public void surfaceCreated(SurfaceHolder holder) {
            if (camera == null) {
            camera = Camera.open();
            }
            try {
                    camera.setPreviewDisplay(previewHolder);
            }
            catch (Throwable t) {
                    Log.e(TAG, "Exception in setPreviewDisplay()", t);
            }
    }

    public void surfaceChanged(SurfaceHolder holder, int format, int width,
int height) {
            Camera.Parameters parameters=camera.getParameters();
            Camera.Size size=getBestPreviewSize(width, height, parameters);

            if (size!=null) {
                    parameters.setPreviewSize(size.width, size.height);
                    camera.setParameters(parameters);
                    camera.startPreview();
                    inPreview=true;
            }
    }

    public void surfaceDestroyed(SurfaceHolder holder) {
            if (camera != null) {
            camera.stopPreview();
            camera.setPreviewCallback(null);
            camera.release();
            camera = null;
        }
    }
```

```
    };
}
```

This is the end of the first Java file. This file works with the GPS and sensors to get updates and then displays them via TextViews and LogCat outputs.

FlatBack.java

Now we are going to work on FlatBack.java. This Activity is called whenever the phone is held parallel to the ground and displays your current location on a map. The class won't make much sense right now because part of the work is done in FixLocation.

Imports, Variable Declarations and onCreate() Method

In the onCreate() in this Activity, we repeat the SensorManager stuff as always in the beginning. We need the sensor inputs here because we want to switch back to the CameraView when the device is no longer parallel to the ground. After that, we get a reference to the MapView (the one in the XML layout), tell Android that we will not be implementing our own zoom controls, pass the MapView to FixLocation, add the location overlay to the MapView, tell it to update, and call the custom method that will zoom it to the user's location.

Listing 6-17. *Flatback.java's imports, declarations and onCreate()*

```
package com.paar.ch6;

import com.google.android.maps.GeoPoint;
import com.google.android.maps.MapActivity;
import com.google.android.maps.MapView;
import com.google.android.maps.MyLocationOverlay;

import android.hardware.Sensor;
import android.hardware.SensorEvent;
import android.hardware.SensorEventListener;
import android.hardware.SensorManager;
import android.os.Bundle;
import android.util.Log;
import android.view.Menu;
import android.view.MenuInflater;
import android.view.MenuItem;
```

```java
public class FlatBack extends MapActivity{
        private MapView mapView;
    private MyLocationOverlay myLocationOverlay;
        final static String TAG = "PAAR";
        SensorManager sensorManager;

        int orientationSensor;
        float headingAngle;
        float pitchAngle;
        float rollAngle;
/** Called when the activity is first created. */
@Override
public void onCreate(Bundle savedInstanceState) {
    super.onCreate(savedInstanceState);

    // main.xml contains a MapView
    setContentView(R.layout.map);

    sensorManager = (SensorManager) getSystemService(SENSOR_SERVICE);
    orientationSensor = Sensor.TYPE_ORIENTATION;
    sensorManager.registerListener(sensorEventListener, sensorManager
.getDefaultSensor(orientationSensor), SensorManager.SENSOR_DELAY_NORMAL);

    // extract MapView from layout
        mapView = (MapView) findViewById(R.id.mapView);
        mapView.setBuiltInZoomControls(true);

        // create an overlay that shows our current location
        myLocationOverlay = new FixLocation(this, mapView);

        // add this overlay to the MapView and refresh it
        mapView.getOverlays().add(myLocationOverlay);
        mapView.postInvalidate();

        // call convenience method that zooms map on our location
        zoomToMyLocation();
}
```

onCreateOptionsMenu() and onOptionsItemSelected() methods

Next are the two Options menu–related methods, which create the Options menu, watch for clicks, distinguish between which option was clicked, and execute the appropriate action on the map.

Listing 6-18. *onCreateOptionsMenu() and onOptionsItemSelected()*

```java
@Override
public boolean onCreateOptionsMenu(Menu menu) {
    MenuInflater inflater = getMenuInflater();
    inflater.inflate(R.menu.map_toggle, menu);
    return true;
}

public boolean onOptionsItemSelected(MenuItem item) {
    // Handle item selection
    switch (item.getItemId()) {
    case R.id.map:
        if (mapView.isSatellite() == true) {
                mapView.setSatellite(false);
                mapView.setStreetView(true);
        }
        return true;
    case R.id.sat:
        if (mapView.isSatellite()==false){
                mapView.setSatellite(true);
                mapView.setStreetView(false);
        }
        return true;
    case R.id.both:
        mapView.setSatellite(true);
        mapView.setStreetView(true);
    default:
        return super.onOptionsItemSelected(item);
    }
}
```

SensorEventListener

Next is the SensorEventListener, which is similar to that in the previous class, except that it checks to see if the phone is no longer parallel to the ground and then calls the custom method that will take us back to the camera preview.

Listing 6-19. *SensorEventListener*

```java
final SensorEventListener sensorEventListener = new SensorEventListener() {
        public void onSensorChanged(SensorEvent sensorEvent) {
                if (sensorEvent.sensor.getType() == Sensor.TYPE_ORIENTATION)
                {
                        headingAngle = sensorEvent.values[0];
                        pitchAngle = sensorEvent.values[1];
                        rollAngle = sensorEvent.values[2];
```

```
                    Log.d(TAG, "Heading: " + String.valueOf(headingAngle));
                    Log.d(TAG, "Pitch: " + String.valueOf(pitchAngle));
                    Log.d(TAG, "Roll: " + String.valueOf(rollAngle));

                    if (pitchAngle > 7 || pitchAngle < -7 || rollAngle > 7
 || rollAngle < -7)
                    {
                            launchCameraView();
                    }
                }
        }

        public void onAccuracyChanged(Sensor arg0, int arg1) {
                // TODO Auto-generated method stub

        }
};
```

launchCameraView() Method

The launchCameraView() method finishes the current activity so that we can get to the camera preview without any problems. An Intent is commented out that seems to do the same thing. I have commented it out because although it does end up launching the camera preview, it does so by creating another instance of that activity, which will give an error because the camera will already be in use by the first instance of the activity. Therefore, it is best to return to the previous instance.

Listing 6-20. *launchCameraView()*

```
public void launchCameraView() {
        finish();
        //Intent cameraView = new Intent(this, ASimpleAppUsingARActivity.class);
        //startActivity(cameraView);
}
```

onResume() and onPause() Methods

Then are the onResume() and onPause() methods, which enable and disable location updates to save resources.

Listing 6-21. *onResume() and onPause()*

```
@Override
    protected void onResume() {
            super.onResume();
```

```
                myLocationOverlay.enableMyLocation();
        }

        @Override
        protected void onPause() {
                super.onPause();
                myLocationOverlay.disableMyLocation();
        }
```

zoomToMyLocation() Method

After this is the custom zoomToMyLocation() method. This method applies a
zoom level of 10 to the current location on the map.

Listing 6-22. *zoomToMyLocation()*

```
private void zoomToMyLocation() {
        GeoPoint myLocationGeoPoint = myLocationOverlay.getMyLocation();
        if(myLocationGeoPoint != null) {
                mapView.getController().animateTo(myLocationGeoPoint);
                mapView.getController().setZoom(10);
        }
}
```

isRouteDisplayed() Method

Finally is the Boolean method isRouteDisplayed(). Because it is not used in the
app, it is set to false.

Listing 6-23. *isRouteDisplayed()*

```
    protected boolean isRouteDisplayed() {
            return false;
    }
}
```

This brings us to the end of FlatBack.java. Notice that most of the actual
location work seems to be done in FixLocation.java. Before you get tired of
Eclipse giving you errors at its references, we'll move on and write that class.

FixLocation.java

Now is the time to get to know what FixLocation is for. The MyLocationOverlay
class has severe bugs in some Android-powered devices, most notable of which
is the Motorola DROID. FixLocation tries to use the standard

MyLocationOverlay, but if it fails to work properly, it implements its own version of the same that will produce the same result. Source code first, followed by the explanation:

Listing 6-24. *FixLocation.java*

```java
package com.paar.ch6;

import android.content.Context;
import android.graphics.Canvas;
import android.graphics.Paint;
import android.graphics.Point;
import android.graphics.Paint.Style;
import android.graphics.drawable.Drawable;
import android.location.Location;

import com.google.android.maps.GeoPoint;
import com.google.android.maps.MapView;
import com.google.android.maps.MyLocationOverlay;
import com.google.android.maps.Projection;


public class FixLocation extends MyLocationOverlay {

        private boolean bugged = false;

        private Drawable drawable;
        private Paint accuracyPaint;
        private Point center;
        private Point left;
        private int width;
        private int height;

        public FixLocation(Context context, MapView mapView) {
                super(context, mapView);
        }

        @Override
        protected void drawMyLocation(Canvas canvas, MapView mapView,
                        Location lastFix, GeoPoint myLocation, long when) {
                if(!bugged) {
                        try {
                                super.drawMyLocation(canvas, mapView, lastFix,
myLocation, when);
                        } catch (Exception e) {
                                // we found a buggy phone, draw the location
icons ourselves

                                bugged = true;
                        }
                }
```

```
                if(bugged) {
                        if(drawable == null) {

                                accuracyPaint = new Paint();
                                accuracyPaint.setAntiAlias(true);
                                accuracyPaint.setStrokeWidth(2.0f);

                                drawable = mapView.getContext()
.getResources().getDrawable(R.drawable.ic_maps_indicator_current_position);
                                width = drawable.getIntrinsicWidth();
                                height = drawable.getIntrinsicHeight();
                                center = new Point();
                                left = new Point();
                        }

                        Projection projection = mapView.getProjection();
                        double latitude = lastFix.getLatitude();
                        double longitude = lastFix.getLongitude();
                        float accuracy = lastFix.getAccuracy();

                        float[] result = new float[1];

                        Location.distanceBetween(latitude, longitude, latitude,
longitude + 1, result);
                        float longitudeLineDistance = result[0];

                        GeoPoint leftGeo = new GeoPoint((int)(latitude*1e6),
 (int)((longitude-accuracy/longitudeLineDistance)*1e6));
                        projection.toPixels(leftGeo, left);
                        projection.toPixels(myLocation, center);
                        int radius = center.x - left.x;

                        accuracyPaint.setColor(0xff6666ff);
                        accuracyPaint.setStyle(Style.STROKE);
                        canvas.drawCircle(center.x, center.y, radius,
accuracyPaint);

                        accuracyPaint.setColor(0x186666ff);
                        accuracyPaint.setStyle(Style.FILL);
                        canvas.drawCircle(center.x, center.y, radius,
accuracyPaint);

                        drawable.setBounds(center.x - width/2, center.y -
height/2, center.x + width/2, center.y + height/2);
                        drawable.draw(canvas);
                }
        }
}
```

To begin with, we have the method that receives the call from FlatBack. We then override the drawMyLocation() method. In the implementation, we check to see whether it is bugged or not. We try to let it run the normal course, but if we get an exception, we set bugged to true and then proceed to execute our own implementation of the work.

If it does turn out to be bugged, we set up the paints, get a reference to the drawable, get the location, calculate the accuracy, and then draw the marker, along with the accuracy circle onto the map. The accuracy circle means that the location is not 100% accurate and that you are somewhere inside that circle.

This brings us to the end of this sample application. Now take a quick look on how to run the application and see some screenshots to go with it.

Running the App

The app should compile without any errors or warnings. If you do happen to get an error, go through the common errors section that follows.

When debugging on a device, you might see an orange triangle like the one shown in Figure 6-2.

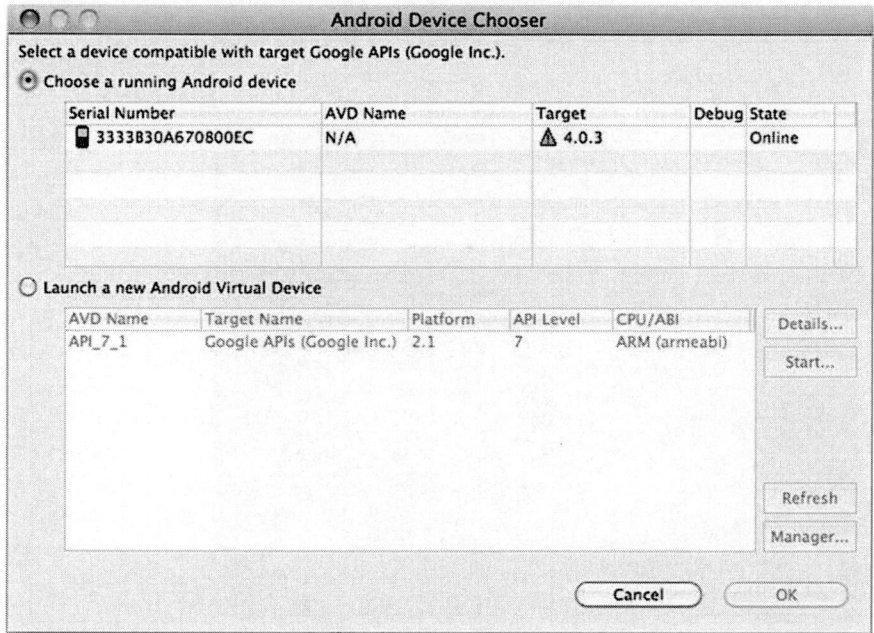

Figure 6-2. *Orange warning triangle*

This triangle simply means that Eclipse could not confirm that the Google APIs are installed on your device. If your Android device came preloaded with Android Market, you can be pretty sure that it has the Google APIs installed.

When you do run the app, you should see something like the screenshots in Figure 6-3 to Figure 6-5.

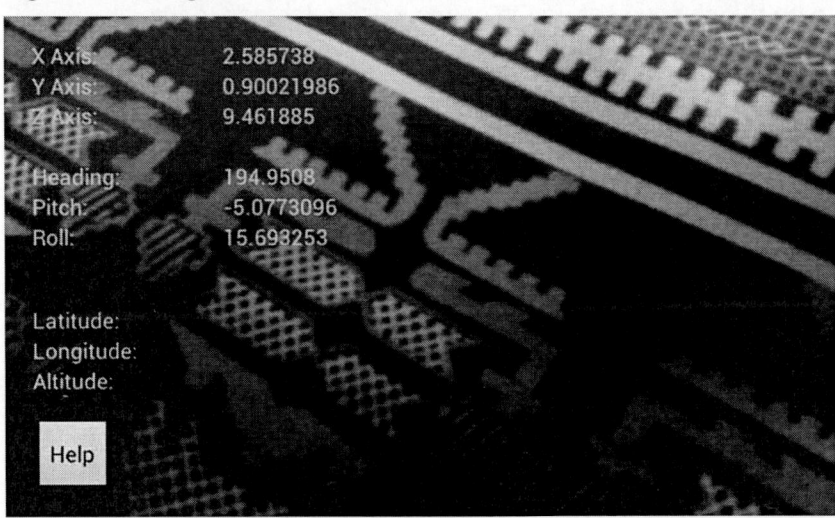

Figure 6-3. *Augmented reality view of the app*

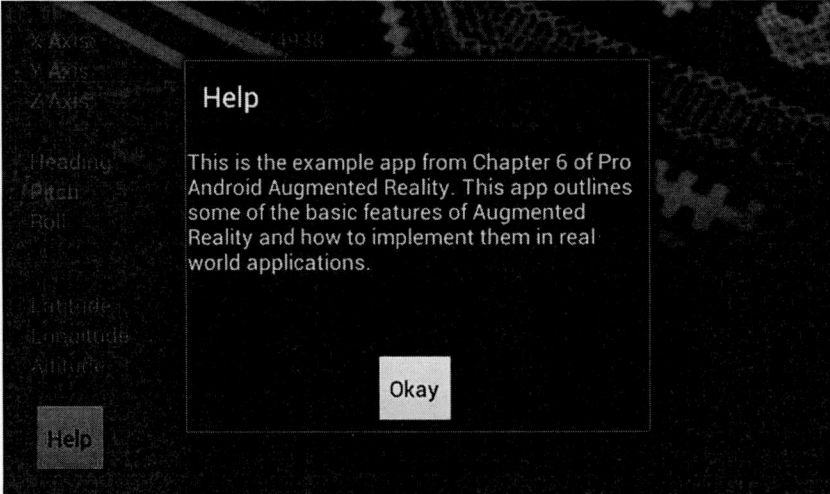

Figure 6-4. *Help dialog box for the app*

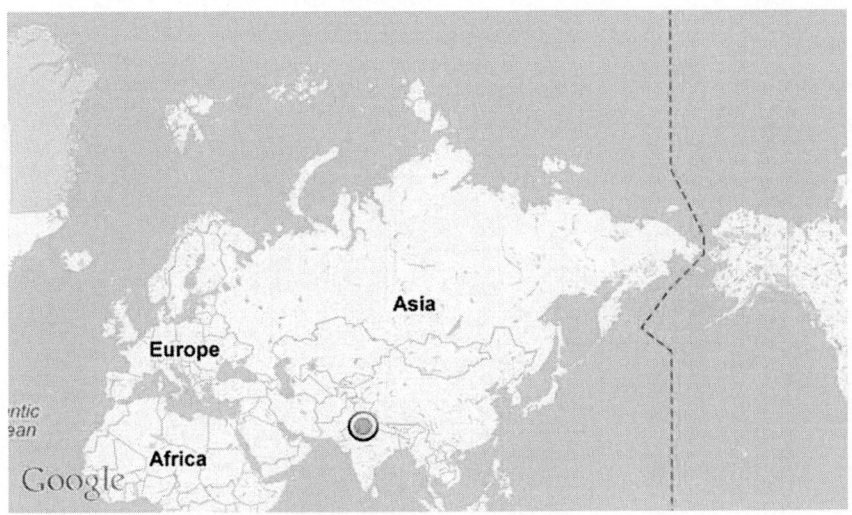

Figure 6-5. *Map shown when device is parallel to the ground*

The LogCat should look similar to Figure 6-6.

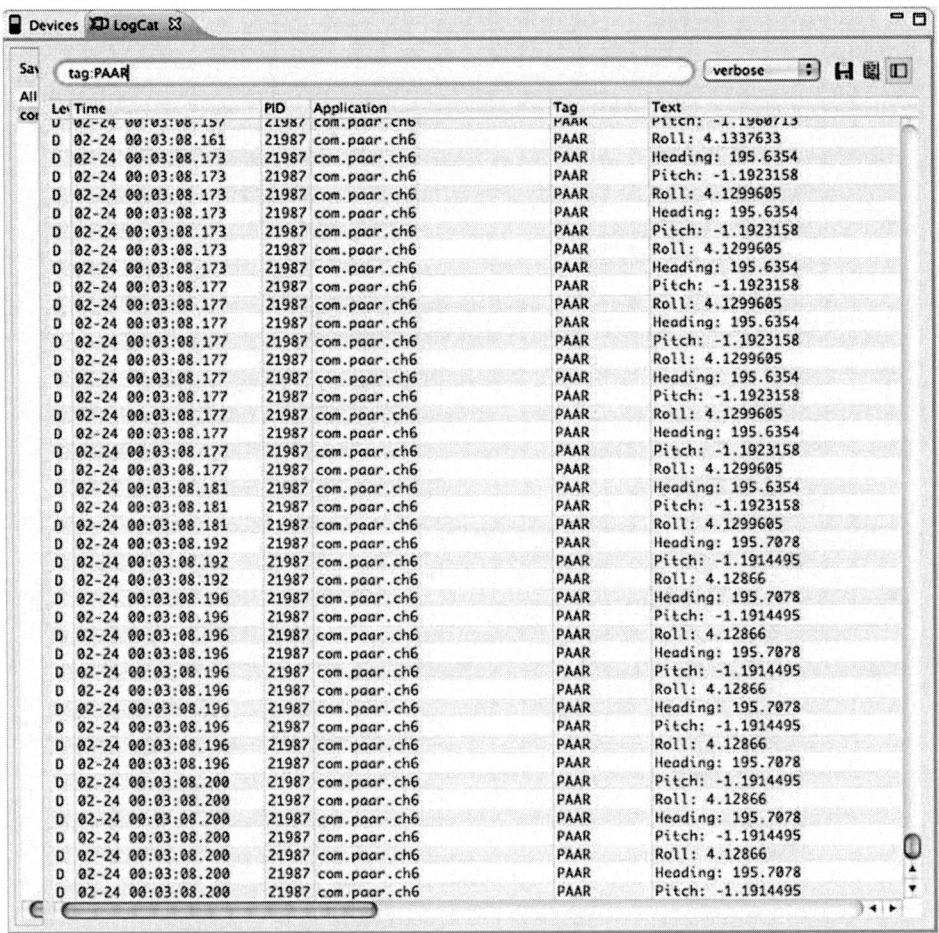

Figure 6-6. *Screenshot of the LogCat for the app*

Common errors

Following are four common errors from the app. For anything else, check with the android-developers Google group or stackoverflow.com for help.

- **Failed to connect to camera service:** The only time I have ever seen this error is when something else is already using the camera. This error can be resolved in several ways, and stackoverflow.com should be able to give you the answers.

- **Anything that looks related to the Map:** This is most likely because you are not building against Google APIs, or because you forgot to declare `<uses-library>` in the AndroidManifest or are using an incorrect API key.

- **Anything that looks related to R.something:** This error is most likely due to a mistake or mismatch in your XML files, or to a missing drawable. You can fix it by checking your XML files. If you are sure that they are correct and that your marker drawable is in place, try building from scratch by either compiling after deleting your /bin directory or using Project -> Clean.

- **Security exceptions:** These will most likely be due to a missing permission in your `AndroidManifest`.

Summary

This brings us to the end of the first example app in this book, which demonstrates how to do the following:

- Augment sensor information over a live camera preview, using the standard Android SDK

- Launch an `Activity` when the device is held in a particular manner, in this case parallel to the ground

- Display the user's current location on a map using the Google Maps APIs

- Implement a fix in case the Maps API is broken on a device

This app will be built upon in the next chapter to act as a simple navigational app with AR.

A Basic Navigational App Using Augmented Reality, the GPS, and Maps

In Chapter 6, we designed a simple AR app that would display sensor data over a camera preview and display a location on a map if the device was held parallel to the ground. In this chapter, we will extend this app so that it can be used for basic navigational purposes.

The New App

The extended version of the app will have the following features:

- When held nonparallel to the ground, the app will display a camera preview with various data overlayed onto it.

- When held parallel to the ground, a map will be launched. The user can locate the desired location on the map and enable the Tap To Set mode. Once the mode is enabled, the user can tap the desired location. This location is saved.

- When the camera preview is displayed again, a bearing to the desired location is calculated from the GPS's data, along with the distance between the two locations.

- The bearing and distance are updated every time a new location fix is received.

This app gives you every calculation you'll need, in case you ever want to extend it to add a compass and do other things.

Now without further ado, let's get to the coding.

Create a new project to begin with. In the example, the package name is com.paar.ch7, and the build target is the Google APIs, for android 2.1. We must target the Google APIs SDK as we are using Google Maps.

First, duplicate the Chapter 6 project. Change the name of the main `Activity` (the one with the camera preview) to whatever you want, as long as you remember to update the manifest to go with it. Also, because this is a new project, you'll probably want another package name as well.

Updated XML files

First, we need to update some of our XML files. Let's start with `strings.xml`:

Listing 7-1. *Updated strings.xml*

```
<?xml version="1.0" encoding="utf-8"?>
<resources>
    <string name="hello">Hello World, ASimpleAppUsingARActivity!</string>
    <string name="app_name">A Slightly More Complex AR App</string>
    <string name="xAxis">X Axis:</string>
    <string name="yAxis">Y Axis:</string>
    <string name="zAxis">Z Axis:</string>
    <string name="heading">Heading:</string>
    <string name="pitch">Pitch:</string>
    <string name="roll">Roll:</string>
    <string name="altitude">Altitude:</string>
    <string name="longitude">Longitude:</string>
    <string name="latitude">Latitude:</string>
    <string name="empty"></string>
    <string name="help">This is the example app from Chapter 7 of Pro Android
Augmented Reality. This app outlines some of the basic features of Augmented
Reality and how to implement them in real world applications. This app includes
a basic system that can be used for navigation. To make use of this system, put
the app in the map mode by holding the device flat. Then enable \"Enable tap to
set\" from the menu option after you have located the place you want to go to.
After that, switch back to camera mode. If a reliable GPS fix is available, you
```

will be given your current bearing to that location. The bearing will be updated every time a new location fix is received.</string>
```
        <string name="helpLabel">Help</string>
```
<string name="go">Go</string>
<string name="bearingLabel">Bearing:</string>
<string name="distanceLabel">Distance:</string>
```
</resources>
```

The "Distance:" over here will be used as the label where we tell the user the distance from his/her current location to the location selected, as the crow flies. The crows's path is the distance in a direct line from Point A to Point B. It does not tell the distance via road or any other such path. If you remember high school physics, it's pretty much like displacement. It is the shortest distance from Point A to Point B, regardless of whether that distance is actually traversable or not.

You'll notice a few new strings and an increase in the size of the help string. Apart from that, our strings.xml is mainly the same. Next, we need to update our map_toggle.xml from the /res/menu folder. We need to add a new option to allow the user to set the location.

Listing 7-2. *Updated map_toggle.xml*

```
<?xml version="1.0" encoding="utf-8"?>
<menu
  xmlns:android="http://schemas.android.com/apk/res/android">
    <item
        android:id="@+id/map"
        android:title="Map View"></item>
    <item
        android:id="@+id/sat"
        android:title="Satellite View"></item>
    <item
        android:id="@+id/both"
        android:title="Map + Satellite View"></item>
    <item
        android:id="@+id/toggleSetDestination"
        android:title="Enable Tap to Set">
    </item>
</menu>
```

Our new menu option is "Enable Tap to Set." This option will be used to allow the user to enable and disable the tap to set the functionality of our app. If we do not add a check, every time the user moves the map around or tries to zoom, a new location will be set. To avoid this, we make an enable/disable option.

Now for the final change in our biggest XML file: main.xml. We need to add two TextViews and move our help button a little. The code that follows shows only the updated parts. Anything not given here is exactly the same as in the previous chapter.

Listing 7-3. *Updated main.xml*

```
// Cut here

    <TextView
        android:id="@+id/altitudeValue"
        android:layout_width="wrap_content"
        android:layout_height="wrap_content"
        android:layout_alignBaseline="@+id/altitudeLabel"
        android:layout_alignBottom="@+id/altitudeLabel"
        android:layout_alignLeft="@+id/longitudeValue"
        android:text="@string/empty" />

    <TextView
        android:id="@+id/textView1"
        android:layout_width="wrap_content"
        android:layout_height="wrap_content"
        android:layout_alignLeft="@+id/altitudeLabel"
        android:layout_below="@+id/altitudeLabel"
        android:text="@string/bearingLabel" />

    <TextView
        android:id="@+id/bearingValue"
        android:layout_width="wrap_content"
        android:layout_height="wrap_content"
        android:layout_alignLeft="@+id/altitudeValue"
        android:layout_below="@+id/altitudeValue"
        android:text="@string/empty" />

    <Button
        android:id="@+id/helpButton"
        android:layout_width="wrap_content"
        android:layout_height="wrap_content"
        android:layout_alignParentBottom="true"
        android:layout_alignParentRight="true"
        android:text="@string/helpLabel" />

    <TextView
        android:id="@+id/distanceLabel"
        android:layout_width="wrap_content"
        android:layout_height="wrap_content"
        android:layout_alignLeft="@+id/textView1"
        android:layout_below="@+id/textView1"
        android:text="@string/distanceLabel" />

    <TextView
```

```
                    android:id="@+id/distanceValue"
                    android:layout_width="wrap_content"
                    android:layout_height="wrap_content"
                    android:layout_alignBottom="@+id/distanceLabel"
                    android:layout_alignLeft="@+id/bearingValue"
                    android:text="@string/empty" />
```

```
</RelativeLayout>
```

Seeing as even what we added follows the pattern of the previous chapter, I hope that this code is pretty self-explanatory. The TextViews with IDs that have "label" in them are the labels for the actual values. These will not be referenced from our Java code. The TextViews with "value" in their IDs will be updated dynamically from our Java code to display the values.

Updated Java files

Now we can get to the main Java code. Two out of three of our Java files need to be updated with new code.

In FixLocation.java, you need to update the package declaration to match the new one. That's the one and only change in that file.

Updates to FlatBack.java

Now let's move on to the next file that we need to update: FlatBack.java:

Listing 7-4. *Updated FlatBack.java*

```
package com.paar.ch7;

import com.google.android.maps.GeoPoint;
import com.google.android.maps.MapActivity;
import com.google.android.maps.MapView;
import com.google.android.maps.MyLocationOverlay;

import android.content.SharedPreferences;
import android.hardware.Sensor;
import android.hardware.SensorEvent;
import android.hardware.SensorEventListener;
import android.hardware.SensorManager;
import android.os.Bundle;
import android.util.Log;
import android.view.Menu;
import android.view.MenuInflater;
import android.view.MenuItem;
```

```
import android.view.MotionEvent;
import android.view.View;
import android.view.View.OnTouchListener;

public class FlatBack extends MapActivity{
    private MapView mapView;
    private MyLocationOverlay myLocationOverlay;
    final static String TAG = "PAAR";
    SensorManager sensorManager;

    SharedPreferences prefs;
    SharedPreferences.Editor editor;

    int orientationSensor;
    float headingAngle;
    float pitchAngle;
    float rollAngle;
    String enteredAddress;
    boolean tapToSet;
/** Called when the activity is first created. */
@Override
public void onCreate(Bundle savedInstanceState) {
    super.onCreate(savedInstanceState);

    // main.xml contains a MapView
    setContentView(R.layout.map);
    prefs = getSharedPreferences("PAARCH7", 0);
    editor = prefs.edit();
    sensorManager = (SensorManager) getSystemService(SENSOR_SERVICE);
    orientationSensor = Sensor.TYPE_ORIENTATION;
    sensorManager.registerListener(sensorEventListener, sensorManager
.getDefaultSensor(orientationSensor), SensorManager.SENSOR_DELAY_NORMAL);

    // extract MapView from layout
            mapView = (MapView) findViewById(R.id.mapView);
            mapView.setBuiltInZoomControls(true);

            // create an overlay that shows our current location
            myLocationOverlay = new FixLocation(this, mapView);

            // add this overlay to the MapView and refresh it
            mapView.getOverlays().add(myLocationOverlay);
            mapView.postInvalidate();

            // call convenience method that zooms map on our location
            zoomToMyLocation();

            mapView.setOnTouchListener(new OnTouchListener() {
```

```
        public boolean onTouch(View arg0, MotionEvent arg1) {

            if(tapToSet == true)
            {
            GeoPoint p = mapView.getProjection().fromPixels((int)
arg1.getX(), (int) arg1.getY());

            Log.d(TAG,"Latitude:" + String.valueOf(p.getLatitudeE6()/1e6));
            Log.d(TAG,"Longitude:" +
String.valueOf(p.getLongitudeE6()/1e6));
            float lat =(float) ((float) p.getLatitudeE6()/1e6);
            float lon = (float) ((float) p.getLongitudeE6()/1e6);
            editor.putFloat("SetLatitude", lat);
            editor.putFloat("SetLongitude", lon);
            editor.commit();
            return true;
            }
            return false;

        }

    });

}

@Override
public boolean onCreateOptionsMenu(Menu menu) {
    MenuInflater inflater = getMenuInflater();
    inflater.inflate(R.menu.map_toggle, menu);
    return true;
}

public boolean onOptionsItemSelected(MenuItem item) {
    // Handle item selection
    switch (item.getItemId()) {
    case R.id.map:
        if (mapView.isSatellite() == true) {
            mapView.setSatellite(false);
            mapView.setStreetView(true);
        }
        return true;
    case R.id.sat:
        if (mapView.isSatellite()==false){
            mapView.setSatellite(true);
            mapView.setStreetView(false);
        }
        return true;
    case R.id.both:
        mapView.setSatellite(true);
```

```
            mapView.setStreetView(true);
    case R.id.toggleSetDestination:
        if(tapToSet == false)
        {
            tapToSet = true;
            item.setTitle("Disable Tap to Set");
        }
        else if(tapToSet == true)
        {
            tapToSet = false;
            item.setTitle("Enable Tap to Set");
            mapView.invalidate();
        }
    default:
        return super.onOptionsItemSelected(item);
    }
}

final SensorEventListener sensorEventListener = new SensorEventListener() {
    public void onSensorChanged(SensorEvent sensorEvent) {
        if (sensorEvent.sensor.getType() == Sensor.TYPE_ORIENTATION)
        {
            headingAngle = sensorEvent.values[0];
            pitchAngle = sensorEvent.values[1];
            rollAngle = sensorEvent.values[2];

            Log.d(TAG, "Heading: " + String.valueOf(headingAngle));
            Log.d(TAG, "Pitch: " + String.valueOf(pitchAngle));
            Log.d(TAG, "Roll: " + String.valueOf(rollAngle));

            if (pitchAngle > 7 || pitchAngle < -7 || rollAngle > 7 || rollAngle
< -7)
            {
            launchCameraView();
            }
        }
}

    public void onAccuracyChanged(Sensor arg0, int arg1) {

    }
};

public void launchCameraView() {
    finish();
}

@Override
    protected void onResume() {
            super.onResume();
```

```
                myLocationOverlay.enableMyLocation();
    }

    @Override
    protected void onPause() {
            super.onPause();
            myLocationOverlay.disableMyLocation();
    }


    private void zoomToMyLocation() {
            GeoPoint myLocationGeoPoint = myLocationOverlay.getMyLocation();
            if(myLocationGeoPoint != null) {
                    mapView.getController().animateTo(myLocationGeoPoint);
                    mapView.getController().setZoom(10);
            }
    }

    protected boolean isRouteDisplayed() {
            return false;
    }
}
```

Let's look at what's changed. First, we have some new variables at the top:

```
boolean tapToSet;
SharedPreferences prefs;
SharedPreferences.Editor editor;
```

The boolean tapToSet will tell us if the Tap To Set mode is enabled or not. The other two are the SharedPreferences related variables. We will be using SharedPreferences to store the user's set value because we will be accessing it from both activities of our class. Sure, we could use startActivityForResult() when launching the MapActivity and get the user's set value that way, but by using SharedPreferences, we can also keep the user's last used location, in case the app is started later and a new location is not set.

Next, we have added some new stuff to our onCreate() method. These two lines are responsible for getting access to our SharedPreferences and allowing us to edit them later on:

```
prefs = getSharedPreferences("PAARCH7", 0);
editor = prefs.edit();
```

PAARCH7 is the name of our preferences file, standing for **Pro Android Augmented Reality Chapter 7**. If you extend this app on your own and use SharedPreferences from multiple places at once, keep in mind that when editing the same preference file, the changes are visible to everyone instantaneously. On the first run, the PAARCH7 file does not exist, so Android creates it. The little

0 right after the comma tells Android that this file is private. The next line assigns the editor to be able to edit our preferences.

Now we have some more changes in our onCreate() method. We assign an onTouchListener() to our MapView:

```
mapView.setOnTouchListener(new OnTouchListener() {

        public boolean onTouch(View arg0, MotionEvent arg1) {

                if(tapToSet == true)
                {
                GeoPoint p =
mapView.getProjection().fromPixels((int)arg1.getX(),↵
 (int) arg1.getY());

                Log.d(TAG,"Latitude:" +String.valueOf(p.getLatitudeE6()/1e6));
                Log.d(TAG,"Longitude:" +String.valueOf(p.getLongitudeE6()/1e6));
                float lat =(float) ((float) p.getLatitudeE6()/1e6);
                float lon = (float) ((float) p.getLongitudeE6()/1e6);
                editor.putFloat("SetLatitude", lat);
                editor.putFloat("SetLongitude", lon);
                editor.commit();
                return true;
                }
                return false;

                }

        });
```

In this onTouchListener(), we filter each touch. If Tap To Set mode is enabled, we capture the touch event and get the latitude and longitude. Then we convert the doubles we received from the touched GeoPoint into floats, so that we can write them to our preferences, which is exactly what we do. We put both the floats in our preferences file and then call editor.commit() to write them to the file. We return true if we capture the touch and false if we don't. By returning false, we allow the MapView to continue on its normal course of scrolling around and zooming in and out.

The last thing we need to do is alter our onOptionsItemSelected() method to allow for the Enable Tap To Set option.

```
public boolean onOptionsItemSelected(MenuItem item) {
    // Handle item selection
    switch (item.getItemId()) {
    case R.id.map:
        if (mapView.isSatellite() == true) {
            mapView.setSatellite(false);
```

```
                mapView.setStreetView(true);
        }
        return true;
    case R.id.sat:
        if (mapView.isSatellite()==false){
            mapView.setSatellite(true);
            mapView.setStreetView(false);
        }
        return true;
    case R.id.both:
        mapView.setSatellite(true);
        mapView.setStreetView(true);
    case R.id.toggleSetDestination:
        if(tapToSet == false)
        {
            tapToSet = true;
            item.setTitle("Disable Tap to Set");
        }
        else if(tapToSet == true)
        {
            tapToSet = false;
            item.setTitle("Enable Tap to Set");
            mapView.invalidate();
        }
    default:
        return super.onOptionsItemSelected(item);
    }
}
```

We check to see whether tapToSet is false first. If so, we set it to true and change the title to "Disable Tap to Set." If it is true, we change it to false and change the title back to "Enable Tap to Set."

That wraps up this file.

The main Activity file

Now we are left only with our main file.

We'll begin by looking at the new variables.

Listing 7-5. *Package declaration, imports, and new variables*

package com.paar.ch7;

```
import android.app.Activity;
import android.app.Dialog;
import android.content.Intent;
import android.content.SharedPreferences;
```

```
import android.hardware.Camera;

...

    double bearing;
    double distance;

    float lat;
    float lon;

    Location setLoc;
    Location locationInUse;

    SharedPreferences prefs;

...

    TextView bearingValue;
    TextView distanceValue;
```

The two floats lat and lon will store the values that we saved into our SharedPreferences in the MapActivity when they are read from the file. The Location setLoc will be passed the aforementioned latitude and longitude to create a new Location. We will then use that location to get the user's bearing. locationInUse is a copy of our GPS's location fix. The two TextViews will display our results. The doubles bearing and distance will store our results.

Now we need to make some changes to our onCreate() method.

Listing 7-6. *Updated onCreate()*

```
@Override
public void onCreate(Bundle savedInstanceState) {
    super.onCreate(savedInstanceState);
    setContentView(R.layout.main);
    setLoc = new Location("");

    prefs = getSharedPreferences("PAARCH7", 0);


    locationManager = (LocationManager) getSystemService(LOCATION_SERVICE);
    locationManager.requestLocationUpdates(LocationManager.GPS_PROVIDER, 2000,
 2, locationListener);

    sensorManager = (SensorManager) getSystemService(SENSOR_SERVICE);
    orientationSensor = Sensor.TYPE_ORIENTATION;
    accelerometerSensor = Sensor.TYPE_ACCELEROMETER;
    sensorManager.registerListener(sensorEventListener, sensorManager
.getDefaultSensor(orientationSensor), SensorManager.SENSOR_DELAY_NORMAL);
```

```
        sensorManager.registerListener(sensorEventListener, sensorManager
.getDefaultSensor(accelerometerSensor), SensorManager.SENSOR_DELAY_NORMAL);

        inPreview = false;

        cameraPreview = (SurfaceView)findViewById(R.id.cameraPreview);
        previewHolder = cameraPreview.getHolder();
        previewHolder.addCallback(surfaceCallback);
        previewHolder.setType(SurfaceHolder.SURFACE_TYPE_PUSH_BUFFERS);

        xAxisValue = (TextView) findViewById(R.id.xAxisValue);
        yAxisValue = (TextView) findViewById(R.id.yAxisValue);
        zAxisValue = (TextView) findViewById(R.id.zAxisValue);
        headingValue = (TextView) findViewById(R.id.headingValue);
        pitchValue = (TextView) findViewById(R.id.pitchValue);
        rollValue = (TextView) findViewById(R.id.rollValue);
        altitudeValue = (TextView) findViewById(R.id.altitudeValue);
        longitudeValue = (TextView) findViewById(R.id.longitudeValue);
        latitudeValue = (TextView) findViewById(R.id.latitudeValue);
        bearingValue = (TextView) findViewById(R.id.bearingValue);
        distanceValue = (TextView) findViewById(R.id.distanceValue);
        button = (Button) findViewById(R.id.helpButton);
        button.setOnClickListener(new OnClickListener() {
            public void onClick(View v) {
                showHelp();
            }
        });
}
```

The line prefs = getSharedPreferences("PAARCH7", 0); gets us access to our SharedPreferences. The next new lines (bearingValue = (TextView) findViewById(R.id.bearingValue); and distanceValue = (TextView) findViewById(R.id.distanceValue);) get a reference to our new TextViews and will allow us to update them later on.

Now we must update the LocationListener so that our calculations are updated as and when the location is updated. This is relatively simple.

Listing 7-7. *Updated LocationListener*

```
LocationListener locationListener = new LocationListener() {
    public void onLocationChanged(Location location) {
        locationInUse = location;
        latitude = location.getLatitude();
        longitude = location.getLongitude();
        altitude = location.getAltitude();

        Log.d(TAG, "Latitude: " + String.valueOf(latitude));
        Log.d(TAG, "Longitude: " + String.valueOf(longitude));
```

```
        Log.d(TAG, "Altitude: " + String.valueOf(altitude));

        latitudeValue.setText(String.valueOf(latitude));
        longitudeValue.setText(String.valueOf(longitude));
        altitudeValue.setText(String.valueOf(altitude));

          lat = prefs.getFloat("SetLatitude", 0.0f);
          lon = prefs.getFloat("SetLongitude", 0.0f);


          setLoc.setLatitude(lat);
          setLoc.setLongitude(lon);
          if(locationInUse != null)
          {
          bearing = locationInUse.bearingTo(setLoc);
          distance = locationInUse.distanceTo(setLoc);
          bearingValue.setText(String.valueOf(bearing));
          distanceValue.setText(String.valueOf(distance));
          }
    }
```

Our modifications include getting the values from the SharedPreferences and checking to see whether we have a valid location; if there is a valid location, we calculate and display the bearing and distance. If there isn't one, we do nothing.

We need to repeat somewhat the same thing in our onResume(). This is because when we switch to the MapActivity and set the location, we will come back to the camera preview. This means that the onResume() will be invoked, thus making it the perfect place to update our locations and calculations.

Listing 7-8. *Updated onResume*

```
@Override
public void onResume() {
  super.onResume();
  locationManager.requestLocationUpdates(LocationManager.GPS_PROVIDER, 2000,
 2, locationListener);
  sensorManager.registerListener(sensorEventListener, sensorManager
.getDefaultSensor(orientationSensor), SensorManager.SENSOR_DELAY_NORMAL);
  sensorManager.registerListener(sensorEventListener, sensorManager
.getDefaultSensor(accelerometerSensor), SensorManager.SENSOR_DELAY_NORMAL);
  //Camera camera;

  lat = prefs.getFloat("SetLatitude", 0.0f);
  lon = prefs.getFloat("SetLongitude", 0.0f);

  setLoc.setLatitude(lat);
  setLoc.setLongitude(lon);
  if(locationInUse != null)
```

```
{
bearing = locationInUse.bearingTo(setLoc);
distance = locationInUse.distanceTo(setLoc);
bearingValue.setText(String.valueOf(bearing));
distanceValue.setText(String.valueOf(distance));
}
else
{
    bearingValue.setText("Unable to get your location reliably.");
    distanceValue.setText("Unable to get your location reliably.");
}
}
```

Pretty much the exact same thing, except that we also give a message if we can't get the location to calculate the distance and bearing.

Updated AndroidManifest

This pretty much wraps up this example app. All the files not given here are exactly the same as those in Chapter 6. The final update is to AndroidManifest.xml, in which the Activity declaration has been edited:

Listing 7-9. *Updated AndroidManifest.xml*

```
<?xml version="1.0" encoding="utf-8"?>
<manifest xmlns:android="http://schemas.android.com/apk/res/android"
    package="com.paar.ch7"
    android:versionCode="1"
    android:versionName="1.0" >

    <uses-sdk android:minSdkVersion="7" />
```

The Completed App

Figures 7-1–7-5 show the app in the augmented reality mode, with the Help dialog box open and with the map open.

Figure 7-1. *The app on startup, with no GPS fix*

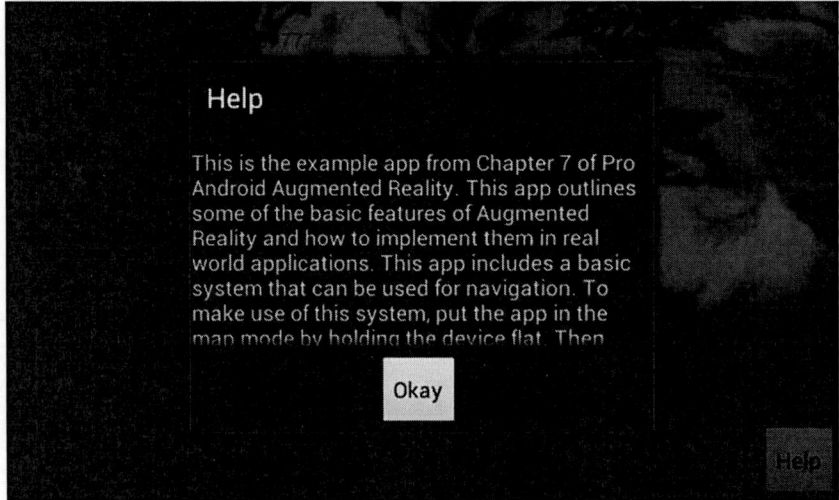

Figure 7-2. *The app with the Help dialog box open*

Figure 7-3. *The app with the map open, showing the options menu*

Figure 7-4. *The app with the user's current location displayed*

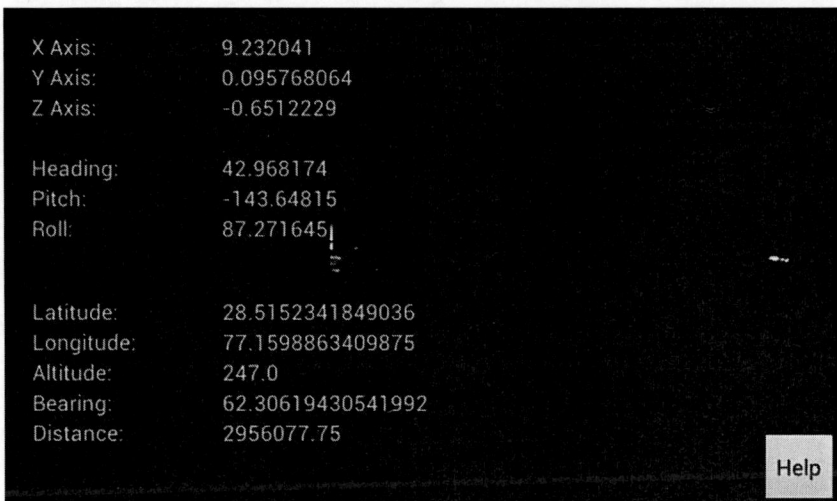

X Axis:	9.232041
Y Axis:	0.095768064
Z Axis:	-0.6512229
Heading:	42.968174
Pitch:	-143.64815
Roll:	87.271645
Latitude:	28.5152341849036
Longitude:	77.1598863409875
Altitude:	247.0
Bearing:	62.30619430541992
Distance:	2956077.75

Figure 7-5. *The app with the bearing and distance to the set location. The location was set to the middle of China, and I was facing north.*

You can get the complete source from this book's page on apress.com or from the GitHub repository.

Summary

This chapter discussed how to make the basic skeleton of a navigational app. We allow the user to select any point on a map to go to, and then we calculate the direction in which the user needs to move as the bearing. Converting this to a publishable app will only require you to draw an arrow pointing the user in the correct direction while in the augmented reality view. However, adding that in the example app will increase its complexity to beyond the scope of this chapter.

In the next chapter, you will learn how to design and implement a marker-based augmented reality viewer.

A 3D Augmented Reality Model Viewer

After completing the informational chapters and going through the previous two example apps, you should now be quite familiar with augmented reality (AR) on Android. This is the second-to-last example app, and the last that is in the realm of a normal, nongame app because the final example app is a game built using AR.

This app uses markers to function and is pretty straightforward. When launched, it will display a list of built-in objects to users to display on the marker or give them the option to select a custom object from the device's memory. The app accepts the objects in wavefront .obj files, along with their .mtl counterparts. If you are unfamiliar with these formats and wavefront in general, I recommend that you read up on it before continuing.

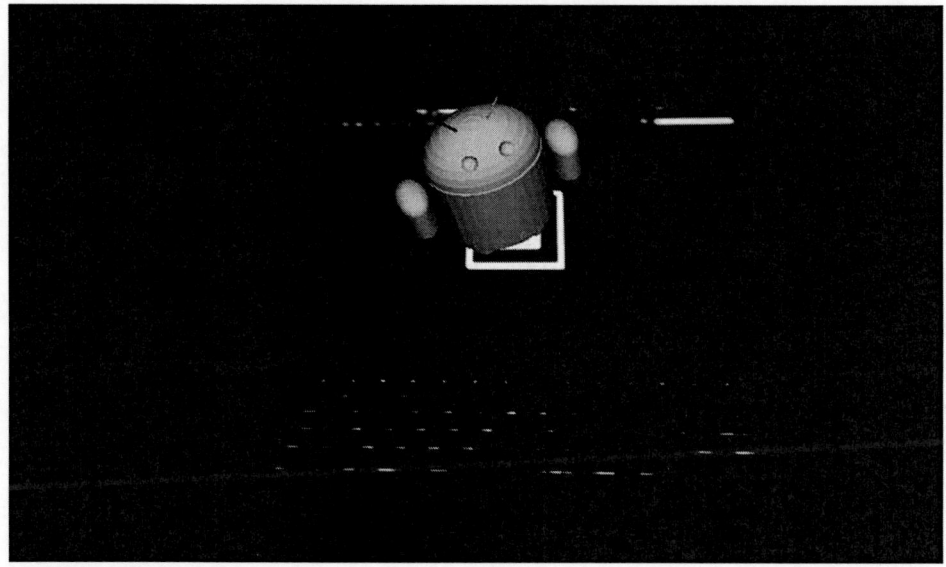

Figure 8-1. *The Android model being displayed.*

Key Features of this App

The following are the key features of this app:

- Allows users to view any of the preloaded models on a marker

- Allows users to view an external model that is located on the SD card, by using OI Filemanager to locate and select it

- Displays all models in 3D on the marker

Once more, start by creating a new project. This project does not extend any of the previous ones, so we'll be starting from scratch. We will have 22 Java files, 8 drawables, 4 layouts, 1 strings.xml, and 31 asset files. Figure 8-2 shows the details of the project.

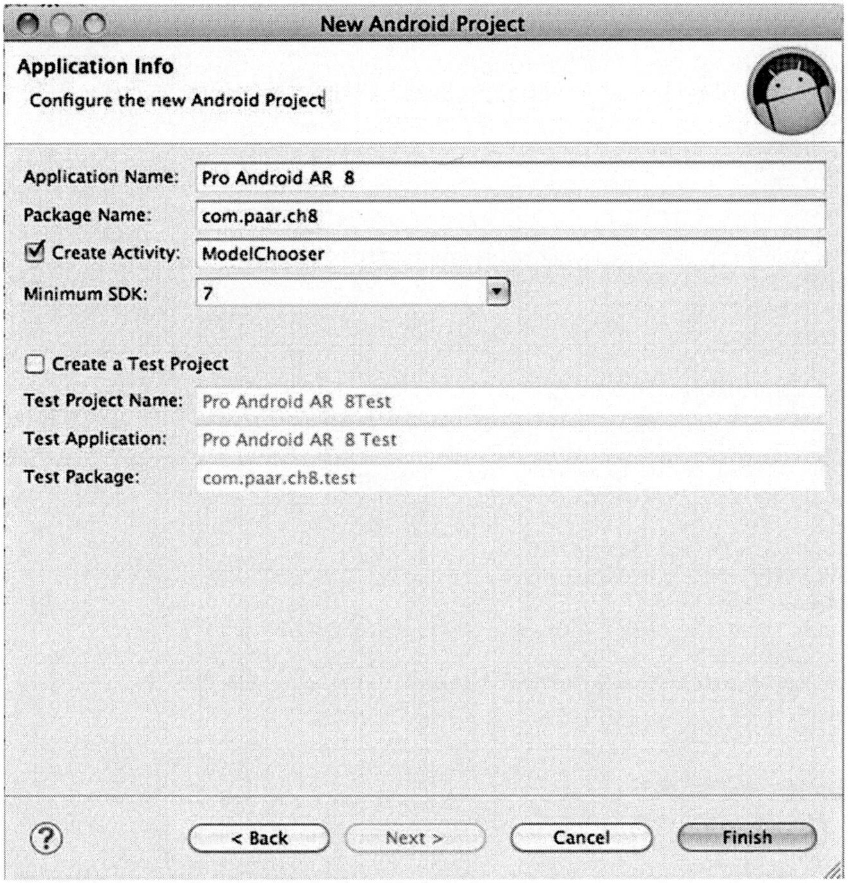

Figure 8-2. *The details of the project in this chapter.*

This project will be using AndAR as an external library to make our AR tasks easier. Marker recognition algorithms are difficult to implement, and this library is a working implementation that we can use safely within the scope of this book. You can obtain a copy of the AndAR library from http://code.google.com/p/andar/downloads/list, but it would be better if you downloaded it from this project's source on GitHub.com or Apress.com because future or older versions of AndAR may not be implemented the same way as the one used in this project.

The Manifest

To begin, here's the AndroidManifest.xml that declares all the permissions and activities in the app.

Listing 8-1. *AndroidManifest.xml*

```xml
<?xml version="1.0" encoding="utf-8"?>
<manifest xmlns:android="http://schemas.android.com/apk/res/android"
    package="com.paar.ch8"
    android:versionCode="1"
    android:versionName="1.0" >

    <uses-sdk android:minSdkVersion="7" />

    <application
        android:icon="@drawable/ic_launcher"
        android:label="@string/app_name" >
        <activity
            android:label="@string/app_name"
            android:name=".ModelChooser" >
            <intent-filter >
                <action android:name="android.intent.action.MAIN" />

                <category android:name="android.intent.category.LAUNCHER" />
            </intent-filter>
        </activity>

<activity android:exported="false"
    android:clearTaskOnLaunch="true"
    android:screenOrientation="landscape"
    android:icon="@drawable/ic_launcher"
    android:name=".ModelViewer">
</activity>
<activity android:exported="false"
    android:icon="@drawable/ic_launcher"
    android:name=".Instructions">
</activity>
            <activity android:label="@string/app_name"
                android:icon="@drawable/ic_launcher"
                android:name=".CheckFileManagerActivity">
        </activity>
    </application>

<uses-permission android:name="android.permission.WRITE_EXTERNAL_STORAGE"/>
<uses-permission android:name="android.permission.CAMERA"/>

<uses-feature android:name="android.hardware.camera" />
<uses-feature android:name="android.hardware.camera.autofocus" />
```

```
<supports-screens android:smallScreens="true"
                  android:normalScreens="true"
                  android:largeScreens="true"
                  android:anyDensity="true" />
</manifest>
```

In this file, we declare the four Activities in our app: ModelChooser, ModelViewer, Instructions and CheckFileManagerActivity. We then tell Android that we will be using the external storage and the camera, and ask for permission. We tell Android that we will be using the camera feature and its autofocus. Finally, we declare the screen sizes that our app will support.

Java Files

Let's begin the Java code by creating the file that will be our main activity.

Main Activity

In my case, this file is called `ModelChooser.java`, which displays when the user first starts the app. It has a list of the preloaded models that can be displayed, an option to load an external, user-provided model from the device memory, and a link to the help file.

onCreate() method

Let's start off its coding by making some changes to the `onCreate()` method of this file.

Listing 8-2. *onCreate() method in ModelChooser.java*

```
@Override
public void onCreate(Bundle savedInstanceState) {
    super.onCreate(savedInstanceState);
    AssetManager am = getAssets();
    Vector<Item> models = new Vector<Item>();
    Item item = new Item();
    item.text = getResources().getString(R.string.choose_a_model);
    item.type = Item.TYPE_HEADER;
    models.add(item);

    try {
        String[] modelFiles = am.list("models");
        List<String> modelFilesList = Arrays.asList(modelFiles);
```

```
        for (int i = 0; i < modelFiles.length; i++) {
        String currFileName = modelFiles[i];
        if(currFileName.endsWith(".obj")) {
            item = new Item();
            String trimmedFileName =
currFileName.substring(0,currFileName.lastIndexOf(".obj"));
            item.text = trimmedFileName;
            models.add(item);
            if(modelFilesList.contains(trimmedFileName+".jpg")) {
            InputStream is = am.open("models/"+trimmedFileName+".jpg");
            item.icon=(BitmapFactory.decodeStream(is));
        } else if(modelFilesList.contains(trimmedFileName+".png")) {
            InputStream is = am.open("models/"+trimmedFileName+".png");
            item.icon=(BitmapFactory.decodeStream(is));
        }
    }
}
}
} catch (IOException e) {
    e.printStackTrace();
}

    item = new Item();
    item.text = getResources().getString(R.string.custom_model);
    item.type = Item.TYPE_HEADER;
    models.add(item);
    item = new Item();
    item.text = getResources().getString(R.string.choose_custom_model);
    item.icon = new Integer(R.drawable.open);
    models.add(item);
    item = new Item();
    item.text = getResources().getString(R.string.help);
    item.type = Item.TYPE_HEADER;
    models.add(item);
    item = new Item();
    item.text = getResources().getString(R.string.instructions);
    item.icon = new Integer(R.drawable.help);
    models.add(item);

    setListAdapter(new ModelChooserListAdapter(models));
}
```

This code may look a little complex, but its task is quite simple. It retrieves a list of all the models we have in our assets folder and creates a nice list out of them. If there is a corresponding image file to go with the model, it displays that image in icon style next to the name of the object; otherwise it simply displays a cross-like image. Apart from adding the models that are shipped with the app, this code also adds the option to select your own model and to access the help files.

Listening for Clicks

Next, we need a method to listen for clicks and do the appropriate work for each click.

Listing 8-3. *onListItemClick() method*

```
@Override
protected void onListItemClick(ListView l, View v, int position, long id) {
    super.onListItemClick(l, v, position, id);
    Item item = (Item) this.getListAdapter().getItem(position);
    String str = item.text;
    if(str.equals(getResources().getString(R.string.choose_custom_model))) {
    //start oi file manager activity
    Intent intent = new Intent(ModelChooser.this,
CheckFileManagerActivity.class);
    startActivity(intent);
    } else if(str.equals(getResources().getString(R.string.instructions))) {
        //show the instructions activity
        startActivity(new Intent(ModelChooser.this, Instructions.class));
    } else {
        //load the selected internal file
        Intent intent = new Intent(ModelChooser.this, ModelViewer.class);
    intent.putExtra("name", str+".obj");
    intent.putExtra("type", ModelViewer.TYPE_INTERNAL);
    intent.setAction(Intent.ACTION_VIEW);
    startActivity(intent);
    }
}
```

This code listens for clicks on any of our list items. When a click is detected, it checks to see which item was clicked. If the user wants to select an external model, we use an intent to check for and launch the OI Filemanager. If the user wants to see the instructions, we launch the instructions activity. If an internal model is selected, we launch the model viewer while setting its action to `ACTION_VIEW` and sending the name of the model as an extra.

List Adapter

If you've been looking closely at the code in the `onCreate`, you will see an error where we are setting the adapter for our list. We'll fix this now by creating an inner class to function as our list's adapter.

Listing 8-4. *The Adapter for our list*

```
    class ModelChooserListAdapter extends BaseAdapter{
```

```java
        private Vector<Item> items;

        public ModelChooserListAdapter(Vector<Item> items) {
            this.items = items;
        }

        public int getCount() {
            return items.size();
        }

        public Object getItem(int position) {
            return items.get(position);
        }

        public long getItemId(int position) {
            return position;
        }

        @Override
        public int getViewTypeCount() {
            //normal items, and the header
            return 2;
        }

        @Override
        public boolean areAllItemsEnabled() {
            return false;
        }

        @Override
        public boolean isEnabled(int position) {
            return !(items.get(position).type==Item.TYPE_HEADER);
        }
    }

        @Override
        public int getItemViewType(int position) {
            return items.get(position).type;
        }


        public View getView(int position, View convertView, ViewGroup parent) {
            View v = convertView;
            Item item = items.get(position);
            if (v == null) {
                LayoutInflater vi =
(LayoutInflater)getSystemService(Context.LAYOUT_INFLATER_SERVICE);
                switch(item.type) {
                case Item.TYPE_HEADER:
                    v = vi.inflate(R.layout.list_header, null);
                        break;
```

```
                case Item.TYPE_ITEM:
                    v = vi.inflate(R.layout.choose_model_row, null);
                        break;
                }
            }
        if(item != null) {
            switch(item.type) {
                case Item.TYPE_HEADER:
                    TextView headerText = (TextView)
v.findViewById(R.id.list_header_title);
                    if(headerText != null) {
                        headerText.setText(item.text);
                    }
                    break;
                case Item.TYPE_ITEM:
                    Object iconImage = item.icon;
                    ImageView icon = (ImageView)
v.findViewById(R.id.choose_model_row_icon);
                    if(icon!=null) {
                        if(iconImage instanceof Integer) {

icon.setImageResource(((Integer)iconImage).intValue());
                        } else if(iconImage instanceof Bitmap) {
                            icon.setImageBitmap((Bitmap)iconImage);
                        }
                    }
            TextView text = (TextView)
v.findViewById(R.id.choose_model_row_text);
            if(text!=null)
            text.setText(item.text);
        break;
        }
            }
            return v;
        }

    }
```

In a nutshell, this code is responsible for actually pulling the icon images, names, and so on; and then creating a list out of them. There is nothing remarkable about it. It's more or less standard Android code when working with lists.

The following is another extremely small inner class that deals with our items.

Listing 8-5. *The inner class Item*

```
class Item {
    private static final int TYPE_ITEM=0;
    private static final int TYPE_HEADER=1;
```

```
        private int type = TYPE_ITEM;
        private Object icon = new Integer(R.drawable.missingimage);
        private String text;
    }
```

These five variables are used to set up each row in our list. TYPE_ITEM is a
constant that we can use to denote a row with a model in it instead of using
integers. TYPE_HEADER is the same as TYPE_ITEM, except that it is for headers.
The type variable is used to store the type of the item that is currently being
worked upon. It is set to TYPE_ITEM by default. The icon variable is used to
denote the icon used whenever a corresponding image is not available for a
model. The text variable is used to store the text of the current item being
worked upon.

This brings us to the end of the main ModelChooser class. Don't forget to insert
a final "}" to close the entire outer class.

Now that we've created our main Activity, let's tackle the remaining 21 Java files
in alphabetical order to keep track of them easily and to make it all a tad bit
easier.

AssetsFileUtility.java

We now need to create a file called AssetsFileUtility, which will be
responsible for reading in the data we have stored in our /assets folder. The
/assets folder is a place in which you can store any file you want and then later
retrieve it as a raw byte stream. In the capability to store raw files, it is similar to
/res/raw. However, a file stored in /res/raw can be localized and accessed
through a resource id such as R.raw.filename. The /assets folder offers no
localization or resource id access.

Listing 8-6. *AssetsFileUtility.java*

```
public class AssetsFileUtility extends BaseFileUtil {
    private AssetManager am;

    public AssetsFileUtility(AssetManager am) {
        this.am = am;
    }

    @Override
    public Bitmap getBitmapFromName(String name) {
        InputStream is = getInputStreamFromName(name);
        return (is==null)?null:BitmapFactory.decodeStream(is);
    }
```

```
@Override
public BufferedReader getReaderFromName(String name) {
    InputStream is = getInputStreamFromName(name);
    return (is==null)?null:new BufferedReader(new InputStreamReader(is));
}

private InputStream getInputStreamFromName(String name) {
    InputStream is;
    if(baseFolder != null) {
        try {
            is = am.open(baseFolder+name);
        } catch (IOException e) {
            e.printStackTrace();
            return null;
        }
    } else {
        try {
            is = am.open(name);
        } catch (IOException e) {
            e.printStackTrace();
            return null;
        }
    }
    return is;
}

}
```

This code helps us retrieve a file from the /assets folder. It handles most of the work, such as creating InputStreamReaders, and so on. You will get an IOException if the file you are trying to read doesn't exist or is in some other way invalid (for example, by having an invalid file extension).

BaseFileUtil.java

Next up is a miniature class called BaseFileUtil.java. This file is the base of others such as AssetsFileUtility. It allows us to conveniently update the folder in which the model being viewed is located.

Listing 8-7. *BaseFileUtil.java*

```
public abstract class BaseFileUtil {
    protected String baseFolder = null;

    public String getBaseFolder() {
        return baseFolder;
    }
```

```
public void setBaseFolder(String baseFolder) {
    this.baseFolder = baseFolder;
}

public abstract BufferedReader getReaderFromName(String name);
public abstract Bitmap getBitmapFromName(String name);

}
```

CheckFileManagerActivity.java

Next up on our alphabetical list is CheckFileManagerActivity., which is called when the user wants to supply his own object to be augmented by the app. By allowing the user to view his own models, we effectively make this app into a full-fledged 3D AR viewer. The user can create designs for a chair, for example, and see how it will look in his house before having it built. This extends the usability for our app immensely. Currently, the app only supports OI Filemanager for selecting new files, but you could modify the code to allow the app to work with other file managers as well. I chose OI as the default one because it comes preinstalled on a lot of devices, and is often installed if not.

Code Listing

Let's take a look at CheckFileManagerActivity.java section by section.

Declarations

First are the declarations needed in this class.

Listing 8-8. *CheckFileManagerActivity.java declarations*

```
public class CheckFileManagerActivity extends Activity {

    private final int PICK_FILE = 1;
    private final int VIEW_MODEL = 2;
    public static final int RESULT_ERROR = 3;

    private final int INSTALL_INTENT_DIALOG=1;

    private PackageManager packageManager;
    private Resources res;
    private TextView infoText;

    private final int TOAST_TIMEOUT = 3;
```

onCreate() and onResume()

Immediately following the declarations are the onCreate() and onResume() methods.

The first thing we do is check whether the OI File Manager is installed. If it isn't, we ask the user to install it. If the File Manager is available, we allow the user to select a file. See Listing 8-9.

Listing 8-9. *onCreate() and onResume()*

```
@Override
final public void onCreate(Bundle savedInstanceState) {
    super.onCreate(savedInstanceState);
    setContentView(R.layout.main);
    Context context = this;
    packageManager= context.getPackageManager();
    res = this.getResources();
    infoText = (TextView) findViewById(R.id.InfoText);
    if (isPickFileIntentAvailable()) {
        selectFile();
    } else {
        installPickFileIntent();
    }
}


@Override
protected void onResume() {
    super.onResume();
}
```

onActivityResult()

If the file selected is not a valid model file, we display a toast telling the user that and ask him to select again. If the selected file is a valid model file, we pass control to the Model Viewer, which will then have the file parsed and display it. If the user cancels the operation, we return the app to the Model Chooser screen.

Listing 8-10. *onActivityResult()*

```
@Override
protected void onActivityResult(int requestCode, int resultCode, Intent ➡
data) {
    super.onActivityResult(requestCode, resultCode, data);
    switch (requestCode) {
    default:
    case PICK_FILE:
```

```java
        switch(resultCode) {
        case Activity.RESULT_OK:
        //does file exist??
        File file =  new File(URI.create(data.getDataString()));
        if (!file.exists()) {
            //notify user that this file doesn't exist
            Toast.makeText(this, res.getText(R.string.file_doesnt_exist),
TOAST_TIMEOUT).show();
            selectFile();
} else {
    String fileName = data.getDataString();
if(!fileName.endsWith(".obj")) {
    Toast.makeText(this, res.getText(R.string.wrong_file),
TOAST_TIMEOUT).show();
    selectFile();
} else {
    //hand over control to the model viewer
    Intent intent = new Intent(CheckFileManagerActivity.this,
ModelViewer.class);
    intent.putExtra("name", data.getDataString());
    intent.putExtra("type", ModelViewer.TYPE_EXTERNAL);
    intent.setAction(Intent.ACTION_VIEW);
    startActivityForResult(intent, VIEW_MODEL);
}
}
break;
default:
case Activity.RESULT_CANCELED:
    //back to the main activity
    Intent intent = new Intent(CheckFileManagerActivity.this,
ModelChooser.class);
    startActivity(intent);
break;
}
break;
case VIEW_MODEL:
switch(resultCode) {
case Activity.RESULT_OK:
    //model viewer returned...let the user view a new file
    selectFile();
break;
case Activity.RESULT_CANCELED:
    selectFile();
break;
case RESULT_ERROR:
    //something went wrong ... notify the user
    if(data != null) {
        Bundle extras = data.getExtras();
        String errorMessage = extras.getString("error_message");
        if(errorMessage != null)
```

```
        Toast.makeText(this, extras.getString("error_message"),
TOAST_TIMEOUT).show();
        }
selectFile();
break;
}
}
 }
```

selectFile()

The selectFile() method allows the user to select a model file.

Listing 8-11. *selectFile()*

```
    /** Let the user select a File. The selected file will be handled in
     *  {@link
edu.dhbw.andobjviewer.CheckFileManagerActivity#onActivityResult(int, int,
Intent)} */
    private void selectFile() {
            //let the user select a model file
        Intent intent = new Intent("org.openintents.action.PICK_FILE");
        intent.setData(Uri.parse("file:///sdcard/"));
        intent.putExtra("org.openintents.extra.TITLE", res.getText(
            R.string.select_model_file));
        startActivityForResult(intent, PICK_FILE);
    }
```

isPickFileIntentAvailable() and installPickFileIntent()

The isPickFileIntentAvailable() and installPickFileIntent() methods are called in the onCreate method().

Listing 8-12. *isPickFileIntentAvailable() and installPickFileIntent()*

```
    private boolean isPickFileIntentAvailable() {
        return packageManager.queryIntentActivities(
            new Intent("org.openintents.action.PICK_FILE"), 0).size() > 0;
    }

    private boolean installPickFileIntent() {
            Uri marketUri =
Uri.parse("market://search?q=pname:org.openintents.filemanager");
        Intent marketIntent = new Intent(Intent.ACTION_VIEW).setData(marketUri);
        if (!(packageManager
            .queryIntentActivities(marketIntent, 0).size() > 0)) {
            //no Market available
            //show info to user and exit
```

```
            infoText.setText(res.getText(R.string.android_markt_not_avail));
            return false;
        } else {
            //notify user and start Android market

            showDialog(INSTALL_INTENT_DIALOG);
                return true;
        }
    }
```

onCreateDialog()

The final method in CheckFileManagerActivity.java is onCreateDialog().

Listing 8-13. *onCreateDialog()*

```
    @Override
    protected Dialog onCreateDialog(int id) {
        Dialog dialog = null;
        switch(id){
            case INSTALL_INTENT_DIALOG:
                AlertDialog alertDialog = new
AlertDialog.Builder(this).create();

alertDialog.setMessage(res.getText(R.string.pickfile_intent_required));
                alertDialog.setButton("OK", new
DialogInterface.OnClickListener() {
                    public void onClick(DialogInterface dialog, int which) {
                        //launch android market
                    Uri marketUri =
Uri.parse("market://search?q=pname:org.openintents.filemanager");
                        Intent marketIntent = new
Intent(Intent.ACTION_VIEW).setData(marketUri);
                        startActivity(marketIntent);
                        return;
                } });
            dialog = alertDialog;
             break;
        }
        return dialog;
    }

}
```

Configuration File

Next in our list is the `Config.java` file. This is literally the smallest Java file you will ever see. Excluding the package name, it is only three lines in size.

Listing 8-14. *Config.java*

```java
public class Config {
    public final static boolean DEBUG = false;
}
```

This file is technically the configuration file, even though it has only one option. Setting DEBUG to true will put the app in DEBUG mode. If you ever decide to extend the app, you can add other configuration options here, such as flags for which market you're publishing the apk to.

Working with Numbers

Next is the `FixedPointUtilities` class, which handles some of our mathematical functions, mostly converting arrays etc. It is very important for keeping our model looking the way it should.

Listing 8-15. *FixedPointUtilities.java*

```java
public class FixedPointUtilities {
    public static final int ONE = 0x10000;

    public static int toFixed(float val) {
        return (int)(val * 65536F);
    }

    public static int[] toFixed(float[] arr) {
        int[] res = new int[arr.length];
        toFixed(arr, res);
        return res;
    }

    public static void toFixed(float[] arr, int[] storage)
    {
        for (int i=0;i<storage.length;i++) {
            storage[i] = toFixed(arr[i]);
        }
    }


    public static float toFloat(int val) {
        return ((float)val)/65536.0f;
```

```
    }

    public static float[] toFloat(int[] arr) {
        float[] res = new float[arr.length];
        toFloat(arr, res);
        return res;
    }

    public static void toFloat(int[] arr, float[] storage)
    {
        for (int i=0;i<storage.length;i++) {
            storage[i] = toFloat(arr[i]);
        }
    }

    public static int multiply (int x, int y) {
        long z = (long) x * (long) y;
        return ((int) (z >> 16));
    }

    public static int divide (int x, int y) {
        long z = (((long) x) << 32);
        return (int) ((z / y) >> 16);
    }

    public static int sqrt (int n) {
        int s = (n + 65536) >> 1;
        for (int i = 0; i < 8; i++) {
            s = (s + divide(n, s)) >> 1;
        }
        return s;
    }
}
```

Now let's look at the methods in this class. The first method converts a single float value to a 16.16 fixed point value.

```
    public static int toFixed(float val) {
        return (int)(val * 65536F);
    }
```

The second method does the same thing, only it does it to an array of floats.

```
    public static int[] toFixed(float[] arr) {
        int[] res = new int[arr.length];
        toFixed(arr, res);
```

```
        return res;
    }
```

The third method is called by the second method to help in its work.

```
    public static void toFixed(float[] arr, int[] storage)
    {
        for (int i=0;i<storage.length;i++) {
            storage[i] = toFixed(arr[i]);
        }
    }
```

The fourth method converts a single fixed-point value into a float.

```
    public static float toFloat(int val) {
        return ((float)val)/65536.0f;
    }
```

The fifth method does the same to an array of fixed-point values, and it calls the sixth method to help it.

```
    public static float[] toFloat(int[] arr) {
        float[] res = new float[arr.length];
        toFloat(arr, res);
        return res;
    }

    public static void toFloat(int[] arr, float[] storage)
    {
        for (int i=0;i<storage.length;i++) {
            storage[i] = toFloat(arr[i]);
        }
    }
```

The seventh method multiplies two fixed point values, while the eighth method divides two fixed point values.

```
    public static int multiply (int x, int y) {
        long z = (long) x * (long) y;
        return ((int) (z >> 16));
    }

    public static int divide (int x, int y) {
        long z = (((long) x) << 32);
        return (int) ((z / y) >> 16);
    }
```

The ninth and last method finds the square root of a fixed point value.

```
    public static int sqrt (int n) {
        int s = (n + 65536) >> 1;
        for (int i = 0; i < 8; i++) {
            s = (s + divide(n, s)) >> 1;
```

```
        }
        return s;
    }
```

These methods are called from MatrixUtils.java. Our models are essentially a huge number of vertices. When we parse them, we need to deal with those vertices, and this helps us do so.

Group.java

Next, we have a class called `Group.java`. This class is mainly required for and used in parsing the .obj files and their .mtl counterparts; and making proper, user-friendly graphics out of them. This is a relatively small part of our object parsing, but is still important.

In OpenGL, every graphic is a set of coordinates called vertices. When three or more of these vertices are joined by lines, they are called faces. Several faces are often grouped together. Faces may or may not have a texture. A texture alters the way light is reflected off a particular face. This class deals with the creation of groups, associating each group to a material, and setting its texture.

Listing 8-16. *Group.java*

```java
public class Group implements Serializable {
    private String materialName = "default";
    private transient Material material;

    private boolean textured = false;
    public transient FloatBuffer vertices = null;
    public transient FloatBuffer texcoords = null;
    public transient FloatBuffer normals = null;
    public int vertexCount = 0;

    public ArrayList<Float> groupVertices = new ArrayList<Float>(500);
    public ArrayList<Float> groupNormals = new ArrayList<Float>(500);
    public ArrayList<Float> groupTexcoords = new ArrayList<Float>();

    public Group() {
    }

    public void setMaterialName(String currMat) {
        this.materialName = currMat;
    }

    public String getMaterialName() {
        return materialName;
    }
```

```java
    public Material getMaterial() {
        return material;
    }

    public void setMaterial(Material material) {
        if(texcoords != null && material != null && material.hasTexture()) {
            textured = true;
        }
        if(material != null)
            this.material = material;
    }

    public boolean containsVertices() {
        if(groupVertices != null)
            return groupVertices.size()>0;
        else if(vertices != null)
            return vertices.capacity()>0;
        else
            return false;
    }

    public void setTextured(boolean b) {
        textured = b;
    }

    public boolean isTextured() {
        return textured;
    }

    public void finalize() {
        if (groupTexcoords.size() > 0) {
            textured = true;
            texcoords = MemUtil.makeFloatBuffer(groupTexcoords.size());
            for (Iterator<Float> iterator = groupTexcoords.iterator();
iterator.hasNext();) {
                Float curVal = iterator.next();
                texcoords.put(curVal.floatValue());
            }
            texcoords.position(0);
            if(material != null && material.hasTexture()) {
            textured = true;
            } else {
                textured = false;
            }
        }
        groupTexcoords = null;
        vertices = MemUtil.makeFloatBuffer(groupVertices.size());
        vertexCount = groupVertices.size()/3;//three floats pers vertex
        for (Iterator<Float> iterator = groupVertices.iterator();
iterator.hasNext();) {
```

```
        Float curVal = iterator.next();
        vertices.put(curVal.floatValue());
    }
    groupVertices = null;
    normals = MemUtil.makeFloatBuffer(groupNormals.size());
    for (Iterator<Float> iterator = groupNormals.iterator();
iterator.hasNext();) {
        Float curVal = iterator.next();
        normals.put(curVal.floatValue());
    }
    groupNormals = null;
    vertices.position(0);
    normals.position(0);
    }
}
```

The code mostly deals with adding texture and "material" to the graphic we are parsing. It sets the texture to be used for the graphic and the material. Of course, this material is only virtual and is not technically speaking actual material.

Instructions.java

Next is another very simple file. This file is called `Instructions.java` and contains the `Activity` that displays our app's instructions by displaying an HTML file located in our `/assets/help` in a `WebView`.

Listing 8-17. *Instructions.java*

```
public class Instructions extends Activity {

    private WebView mWebView;

    @Override
    protected void onCreate(Bundle savedInstanceState) {
        super.onCreate(savedInstanceState);
        setContentView(R.layout.instructions_layout);
        mWebView = (WebView) findViewById(R.id.instructions_webview);

        WebSettings webSettings = mWebView.getSettings();
        webSettings.setSupportZoom(true);
        webSettings.setBuiltInZoomControls(true);

        WebChromeClient client = new WebChromeClient();
        mWebView.setWebChromeClient(client);
```

```
mWebView.loadUrl("file:///android_asset/help/"+getResources().getString(R.string
.help_file));
    }
}
```

The Activity starts, and a single WebView is set as its view. The WebView is then passed an HTML file that contains our help and is stored in the assets.

Working with Light

Now we get to some of the more complex stuff. Our models are rendered using OpenGL. To make them look even better, we also implement various lighting techniques. For this lighting, we have a class called LightingRenderer.

Listing 8-18. *LightingRenderer.java*

```
public class LightingRenderer implements OpenGLRenderer {

    private float[] ambientlight0 = {.3f, .3f, .3f, 1f};
    private float[] diffuselight0 = {.7f, .7f, .7f, 1f};
    private float[] specularlight0 = {0.6f, 0.6f, 0.6f, 1f};
    private float[] lightposition0 = {100.0f,-200.0f,200.0f,0.0f};

    private FloatBuffer lightPositionBuffer0 =
GraphicsUtil.makeFloatBuffer(lightposition0);
    private FloatBuffer specularLightBuffer0 =
GraphicsUtil.makeFloatBuffer(specularlight0);
    private FloatBuffer diffuseLightBuffer0 =
GraphicsUtil.makeFloatBuffer(diffuselight0);
    private FloatBuffer ambientLightBuffer0 =
GraphicsUtil.makeFloatBuffer(ambientlight0);


    private float[] ambientlight1 = {.3f, .3f, .3f, 1f};
    private float[] diffuselight1 = {.7f, .7f, .7f, 1f};
    private float[] specularlight1 = {0.6f, 0.6f, 0.6f, 1f};
    private float[] lightposition1 = {20.0f,-40.0f,100.0f,1f};

    private FloatBuffer lightPositionBuffer1 =
GraphicsUtil.makeFloatBuffer(lightposition1);
    private FloatBuffer specularLightBuffer1 =
GraphicsUtil.makeFloatBuffer(specularlight1);
    private FloatBuffer diffuseLightBuffer1 =
GraphicsUtil.makeFloatBuffer(diffuselight1);
    private FloatBuffer ambientLightBuffer1 =
GraphicsUtil.makeFloatBuffer(ambientlight1);
```

```java
    private float[] ambientlight2 = {.4f, .4f, .4f, 1f};
    private float[] diffuselight2 = {.7f, .7f, .7f, 1f};
    private float[] specularlight2 = {0.6f, 0.6f, 0.6f, 1f};
    private float[] lightposition2 = {5f,-3f,-20f,1.0f};

    private FloatBuffer lightPositionBuffer2 =
GraphicsUtil.makeFloatBuffer(lightposition2);
    private FloatBuffer specularLightBuffer2 =
GraphicsUtil.makeFloatBuffer(specularlight2);
    private FloatBuffer diffuseLightBuffer2 =
GraphicsUtil.makeFloatBuffer(diffuselight2);
    private FloatBuffer ambientLightBuffer2 =
GraphicsUtil.makeFloatBuffer(ambientlight2);

    private float[] ambientlight3 = {.4f, .4f, .4f, 1f};
    private float[] diffuselight3 = {.4f, .4f, .4f, 1f};
    private float[] specularlight3 = {0.6f, 0.6f, 0.6f, 1f};
    private float[] lightposition3 = {0,0f,-1f,0.0f};

    private FloatBuffer lightPositionBuffer3 =
GraphicsUtil.makeFloatBuffer(lightposition3);
    private FloatBuffer specularLightBuffer3 =
GraphicsUtil.makeFloatBuffer(specularlight3);
    private FloatBuffer diffuseLightBuffer3 =
GraphicsUtil.makeFloatBuffer(diffuselight3);
    private FloatBuffer ambientLightBuffer3 =
GraphicsUtil.makeFloatBuffer(ambientlight3);

    public final void draw(GL10 gl) {

    }

    public final void setupEnv(GL10 gl) {
        gl.glLightfv(GL10.GL_LIGHT0, GL10.GL_AMBIENT, ambientLightBuffer0);
        gl.glLightfv(GL10.GL_LIGHT0, GL10.GL_DIFFUSE, diffuseLightBuffer0);
        gl.glLightfv(GL10.GL_LIGHT0, GL10.GL_SPECULAR, specularLightBuffer0);
        gl.glLightfv(GL10.GL_LIGHT0, GL10.GL_POSITION, lightPositionBuffer0);
        gl.glEnable(GL10.GL_LIGHT0);
        gl.glLightfv(GL10.GL_LIGHT1, GL10.GL_AMBIENT, ambientLightBuffer1);
        gl.glLightfv(GL10.GL_LIGHT1, GL10.GL_DIFFUSE, diffuseLightBuffer1);
        gl.glLightfv(GL10.GL_LIGHT1, GL10.GL_SPECULAR, specularLightBuffer1);
        gl.glLightfv(GL10.GL_LIGHT1, GL10.GL_POSITION, lightPositionBuffer1);
        gl.glEnable(GL10.GL_LIGHT1);
        gl.glLightfv(GL10.GL_LIGHT2, GL10.GL_AMBIENT, ambientLightBuffer2);
        gl.glLightfv(GL10.GL_LIGHT2, GL10.GL_DIFFUSE, diffuseLightBuffer2);
        gl.glLightfv(GL10.GL_LIGHT2, GL10.GL_SPECULAR, specularLightBuffer2);
        gl.glLightfv(GL10.GL_LIGHT2, GL10.GL_POSITION, lightPositionBuffer2);
        gl.glEnable(GL10.GL_LIGHT2);
        gl.glLightfv(GL10.GL_LIGHT3, GL10.GL_AMBIENT, ambientLightBuffer3);
        gl.glLightfv(GL10.GL_LIGHT3, GL10.GL_DIFFUSE, diffuseLightBuffer3);
```

```
        gl.glLightfv(GL10.GL_LIGHT3, GL10.GL_SPECULAR, specularLightBuffer3);
        gl.glLightfv(GL10.GL_LIGHT3, GL10.GL_POSITION, lightPositionBuffer3);
        gl.glEnable(GL10.GL_LIGHT3);
        initGL(gl);
    }

    public final void initGL(GL10 gl) {
        gl.glDisable(GL10.GL_COLOR_MATERIAL);
        gl.glShadeModel(GL10.GL_SMOOTH);
        gl.glEnable(GL10.GL_LIGHTING);
        //gl.glEnable(GL10.GL_CULL_FACE);
        gl.glEnable(GL10.GL_DEPTH_TEST);
        gl.glEnable(GL10.GL_NORMALIZE);
        gl.glEnable(GL10.GL_RESCALE_NORMAL);
    }
}
```

We create floats that store the values for the lighting in different parts and circumstances and then create FloatBuffers out of them. All this is then applied to our app in the setupEnv() method and finally put out by the initGL method. This code is much closer to AR than the rest of the code seen so far in this chapter and is very important to make sure that our graphic's lighting is good and it looks realistic. OpenGL supports a total of eight different lighting configurations, and we create four of them (GL_LIGHT0-8). We have different ambient, specular, and diffusion light settings for all of them, which allows us to give the model four different kind of looks. All the lights are set to GL_SMOOTH, which takes more computational power, but results in a more realistic model.

Creating a Material

Now we come to our Material class. This class is the material mentioned earlier that was used in the Group class. In the real world, light is reflected off the material of an object. Some kinds of material reflect green shades, some red, some blue, and so on. Similarly, in OpenGL we create so-called material objects that then in turn make our final model up. Each material object is set to reflect a particular shade of light. When this is combined with our lighting effects, we get a combination of the two lights. For example, a red material ball will appear black with a blue lighting source because the red material will not reflect a shade of blue; it will reflect only a shade of red. This class handles all the OpenGL code related to materials.

Listing 8-19. *Material.java*

```
public class Material implements Serializable {

    private float[] ambientlightArr = {0.2f, 0.2f, 0.2f, 1.0f};
```

```java
    private float[] diffuselightArr = {0.8f, 0.8f, 0.8f, 1.0f};
    private float[] specularlightArr = {0.0f, 0.0f, 0.0f, 1.0f};

    public transient FloatBuffer ambientlight = MemUtil.makeFloatBuffer(4);
    public transient FloatBuffer diffuselight = MemUtil.makeFloatBuffer(4);
    public transient FloatBuffer specularlight = MemUtil.makeFloatBuffer(4);
    public float shininess = 0;
    public int STATE = STATE_DYNAMIC;
    public static final int STATE_DYNAMIC = 0;
    public static final int STATE_FINALIZED = 1;

    private transient Bitmap texture = null;
    private String bitmapFileName = null;
    private transient BaseFileUtil fileUtil = null;

    private String name = "defaultMaterial";

    public Material() {

    }

    public Material(String name) {
        this.name = name;
        //fill with default values
        ambientlight.put(new float[]{0.2f, 0.2f, 0.2f, 1.0f});
        ambientlight.position(0);
        diffuselight.put(new float[]{0.8f, 0.8f, 0.8f, 1.0f});
        diffuselight.position(0);
        specularlight.put(new float[]{0.0f, 0.0f, 0.0f, 1.0f});
        specularlight.position(0);
    }

    public String getName() {
        return name;
    }

    public void setName(String name) {
        this.name = name;
    }

    public void setFileUtil(BaseFileUtil fileUtil) {
        this.fileUtil = fileUtil;
    }

    public String getBitmapFileName() {
        return bitmapFileName;
    }

    public void setBitmapFileName(String bitmapFileName) {
        this.bitmapFileName = bitmapFileName;
```

```java
}

public void setAmbient(float[] arr) {
    ambientlightArr = arr;
}

public void setDiffuse(float[] arr) {
    diffuselightArr = arr;
}

public void setSpecular(float[] arr) {
    specularlightArr = arr;
}

public void setShininess(float ns) {
    shininess = ns;
}

public void setAlpha(float alpha) {
    ambientlight.put(3, alpha);
    diffuselight.put(3, alpha);
    specularlight.put(3, alpha);
}

public Bitmap getTexture() {
    return texture;
}

public void setTexture(Bitmap texture) {
    this.texture = texture;
}

public boolean hasTexture() {
    if(STATE == STATE_DYNAMIC)
        return this.bitmapFileName != null;
    else if(STATE == STATE_FINALIZED)
        return this.texture != null;
    else
        return false;
}

public void finalize() {
    ambientlight = MemUtil.makeFloatBuffer(ambientlightArr);
    diffuselight = MemUtil.makeFloatBuffer(diffuselightArr);
    specularlight = MemUtil.makeFloatBuffer(specularlightArr);
    ambientlightArr = null;
    diffuselightArr = null;
    specularlightArr = null;
    if(fileUtil != null && bitmapFileName != null) {
        texture = fileUtil.getBitmapFromName(bitmapFileName);
```

```
        }
      }
   }
```

This class helps us create new materials as and when required. There is a default material specified, but the setter methods such as setAmbient(), setDiffuse(), setSpecular(), and setShininess() allow us to specify the reflection values of the new array, along with its ambient light, and so on. The finalize method converts the lighting to FloatBuffers and assigns a value to texture.

MemUtil.java

Next up we have a rather small class that is used to create FloatBuffers. This is our MemUtil class.

Listing 8-20. *MemUtil.java*

```java
public class MemUtil {

    public static FloatBuffer makeFloatBufferFromArray(float[] arr) {
        ByteBuffer bb = ByteBuffer.allocateDirect(arr.length*4);
        bb.order(ByteOrder.nativeOrder());
        FloatBuffer fb = bb.asFloatBuffer();
        fb.put(arr);
        fb.position(0);
        return fb;
    }

    public static FloatBuffer makeFloatBuffer(int size) {
        ByteBuffer bb = ByteBuffer.allocateDirect(size*4);
        bb.order(ByteOrder.nativeOrder());
        FloatBuffer fb = bb.asFloatBuffer();
        fb.position(0);
        return fb;
    }

    public static FloatBuffer makeFloatBuffer(float[] arr) {
        ByteBuffer bb = ByteBuffer.allocateDirect(arr.length*4);
        bb.order(ByteOrder.nativeOrder());
        FloatBuffer fb = bb.asFloatBuffer();
        fb.put(arr);
        fb.position(0);
        return fb;
    }

}
```

This class is pretty straightforward and doesn't need much explanation, as it is pretty much standard Java. We need the floatbuffers as OpenGL only accepts floatbuffer arguments in its lighting and material implementations.

Model.java

Now we have a class that is very important to our app, `Model.java`.

Listing 8-21. *Model.java*

```java
public class Model implements Serializable{

    public float xrot = 90;
    public float yrot = 0;
    public float zrot = 0;
    public float xpos = 0;
    public float ypos = 0;
    public float zpos = 0;
    public float scale = 4f;
    public int STATE = STATE_DYNAMIC;
    public static final int STATE_DYNAMIC = 0;
    public static final int STATE_FINALIZED = 1;

    private Vector<Group> groups = new Vector<Group>();
    protected HashMap<String, Material> materials = new HashMap<String,
Material>();
    public Model() {
        materials.put("default",new Material("default"));
    }
    public void addMaterial(Material mat) {
        materials.put(mat.getName(), mat);
    }
    public Material getMaterial(String name) {
        return materials.get(name);
    }
    public void addGroup(Group grp) {
        if(STATE == STATE_FINALIZED)
            grp.finalize();
        groups.add(grp);
    }
    public Vector<Group> getGroups() {
         return groups;
    }
    public void setFileUtil(BaseFileUtil fileUtil) {
        for (Iterator iterator = materials.values().iterator();
iterator.hasNext();) {
            Material mat = (Material) iterator.next();
            mat.setFileUtil(fileUtil);
```

```java
        }
    }
    public HashMap<String, Material> getMaterials() {
        return materials;
    }
    public void setScale(float f) {
        this.scale += f;
        if(this.scale < 0.0001f)
            this.scale = 0.0001f;
    }
    public void setXrot(float dY) {
        this.xrot += dY;
    }
    public void setYrot(float dX) {
        this.yrot += dX;
    }
    public void setXpos(float f) {
        this.xpos += f;
    }
    public void setYpos(float f) {
        this.ypos += f;
    }
    public void finalize() {
        if(STATE != STATE_FINALIZED) {
            STATE = STATE_FINALIZED;
            for (Iterator iterator = groups.iterator(); iterator.hasNext();) {
                Group grp = (Group) iterator.next();
                grp.finalize();
                grp.setMaterial(materials.get(grp.getMaterialName()));
            }
            for (Iterator<Material> iterator = materials.values().iterator();
iterator.hasNext();) {
                Material mtl = iterator.next();
                mtl.finalize();
            }
        }
    }
}
```

This class does a lot of the groundwork for creating our models. Let's look at this one method by method. The Model() method is the constructor and sets the default material for our models. The addMaterial() method adds a material to our app. The addGroup() method adds another group to our groups, also finalizing it if needed. The setFileUtil() method takes a BaseFileUtil as an argument and then uses it to set the fileUtil for all our materials. The setScale() method allows us to pass a float to be set as the scale. It also makes sure that the scale is a nonzero and positive value. This scale value is used to scale the model. The setXrot() and setYrot() methods allow us to set the rotation on our model for the X-axis and Y-axis. The setXpos() and setYpos() methods are used to set the position of the model on the X-axis and Y-axis. The finalize() method finalizes everything and makes it nonalterable.

Model3D.java

Next on our list is Model3D.java, which is responsible for a good amount of the drawing of our models. The explanation comes after the code.

Listing 8-22. *Model3D.java*

```java
public class Model3D extends ARObject implements Serializable{

    private Model model;
    private Group[] texturedGroups;
    private Group[] nonTexturedGroups;
    private HashMap<Material, Integer> textureIDs = new HashMap<Material,
Integer>();

    public Model3D(Model model, String patternName) {
        super("model", patternName, 80.0, new double[]{0,0});
        this.model = model;
        model.finalize();

        Vector<Group> groups = model.getGroups();
        Vector<Group> texturedGroups = new Vector<Group>();
        Vector<Group> nonTexturedGroups = new Vector<Group>();
        for (Iterator<Group> iterator = groups.iterator(); iterator.hasNext();) {
            Group currGroup = iterator.next();
            if(currGroup.isTextured()) {
                texturedGroups.add(currGroup);
            } else {
                nonTexturedGroups.add(currGroup);
            }
        }
        this.texturedGroups = texturedGroups.toArray(new
Group[texturedGroups.size()]);
        this.nonTexturedGroups = nonTexturedGroups.toArray(new
Group[nonTexturedGroups.size()]);
    }

    @Override
    public void init(GL10 gl){
        int[] tmpTextureID = new int[1];

        Iterator<Material> materialI = model.getMaterials().values().iterator();
        while (materialI.hasNext()) {
            Material material = (Material) materialI.next();
```

```java
        if(material.hasTexture()) {

            gl.glGenTextures(1, tmpTextureID, 0);
            gl.glBindTexture(GL10.GL_TEXTURE_2D, tmpTextureID[0]);
            textureIDs.put(material, tmpTextureID[0]);
            GLUtils.texImage2D(GL10.GL_TEXTURE_2D, 0, material.getTexture(),0);
            material.getTexture().recycle();
            gl.glTexParameterx(GL10.GL_TEXTURE_2D, GL10.GL_TEXTURE_MIN_FILTER,
GL10.GL_LINEAR);
            gl.glTexParameterx(GL10.GL_TEXTURE_2D, GL10.GL_TEXTURE_MAG_FILTER,
GL10.GL_LINEAR);
        }
    }
}

@Override
public void draw(GL10 gl) {
    super.draw(gl);

    gl.glScalef(model.scale, model.scale, model.scale);
    gl.glTranslatef(model.xpos, model.ypos, model.zpos);
    gl.glRotatef(model.xrot, 1, 0, 0);
    gl.glRotatef(model.yrot, 0, 1, 0);
    gl.glRotatef(model.zrot, 0, 0, 1);

    gl.glEnableClientState(GL10.GL_VERTEX_ARRAY);
    gl.glEnableClientState(GL10.GL_NORMAL_ARRAY);

    gl.glDisable(GL10.GL_TEXTURE_2D);
    int cnt = nonTexturedGroups.length;
    for (int i = 0; i < cnt; i++) {
        Group group = nonTexturedGroups[i];
        Material mat = group.getMaterial();
        if(mat != null) {
            gl.glMaterialfv(GL10.GL_FRONT_AND_BACK, GL10.GL_SPECULAR,
mat.specularlight);
            gl.glMaterialfv(GL10.GL_FRONT_AND_BACK, GL10.GL_AMBIENT,
mat.ambientlight);
            gl.glMaterialfv(GL10.GL_FRONT_AND_BACK, GL10.GL_DIFFUSE,
mat.diffuselight);
            gl.glMaterialf(GL10.GL_FRONT_AND_BACK, GL10.GL_SHININESS,
mat.shininess);
        }
        gl.glVertexPointer(3,GL10.GL_FLOAT, 0, group.vertices);
        gl.glNormalPointer(GL10.GL_FLOAT,0, group.normals);
        gl.glDrawArrays(GL10.GL_TRIANGLES, 0, group.vertexCount);
    }

    gl.glEnable(GL10.GL_TEXTURE_2D);
    gl.glEnableClientState(GL10.GL_TEXTURE_COORD_ARRAY);
```

```
    cnt = texturedGroups.length;
    for (int i = 0; i < cnt; i++) {
        Group group = texturedGroups[i];
        Material mat = group.getMaterial();
        if(mat != null) {
            gl.glMaterialfv(GL10.GL_FRONT_AND_BACK, GL10.GL_SPECULAR,
mat.specularlight);
            gl.glMaterialfv(GL10.GL_FRONT_AND_BACK, GL10.GL_AMBIENT,
mat.ambientlight);
            gl.glMaterialfv(GL10.GL_FRONT_AND_BACK, GL10.GL_DIFFUSE,
mat.diffuselight);
            gl.glMaterialf(GL10.GL_FRONT_AND_BACK, GL10.GL_SHININESS,
mat.shininess);
            if(mat.hasTexture()) {
                gl.glTexCoordPointer(2,GL10.GL_FLOAT, 0, group.texcoords);
                gl.glBindTexture(GL10.GL_TEXTURE_2D,
textureIDs.get(mat).intValue());
            }
        }
        gl.glVertexPointer(3,GL10.GL_FLOAT, 0, group.vertices);
        gl.glNormalPointer(GL10.GL_FLOAT,0, group.normals);
        gl.glDrawArrays(GL10.GL_TRIANGLES, 0, group.vertexCount);
    }

    gl.glDisableClientState(GL10.GL_VERTEX_ARRAY);
    gl.glDisableClientState(GL10.GL_NORMAL_ARRAY);
    gl.glDisableClientState(GL10.GL_TEXTURE_COORD_ARRAY);
    }
}
```

In our constructor we get our model and then separate the textured groups from the nontextured groups to attain better performance. The init() method loads the textures for all of our materials. The main thing in this class is the draw() method. The first seven gl statements after the super statement do the positioning of our models. The next two statements and the for loop draw all the nontextured parts. The remainder of the method draws the textured parts of our model.

Viewing the Model

Next on our list is ModelViewer.java. This class is responsible for loading and displaying the model the user selected, whether from our provided models or from the SD Card. It is a big class and reasonably complex.

Variable Declarations

Global variables are used to store the location type of the file (inbuilt or external), the menu options, instances of Model and Model3D for each of the models, a progress dialog box and an instance of ARToolkit.

Listing 8-23. *ModelViewer.java Variables*

```
public class ModelViewer extends AndARActivity implements SurfaceHolder.Callback
{
    public static final int TYPE_INTERNAL = 0;
    public static final int TYPE_EXTERNAL = 1;
    public static final boolean DEBUG = false;
    private final int MENU_SCALE = 0;
    private final int MENU_ROTATE = 1;
    private final int MENU_TRANSLATE = 2;
    private final int MENU_SCREENSHOT = 3;

    private int mode = MENU_SCALE;
    private Model model;
    private Model model2;
    private Model model3;
    private Model model4;
    private Model model5;
    private Model3D model3d;
    private Model3D model3d2;
    private Model3D model3d3;
    private Model3D model3d4;
    private Model3D model3d5;
    private ProgressDialog waitDialog;
    private Resources res;
    ARToolkit artoolkit;
```

Constructor

The constructor for this class looks as follows.

Listing 8-24. *The constructor of ModelViewer.java*

```
public ModelViewer() {
    super(false);
}
```

onCreate() Method

The onCreate() method for our file sets the lighting via LightingRenderer.java, gets the resources for the app, assigns an instance of ARToolkit to artoolkit, sets the touch event listener for the surface view, and adds the call back for the surface view.

Listing 8-25. *The onCreate() method*

```
@Override
public void onCreate(Bundle savedInstanceState) {
    super.onCreate(savedInstanceState);
    super.setNonARRenderer(new LightingRenderer());
    res=getResources();
    artoolkit = getArtoolkit();
    getSurfaceView().setOnTouchListener(new TouchEventHandler());
    getSurfaceView().getHolder().addCallback(this);
}
```

Catching Exceptions and Handling Menu Options

uncaughtException() catches any exception that we do not explicitly catch elsewhere. The other two methods are very common standard Android code dealing with creating the menu and listening to the user's activity on it.

Listing 8-26. *Catching Exceptions and using the menu*

```
public void uncaughtException(Thread thread, Throwable ex) {
    System.out.println("");
}
@Override
public boolean onCreateOptionsMenu(Menu menu) {
    menu.add(0, MENU_TRANSLATE, 0, res.getText(R.string.translate))
        .setIcon(R.drawable.translate);
    menu.add(0, MENU_ROTATE, 0, res.getText(R.string.rotate))
        .setIcon(R.drawable.rotate);
    menu.add(0, MENU_SCALE, 0, res.getText(R.string.scale))
        .setIcon(R.drawable.scale);
    menu.add(0, MENU_SCREENSHOT, 0, res.getText(R.string.take_screenshot))
        .setIcon(R.drawable.screenshoticon);
    return true;
}
public boolean onOptionsItemSelected(MenuItem item) {
    switch (item.getItemId()) {
        case MENU_SCALE:
            mode = MENU_SCALE;
            return true;
        case MENU_ROTATE:
            mode = MENU_ROTATE;
            return true;
        case MENU_TRANSLATE:
            mode = MENU_TRANSLATE;
```

```
                return true;
            case MENU_SCREENSHOT:
                new TakeAsyncScreenshot().execute();
                return true;
        }
        return false;
    }
```

surfaceCreated()

surfaceCreated() is called when the SurfaceView is created, it shows a progress dialog box while the model is loading.

Listing 8-27. *surfaceCreated()*

```
    @Override
    public void surfaceCreated(SurfaceHolder holder) {
        super.surfaceCreated(holder);

        if(model == null) {
            waitDialog = ProgressDialog.show(this, "",
getResources().getText(R.string.loading), true);
            waitDialog.show();
            new ModelLoader().execute();
        }
    }
```

TouchEventHandler Inner Class

This inner class intercepts every single touch event that takes place in our Activity. It takes the kind of event and then appropriately scales, translates, or rotates the model.

Listing 8-28. *The inner class TouchEventHandler*

```
    class TouchEventHandler implements OnTouchListener {
        private float lastX=0;
        private float lastY=0;
        public boolean onTouch(View v, MotionEvent event) {
        if(model!=null) {
            switch(event.getAction()) {
                default:
            case MotionEvent.ACTION_DOWN:
                lastX = event.getX();
                lastY = event.getY();
                break;
            case MotionEvent.ACTION_MOVE:
```

```
                    float dX = lastX - event.getX();
                    float dY = lastY - event.getY();
                    lastX = event.getX();
                    lastY = event.getY();
                    if(model != null) {
                        switch(mode) {
                            case MENU_SCALE:
                                model.setScale(dY/100.0f);
                                break;
                            case MENU_ROTATE:
                                model.setXrot(-1*dX);
                                model.setYrot(-1*dY);
                                break;
                            case MENU_TRANSLATE:
                                model.setXpos(dY/10f);
                                model.setYpos(dX/10f);
                                break;
                        }
                    }
                    break;
                case MotionEvent.ACTION_CANCEL:
                case MotionEvent.ACTION_UP:
                    lastX = event.getX();
                    lastY = event.getY();
                    break;
            }
        }
        return true;
    }
}
```

ModelLoader Inner Class

In this ModelLoader inner class, we use a series of if else statements to
determine the model that we need to load. We also set the different markers
required for some of the inbuilt models. The default marker for some of the
inbuilt models, and all external models are called android. If the model is from
an external file, we first trim it before loading it. If it is an inbuilt model, we load it
directly. In onPostExecute(), we register all the models, and dismiss the
progress dialog box.

Listing 8-29. *ModelLoader*

```
private class ModelLoader extends AsyncTask<Void, Void, Void> {
    private String modelName2patternName (String modelName) {
        String patternName = "android";
        if (modelName.equals("plant.obj")) {
            patternName = "marker_rupee16";
```

```
            } else if (modelName.equals("chair.obj")) {
                patternName = "marker_fisch16";
            } else if (modelName.equals("tower.obj")) {
                patternName = "marker_peace16";
            } else if (modelName.equals("bench.obj")) {
                patternName = "marker_at16";
            } else if (modelName.equals("towergreen.obj")) {
                patternName = "marker_hand16";
            }
        return patternName;
}
    @Override
    protected Void doInBackground(Void... params) {
        Intent intent = getIntent();
        Bundle data = intent.getExtras();
        int type = data.getInt("type");
        String modelFileName = data.getString("name");
        BaseFileUtil fileUtil= null;
        File modelFile=null;
        switch(type) {
            case TYPE_EXTERNAL:
                fileUtil = new SDCardFileUtil();
                modelFile =  new File(URI.create(modelFileName));
                modelFileName = modelFile.getName();

fileUtil.setBaseFolder(modelFile.getParentFile().getAbsolutePath());
                break;
            case TYPE_INTERNAL:
                fileUtil = new AssetsFileUtility(getResources().getAssets());
                fileUtil.setBaseFolder("models/");
                break;
        }
        if(modelFileName.endsWith(".obj")) {
            ObjParser parser = new ObjParser(fileUtil);
            try {
                if(Config.DEBUG)
                Debug.startMethodTracing("AndObjViewer");
                if(type == TYPE_EXTERNAL) {
                BufferedReader modelFileReader = new BufferedReader(new
FileReader(modelFile));
                String shebang = modelFileReader.readLine();

                if(!shebang.equals("#trimmed")) {
                File trimmedFile = new File(modelFile.getAbsolutePath()+".tmp");
                BufferedWriter trimmedFileWriter = new BufferedWriter(new
FileWriter(trimmedFile));
                Util.trim(modelFileReader, trimmedFileWriter);
                if(modelFile.delete()) {
                trimmedFile.renameTo(modelFile);
                }
```

```
                }
                }
                if(fileUtil != null) {
                BufferedReader fileReader =
fileUtil.getReaderFromName(modelFileName);
                if(fileReader != null) {
                model = parser.parse("Model", fileReader);
                Log.w("ModelLoader", "model3d = new Model3D(model, " +
modelName2patternName(modelFileName) + ".patt");
                model3d = new Model3D(model, modelName2patternName(modelFileName)
+ ".patt");
                }
                String modelFileName2 = "chair.obj";
                BufferedReader fileReader2 =
fileUtil.getReaderFromName(modelFileName2);
                if(fileReader2 != null) {
                model2 = parser.parse("Chair", fileReader2);
                Log.w("ModelLoader", "model3d = new Model3D(model2, " +
modelName2patternName(modelFileName2) + ".patt");
                model3d2 = new Model3D(model2,
modelName2patternName(modelFileName2) + ".patt");
                } else {
                Log.w("ModelLoader", "no file reader");
                }
                String modelFileName3 = "towergreen.obj";
                BufferedReader fileReader3 =
fileUtil.getReaderFromName(modelFileName3);
                if(fileReader3 != null) {
                model3 = parser.parse("towergreen", fileReader3);
                Log.w("ModelLoader", "model3d = new Model3D(model3, " +
modelName2patternName(modelFileName3) + ".patt");
                model3d3 = new Model3D(model3,
modelName2patternName(modelFileName3) + ".patt");
                } else {
                Log.w("ModelLoader", "no file reader");
                }
                String modelFileName4 = "tower.obj";
                BufferedReader fileReader4 =
fileUtil.getReaderFromName(modelFileName4);
                if(fileReader4 != null) {
                model4 = parser.parse("tower", fileReader4);
                Log.w("ModelLoader", "model3d = new Model3D(model4, " +
modelName2patternName(modelFileName4) + ".patt");
                model3d4 = new Model3D(model4,
modelName2patternName(modelFileName4) + ".patt");
                } else {
                Log.w("ModelLoader", "no file reader");
                }
                String modelFileName5 = "plant.obj";
```

```
                        BufferedReader fileReader5 =
fileUtil.getReaderFromName(modelFileName5);
                if(fileReader5 != null) {
                model5 = parser.parse("Plant", fileReader5);
                Log.w("ModelLoader", "model3d = new Model3D(model5, " +
modelName2patternName(modelFileName5) + ".patt");
                model3d5 = new Model3D(model5,
modelName2patternName(modelFileName5) + ".patt");
                } else {
                Log.w("ModelLoader", "no file reader");
                }
                }
                if(Config.DEBUG)
                Debug.stopMethodTracing();
                } catch (IOException e) {
                    e.printStackTrace();
                } catch (ParseException e) {
                    e.printStackTrace();
                }
                }
        return null;
        }
        @Override
        protected void onPostExecute(Void result) {
            super.onPostExecute(result);
            waitDialog.dismiss();

            try {
                if(model3d!=null) {
                    artoolkit.registerARObject(model3d);
                    artoolkit.registerARObject(model3d2);
                    artoolkit.registerARObject(model3d3);
                    artoolkit.registerARObject(model3d4);
                    artoolkit.registerARObject(model3d5);
                }
            } catch (AndARException e) {
                e.printStackTrace();
            }
            startPreview();
        }
    }
```

TakeAsyncScreenshot Inner Class

In the TakeAsyncScreenshot inner class we call upon AndAR's inbuilt ability to
take a screenshot.

Listing 8-30. *TakeAsyncScreenshot*

```java
class TakeAsyncScreenshot extends AsyncTask<Void, Void, Void> {

    private String errorMsg = null;

    @Override
    protected Void doInBackground(Void... params) {
        Bitmap bm = takeScreenshot();
        FileOutputStream fos;
        try {
            fos = new FileOutputStream("/sdcard/AndARScreenshot"+new
Date().getTime()+".png");
            bm.compress(CompressFormat.PNG, 100, fos);
            fos.flush();
            fos.close();
        } catch (FileNotFoundException e) {
            errorMsg = e.getMessage();
            e.printStackTrace();
        } catch (IOException e) {
            errorMsg = e.getMessage();
            e.printStackTrace();
        }
        return null;
    }

    protected void onPostExecute(Void result) {
        if(errorMsg == null)
            Toast.makeText(ModelViewer.this,
getResources().getText(R.string.screenshotsaved), Toast.LENGTH_SHORT ).show();
        else
            Toast.makeText(ModelViewer.this,
getResources().getText(R.string.screenshotfailed)+errorMsg, Toast.LENGTH_SHORT
).show();
    };
    }
}
```

Parsing .mtl files

Next we have a very important class, `MtlParser.java`. This class is responsible
for parsing the .mtl files that accompany the .obj files of our models.

Listing 8-31. *MtlParser.java*

```java
public class MtlParser {

    private BaseFileUtil fileUtil;
```

```java
public MtlParser(Model model, BaseFileUtil fileUtil) {
    this.fileUtil = fileUtil;
}

public void parse(Model model, BufferedReader is) {
    Material curMat = null;
    int lineNum = 1;
    String line;
    try {
        for (line = is.readLine();
        line != null;
        line = is.readLine(), lineNum++)
        {
            line = Util.getCanonicalLine(line).trim();
            if (line.length() > 0) {
                if (line.startsWith("newmtl ")) {
                    String mtlName = line.substring(7);
                    curMat = new Material(mtlName);
                    model.addMaterial(curMat);
                } else if(curMat == null) {
                } else if (line.startsWith("# ")) {
                } else if (line.startsWith("Ka ")) {
                    String endOfLine = line.substring(3);
                    curMat.setAmbient(parseTriple(endOfLine));
                } else if (line.startsWith("Kd ")) {
                    String endOfLine = line.substring(3);
                    curMat.setDiffuse(parseTriple(endOfLine));
                } else if (line.startsWith("Ks ")) {
                    String endOfLine = line.substring(3);
                    curMat.setSpecular(parseTriple(endOfLine));
                } else if (line.startsWith("Ns ")) {
                    String endOfLine = line.substring(3);
                    curMat.setShininess(Float.parseFloat(endOfLine));
                } else if (line.startsWith("Tr ")) {
                    String endOfLine = line.substring(3);
                    curMat.setAlpha(Float.parseFloat(endOfLine));
                } else if (line.startsWith("d ")) {
                    String endOfLine = line.substring(2);
                    curMat.setAlpha(Float.parseFloat(endOfLine));
                } else if(line.startsWith("map_Kd ")) {
                    String imageFileName = line.substring(7);
                    curMat.setFileUtil(fileUtil);
                    curMat.setBitmapFileName(imageFileName);
                } else if(line.startsWith("mapKd ")) {
                    String imageFileName = line.substring(6);
                    curMat.setFileUtil(fileUtil);
                    curMat.setBitmapFileName(imageFileName);
                }
            }
```

```
        }
    } catch (IOException e) {
        e.printStackTrace();
    }
}

private static float[] parseTriple(String str) {
    String[] colorVals = str.split(" ");
    float[] colorArr = new float[]{
            Float.parseFloat(colorVals[0]),
            Float.parseFloat(colorVals[1]),
            Float.parseFloat(colorVals[2])};
    return colorArr;
}
}
```

The class is not very complex. Basically, the class reads the entire file line by line, and works on every line by seeing what it starts with. The absolute first condition makes sure that the line is actually a line, and not an empty one. After that, the nested if else statements are there.

All the conditions mentioned from now on are from the nested statements, unless mentioned otherwise. The first such condition checks to see whether the line is the first one by seeing if it begins with "newmtl".

```
        if (line.startsWith("newmtl ")) {
            String mtlName = line.substring(7);
            curMat = new Material(mtlName);
            model.addMaterial(curMat);
```

The next condition makes sure that our current material isn't null.

```
        } else if(curMat == null) {
```

The third one is used to ignore comments because they start with a "#" in .mtl files.

```
        } else if (line.startsWith("# ")) {
```

The fourth condition sees whether the line specifies the ambient light for our model, and sets it if it does.

```
        } else if (line.startsWith("Ka ")) {
            String endOfLine = line.substring(3);
            curMat.setAmbient(parseTriple(endOfLine));
```

The fifth condition sees whether the line specifies the diffuse light for our model and sets it if it does.

```
        } else if (line.startsWith("Kd ")) {
            String endOfLine = line.substring(3);
            curMat.setDiffuse(parseTriple(endOfLine));
```

The sixth condition sees whether the line specifies the specular light for our model and sets it if it does.

```
        } else if (line.startsWith("Ks ")) {
            String endOfLine = line.substring(3);
            curMat.setSpecular(parseTriple(endOfLine));
```

The seventh condition checks whether the line specifies the shininess for our model and sets it if it does.

```
        } else if (line.startsWith("Ns ")) {
            String endOfLine = line.substring(3);
            curMat.setShininess(Float.parseFloat(endOfLine));
```

The eighth and ninth conditions check whether the line specifies the alpha values for our model and sets it if it does.

```
        } else if (line.startsWith("Tr ")) {
            String endOfLine = line.substring(3);
            curMat.setAlpha(Float.parseFloat(endOfLine));
        } else if (line.startsWith("d ")) {
            String endOfLine = line.substring(2);
            curMat.setAlpha(Float.parseFloat(endOfLine));
```

The tenth and eleventh conditions check whether the line specifies the image for this model and sets it if it does.

```
        } else if(line.startsWith("map_Kd ")) {
            String imageFileName = line.substring(7);
            curMat.setFileUtil(fileUtil);
            curMat.setBitmapFileName(imageFileName);
        } else if(line.startsWith("mapKd ")) {
            String imageFileName = line.substring(6);
            curMat.setFileUtil(fileUtil);
            curMat.setBitmapFileName(imageFileName);
```

The catch statement in the end of the methods catches the IOException that will be triggered by something like the file not being found or if the file has unfavorable permissions.

```
    } catch (IOException e) {
        e.printStackTrace();
    }
```

The float parseTriple() is repeatedly called to help in parsing the file.

```
private static float[] parseTriple(String str) {
    String[] colorVals = str.split(" ");
    float[] colorArr = new float[]{
```

```
                Float.parseFloat(colorVals[0]),
                Float.parseFloat(colorVals[1]),
                Float.parseFloat(colorVals[2])};
        return colorArr;
    }
```

Parsing the .obj files

Next up is another very important class, `ObjParser.java`. It parses the .obj files, at least to an extent. It does not support the full .obj specification. It supports the following:

- Vertices

- Vertice normals

- Texture Coordinates

- Basic Materials

- Limited Texture Support (through the map_Kd, no options)

- Faces (may not omit the face normal)

This kind of support is enough for our models.

Listing 8-32. *ObjParser.java*

```
public class ObjParser {
    private final int VERTEX_DIMENSIONS = 3;
    private final int TEXTURE_COORD_DIMENSIONS = 2;

    private BaseFileUtil fileUtil;

    public ObjParser(BaseFileUtil fileUtil) {
        this.fileUtil = fileUtil;
    }

    public Model parse(String modelName, BufferedReader is) throws IOException,
ParseException {
        ArrayList<float[]> vertices = new ArrayList<float[]>(1000);
        ArrayList<float[]> normals = new ArrayList<float[]>(1000);
        ArrayList<float[]> texcoords = new ArrayList<float[]>();

        Model model = new Model();
        Group curGroup = new Group();
        MtlParser mtlParser = new MtlParser(model,fileUtil);
        SimpleTokenizer spaceTokenizer = new SimpleTokenizer();
        SimpleTokenizer slashTokenizer = new SimpleTokenizer();
        slashTokenizer.setDelimiter("/");
```

```
String line;
int lineNum = 1;
for (line = is.readLine();
line != null;
line = is.readLine(), lineNum++)
{
if (line.length() > 0) {
    if (line.startsWith("#")) {
    } else if (line.startsWith("v ")) {
        String endOfLine = line.substring(2);
        spaceTokenizer.setStr(endOfLine);
        vertices.add(new float[]{
            Float.parseFloat(spaceTokenizer.next()),
            Float.parseFloat(spaceTokenizer.next()),
            Float.parseFloat(spaceTokenizer.next())});
        }
    else if (line.startsWith("vt ")) {
        String endOfLine = line.substring(3);
        spaceTokenizer.setStr(endOfLine);
        texcoords.add(new float[]{
            Float.parseFloat(spaceTokenizer.next()),
            Float.parseFloat(spaceTokenizer.next())});
        }
    else if (line.startsWith("f ")) {
        String endOfLine = line.substring(2);
        spaceTokenizer.setStr(endOfLine);
        int faces = spaceTokenizer.delimOccurCount()+1;
        if(faces != 3) {
            throw new ParseException(modelName, lineNum, "only triangle faces
are supported");
            }
            for (int i = 0; i < 3; i++) {
                String face = spaceTokenizer.next();
                slashTokenizer.setStr(face);
                int vertexCount = slashTokenizer.delimOccurCount()+1;
                int vertexID=0;
                int textureID=-1;
                int normalID=0;
                if(vertexCount == 2) {
                    vertexID = Integer.parseInt(slashTokenizer.next())-1;
                    normalID = Integer.parseInt(slashTokenizer.next())-1;
                    throw new ParseException(modelName, lineNum, "vertex normal
needed.");
                } else if(vertexCount == 3) {
                vertexID = Integer.parseInt(slashTokenizer.next())-1;
                String texCoord = slashTokenizer.next();
                if(!texCoord.equals("")) {
                    textureID = Integer.parseInt(texCoord)-1;
                }
```

```
            normalID = Integer.parseInt(slashTokenizer.next())-1;
            } else {
            throw new ParseException(modelName, lineNum, "a faces needs
reference a vertex, a normal vertex and optionally a texture coordinate per
vertex.");
            }
            float[] vec;
            try {
                vec = vertices.get(vertexID);
            } catch (IndexOutOfBoundsException ex) {
            throw new ParseException(modelName, lineNum, "non existing vertex
referenced.");
            }
        if(vec==null)
        throw new ParseException(modelName, lineNum, "non existing vertex
referenced.");
        for (int j = 0; j < VERTEX_DIMENSIONS; j++)
        curGroup.groupVertices.add(vec[j]);
        if(textureID != -1) {
        try {
        vec = texcoords.get(textureID);
        } catch (IndexOutOfBoundsException ex) {
        throw new ParseException(modelName, lineNum, "non existing texture
coord referenced.");
            }
        if(vec==null)
        throw new ParseException(modelName, lineNum,  "non existing texture
coordinate referenced.");
        for (int j = 0; j < TEXTURE_COORD_DIMENSIONS; j++)
            curGroup.groupTexcoords.add(vec[j]);
        }
        try {
        vec = normals.get(normalID);
        } catch (IndexOutOfBoundsException ex) {
        throw new ParseException(modelName, lineNum, "non existing normal
vertex referenced.");
        }
        if(vec==null)
        throw new ParseException(modelName, lineNum, "non existing normal
vertex referenced.");
        for (int j = 0; j < VERTEX_DIMENSIONS; j++)
            curGroup.groupNormals.add(vec[j]);
        }
        }
    else if (line.startsWith("vn ")) {
        String endOfLine = line.substring(3);
        spaceTokenizer.setStr(endOfLine);
        normals.add(new float[]{
            Float.parseFloat(spaceTokenizer.next()),
            Float.parseFloat(spaceTokenizer.next()),
```

```
            Float.parseFloat(spaceTokenizer.next())});
    } else if (line.startsWith("mtllib ")) {
        String filename = line.substring(7);
        String[] files = Util.splitBySpace(filename);
        for (int i = 0; i < files.length; i++) {
        BufferedReader mtlFile = fileUtil.getReaderFromName(files[i]);
        if(mtlFile != null)
            mtlParser.parse(model, mtlFile);
        }
    } else if(line.startsWith("usemtl ")) {
        if(curGroup.groupVertices.size()>0) {
            model.addGroup(curGroup);
            curGroup = new Group();
        }
        curGroup.setMaterialName(line.substring(7));
    } else if(line.startsWith("g ")) {
        if(curGroup.groupVertices.size()>0) {
            model.addGroup(curGroup);
            curGroup = new Group();
        }
    }
    }
}
if(curGroup.groupVertices.size()>0) {
    model.addGroup(curGroup);
}
Iterator<Group> groupIt = model.getGroups().iterator();
while (groupIt.hasNext()) {
    Group group = (Group) groupIt.next();
    group.setMaterial(model.getMaterial(group.getMaterialName()));
}
return model;
}
}
```

This file goes through the .obj files line by line. There are a series of if else blocks that parse the file. The following happens at each line:

1. Comments (starting with a #) are ignored

2. Vertices (starting with v) are added to the vertices ArrayList.

3. Texture Coordinates (starting with vt) are added to the texcoords ArrayList.

4. Faces (starting with f) are added to groups.

5. Normals (starting with vn) are added to the normals ArrayList.

6. Corresponding .mtl files (starting with mtllib) are parsed.

7. New materials are added and corresponding groups created (starting with usemtl).

8. New groups are created (starting with g).

Upon completion, it returns a model.

ParseException

Next is the ParseException.java class that is the ParseException that is repeatedly thrown in ObjParser.java. It is a custom exception that we have written to allow us to easily put across problems that occur during the parsing process.

Listing 8-33. *ParseException.java*

```
public class ParseException extends Exception {
    public ParseException(String file,int lineNumber, String msg) {
        super("Parse error in file "+file+"on line "+lineNumber+":"+msg);
    }
}
```

It's very simple; it just outputs a message, filling in the message specific details via parameters.

Rendering

Next is the Renderer.java file, which handles a lot of the drawing work for our graphic, including some tricky 3D stuff.

Listing 8-34. *Renderer.java*

```
public class Renderer implements GLSurfaceView.Renderer {

    private final Vector<Model3D> models;
    private final Vector3D cameraPosition = new Vector3D(0, 3, 50);
    long frame,time,timebase=0;
    public Renderer(Vector<Model3D> models) {
        this.models = models;
    }
    public void addModel(Model3D model) {
        if(!models.contains(model)) {
            models.add(model);
        }
    }
    public void onDrawFrame(GL10 gl) {
        if(ModelViewer.DEBUG) {
```

```
            frame++;
            time=System.currentTimeMillis();
            if (time - timebase > 1000) {
                Log.d("fps: ", String.valueOf(frame*1000.0f/(time-timebase)));
                timebase = time;
                frame = 0;
            }
        }
        gl.glClear(GL10.GL_COLOR_BUFFER_BIT | GL10.GL_DEPTH_BUFFER_BIT);
        gl.glLoadIdentity();
        GLU.gluLookAt(gl, cameraPosition.x, cameraPosition.y, cameraPosition.z,
                0, 0, 0, 0, 1, 0);
        for (Iterator<Model3D> iterator = models.iterator(); iterator.hasNext();)
{
            Model3D model = iterator.next();
            model.draw(gl);
        }
    }

    public void onSurfaceChanged(GL10 gl, int width, int height) {
        gl.glViewport(0,0,width,height);
        gl.glMatrixMode(GL10.GL_PROJECTION);
        gl.glLoadIdentity();
        GLU.gluPerspective(gl, 45.0f, ((float)width)/height, 0.11f, 100f);
        gl.glMatrixMode(GL10.GL_MODELVIEW);
        gl.glLoadIdentity();
    }

    public void onSurfaceCreated(GL10 gl, EGLConfig config) {
        gl.glClearColor(1,1,1,1);

        gl.glClearDepthf(1.0f);
        gl.glEnable(GL10.GL_DEPTH_TEST);
        gl.glDepthFunc(GL10.GL_LEQUAL);

        gl.glEnable(GL10.GL_TEXTURE_2D);

        gl.glShadeModel(GL10.GL_SMOOTH);
        gl.glDisable(GL10.GL_COLOR_MATERIAL);
        gl.glEnable(GL10.GL_BLEND);
        gl.glBlendFunc(GL10.GL_SRC_ALPHA, GL10.GL_ONE_MINUS_SRC_ALPHA);
        gl.glEnable(GL10.GL_LIGHTING);
        float[] ambientlight = {.6f, .6f, .6f, 1f};
        float[] diffuselight = {1f, 1f, 1f, 1f};
        float[] specularlight = {1f, 1f, 1f, 1f};
        gl.glLightfv(GL10.GL_LIGHT0, GL10.GL_AMBIENT,
MemUtil.makeFloatBuffer(ambientlight));
        gl.glLightfv(GL10.GL_LIGHT0, GL10.GL_DIFFUSE,
MemUtil.makeFloatBuffer(diffuselight));
```

```
    gl.glLightfv(GL10.GL_LIGHT0, GL10.GL_SPECULAR,
MemUtil.makeFloatBuffer(specularlight));
    gl.glEnable(GL10.GL_LIGHT0);

    for (Iterator<Model3D> iterator = models.iterator(); iterator.hasNext();)
{
        Model3D model = iterator.next();
        model.init(gl);
    }
  }
}
```

The constructor stores the models that are passed to it locally. The addModel()
method adds a model to our list. The onDrawFrame() logs the frame rate if the
app is set to Debug mode. Regardless of the mode of the app, the
onDrawFrame() method also updates what the user is shown. The
onSurfaceChanged() method is called whenever the surface changes and
applies changes related to the new width and height. The onSurfaceCreated()
method does the initial setup work when the surface is first created.

SDCardFileUtil.java

Next is the SDCardFileUtil.java. This is an extension of BaseFileUtil and
handles the reading of the files.

Listing 8-35. *SDCardFileUtil.java*

```
public class SDCardFileUtil extends BaseFileUtil {
    public BufferedReader getReaderFromName(String name) {
    if (baseFolder != null) {
       try {
       return new BufferedReader(new FileReader(new File(baseFolder, name)));
       } catch (FileNotFoundException e) {
       return null;
       }
       } else {
       try {
       return new BufferedReader(new FileReader(new File(name)));
       } catch (FileNotFoundException e) {
       return null;
       }
       }
    }

    public Bitmap getBitmapFromName(String name) {
        if (baseFolder != null) {
            String path = new File(baseFolder,name).getAbsolutePath();
```

```
        return BitmapFactory.decodeFile(path);
    } else {
        return BitmapFactory.decodeFile(name);
    }
  }
}
}
```

The first method attempts to get a BufferedReader by the file name, and the second one tries to get a Bitmap by the name.

SimpleTokenizer.java

Next is the SimpleTokenizer.java class, which class is used as a Tokenizer in many places to delimit strings.

Listing 8-36. *SimpleTokenizer.java*

```java
public class SimpleTokenizer {
    String str = "";
    String delimiter = " ";
    int delimiterLength = delimiter.length();
    int i =0;
    int j =0;
    public final String getStr() {
        return str;
    }
    public final void setStr(String str) {
        this.str = str;
        i =0;
        j =str.indexOf(delimiter);
    }
    public final String getDelimiter() {
        return delimiter;
    }
    public final void setDelimiter(String delimiter) {
        this.delimiter = delimiter;
        delimiterLength = delimiter.length();
    }
    public final boolean hasNext() {
        return j >= 0;
    }
    public final String next() {
        if(j >= 0) {
            String result = str.substring(i,j);
            i = j + 1;
            j = str.indexOf(delimiter, i);
            return result;
        } else {
```

```
            return str.substring(i);
        }
    }
    public final String last() {
        return str.substring(i);
    }

    public final int delimOccurCount() {
        int result = 0;
        if (delimiterLength > 0) {
            int start = str.indexOf(delimiter);
            while (start != -1) {
                result++;
                start = str.indexOf(delimiter, start + delimiterLength);
            }
        }
        return result;
    }
}
```

It's a simple class. Everything is from the standard Java package, and nothing needs to be imported. Strictly speaking, there is no Android API used in this class. You could copy paste it into a normal Java project and it would work perfectly.

Util.java

Next is Util.java. This class optimizes our .obj files so that they can be parsed faster next time.

Listing 8-37. *Util.java*

```
public class Util {
    private static final Pattern trimWhiteSpaces = Pattern.compile("[\\s]+");
    private static final Pattern removeInlineComments = Pattern.compile("#");
    private static final Pattern splitBySpace = Pattern.compile(" ");

    public static final String getCanonicalLine(String line) {
        line = trimWhiteSpaces.matcher(line).replaceAll(" ");
        if(line.contains("#")) {
            String[] parts = removeInlineComments.split(line);
            if(parts.length > 0)
                line = parts[0];
        }
        return line;
    }
    public static String[] splitBySpace(String str) {
        return splitBySpace.split(str);
```

```java
        }

    public static void trim(BufferedReader in, BufferedWriter out) throws
IOException {
        String line;
        out.write("#trimmed\n");
        for (line = in.readLine();
        line != null;
        line = in.readLine()) {
            line = getCanonicalLine(line);
            if(line.length()>0) {
                out.write(line.trim());
                out.write('\n');
            }
        }
        in.close();
        out.close();
    }

    public final static List<String> fastSplit(final String text, char
separator, final boolean emptyStrings) {
        final List<String> result = new ArrayList<String>();

        if (text != null && text.length() > 0) {
            int index1 = 0;
            int index2 = text.indexOf(separator);
            while (index2 >= 0) {
                String token = text.substring(index1, index2);
                result.add(token);
                index1 = index2 + 1;
                index2 = text.indexOf(separator, index1);
            }

            if (index1 < text.length() - 1) {
                result.add(text.substring(index1));
            }
        }

        return result;
    }

}
```

This is, once again, standard Java. It simply removes whitespaces, inline comments etc. for faster parsing next time.

3D Vectors

Now we come to that last of the Java files, `Vector3D.java`. This file works with a three-dimensional vector. This class is used to position our virtual OpenGL camera. This camera is very different from the hardware camera we've been using all along. It is a virtual camera from which we see our model.

Listing 8-38. *Vector3D.java*

```
public class Vector3D implements Serializable {
    public float x=0;
    public float y=0;
    public float z=0;

    public Vector3D(float x, float y, float z) {
        super();
        this.x = x;
        this.y = y;
        this.z = z;
    }
    public float getX() {
        return x;
    }

    public void setX(float x) {
        this.x = x;
    }

    public float getY() {
        return y;
    }

    public void setY(float y) {
        this.y = y;
    }

    public float getZ() {
        return z;
    }

    public void setZ(float z) {
        this.z = z;
    }

}
```

All the methods are getting x, y, or z or setting them. That's all there is to it.

XML Files

Now that we are done with the all the Java files, we can move on to the XML files.

Strings.xml

Let's start with the `strings.xml`.

Listing 8-39. *strings.xml*

```xml
<?xml version="1.0" encoding="utf-8"?>
<resources>
<string name="app_name">PAAR Chapter 8</string>
<string name="select_model_file">Select a model file:</string>
<string name="android_markt_not_avail">Android market is not available, you need
install to OI File manager manually.</string>
<string name="pickfile_intent_required">You need to install the OI File Manager
in order to use this application.</string>
<string name="file_doesnt_exist">This file doesn\'t exist!</string>
<string name="unknown_file_type">Unknown file type!</string>
<string name="rotate">rotate</string>
<string name="translate">translate</string>
<string name="scale">scale</string>

<string name="loading">Loading. Please wait...</string>
<string name="app_description">AndAR Model Viewer allows you to view wavefront
obj models on an Augmented Reality marker.</string>
<string name="take_screenshot">Take a screenshot</string><string
name="screenshotsaved">Screenshot saved!</string><string
name="screenshotfailed">Failed to save screenshot: </string>
<string name="choose_custom_model">Select a model file</string>
<string name="instructions">Instructions</string>
<string name="wrong_file">Select an obj model file. (.obj)</string>
<string name="choose_a_model">Choose a model:</string>
<string name="help">Help:</string>
<string name="custom_model">Custom model:</string>
<string name="help_file">index.html</string>
</resources>
```

This file contains all the predefined strings for our app. Each string's contents and name should provide you with an exact description of what they do.

Layout for the Rows

Now let's see the layout files. We have choose_model_row.xml, which is used in the ModelChooser.

Listing 8-40. *choose_model_row.xml*

```
<?xml version="1.0" encoding="utf-8"?>
<LinearLayout xmlns:android="http://schemas.android.com/apk/res/android"
    android:layout_width="fill_parent"
    android:layout_height="?android:attr/listPreferredItemHeight"
    android:padding="6dip">
<ImageView
        android:id="@+id/choose_model_row_icon"
        android:layout_width="wrap_content"
        android:layout_height="fill_parent"
        android:layout_marginRight="6dip"
        android:src="@drawable/ic_launcher" />
<TextView xmlns:android="http://schemas.android.com/apk/res/android"
        android:id="@+id/choose_model_row_text"
    android:layout_width="fill_parent"
    android:layout_height="wrap_content"
    android:textAppearance="?android:attr/textAppearanceLarge"
    android:gravity="center_vertical"
    android:paddingLeft="6dip"
    android:minHeight="?android:attr/listPreferredItemHeight"
/>
</LinearLayout>
```

We have an ImageView for the icon, and a TextView for the name put together side by side. That's the entire layout for our rows.

instructions_layout.xml

Next is the instructions_layout.xml, which is the XML file behind our instructions Activity.

Listing 8-41. *instructions_layout.xml*

```
<?xml version="1.0" encoding="utf-8"?>
<LinearLayout xmlns:android="http://schemas.android.com/apk/res/android"
    android:orientation="vertical"
    android:layout_width="fill_parent"
    android:layout_height="fill_parent"
    >
<WebView
        android:id="@+id/instructions_webview"
        android:layout_width="fill_parent"
```

```
        android:layout_height="0dip"
        android:layout_weight="1"
        />
</LinearLayout>
```

Here we have a linear layout that is completely filled by a WebView to display the instructions HTML file.

List Header

Next we have `list_header.xml`, which is, as the name may have given away, the header for our list.

Listing 8-42. *list_header.xml*

```
<?xml version="1.0" encoding="utf-8"?>
<TextView
    xmlns:android="http://schemas.android.com/apk/res/android"
    android:id="@+id/list_header_title"
    android:layout_width="fill_parent"
    android:layout_height="wrap_content"
    android:paddingTop="2dip"
    android:paddingBottom="2dip"
    android:paddingLeft="5dip"
    style="?android:attr/listSeparatorTextViewStyle" />
```

main.xml

Finally we have `main.xml`, which is used to display the information.

Listing 8-43. *main.xml*

```
<?xml version="1.0" encoding="utf-8"?>
<LinearLayout xmlns:android="http://schemas.android.com/apk/res/android"
    android:orientation="vertical"
    android:layout_width="fill_parent"
    android:layout_height="fill_parent"
    >
<TextView
    android:layout_width="wrap_content"
    android:layout_height="wrap_content"
    android:id="@+id/InfoText">
</TextView>
</LinearLayout>
```

HTML Help File

This brings us to the end of the XML files. Now all that is left is one HTML file, which is our instructions file. It is located in /assets/help/.

Listing 8-44. *index.html*

```
<html>
    <head>
        <style type="text/css">
        h1 {font-size:20px;}
        h2 {font-size:16px;}
        </style>
    </head>
    <body>
        <p>This is the 3rd example application from the book Pro Android
Augmented Reality by Raghav Sood, published by Apress. It projects models on a
marker.
        You may either use the internal models or supply your own models in the
<a href="http://en.wikipedia.org/wiki/Obj">wavefront obj format.</a></p>
            <ol
                    <li><a href="#firststeps">First steps</a></li>
                    <li><a href="#screenshot">Taking a screenshot</a></li>
                    <li><a href="#transforming">Transforming the
model</a></li>
                    <li><a href="#custommodels">Custom models</a></li>
            </ol>
            <h2><a name="firststeps">First steps</a></h2>
            <ul>
                    <li>First print out the marker, upon which the models
will be projected. The marker is located in the assets folder of the project
source.</li>
            </ul>
            <ul>
                    <li>Select one of the internal models.</li>
                    <li>The app will start loading the model.</li>
                    <li>After it has finished, you will see a live video
stream from the camera.</li>
                    <li>Now point the camera to the marker, you should see
the model you selected.</li>
            </ul>
            <h2><a name="screenshot">Taking a screenshot</a></h2>
            <ul>
                    <li>First press the menu key.</li>
                    <li>Next press the button "Take a screenshot".</li>
                    <li>The application will now process the image. It
will notfiy you, when it's finished.</li>
```

```
                    <li>The screenshot you just took can be found in the
root folder of your sd-card. It will be named something like
<i>AndARScreenshot1234.png</i></li>
        </ul>
        <h2><a name="transforming">Transforming the model</a></h2>
        <ul>
                    <li>Press the menu key and select the desired
transformation mode. You may either scale, rotate or translate the model.</li>
                    <li>Scale: Slide you finger up and down the touch
screen. This will enlarge and shorten the model, respectively.</li>
                    <li>Rotate: Slide your finger horizontally and
vertically, this will rotate your model correspondingly. </li>
                    <li>Translate: Slide your finger horizontally and
vertically, this will translate your model correspondingly. </li>
        </ul>
        <h2><a name="custommodels">Custom models</a></h2>
        The application is capable of showing custom wavefront obj models.
Most 3d modelling software out there can export this format(e.g. 3ds max,
Blender).
        There are currently some restrictions to the models:
        <ul>
        <li>Every face must have normals specified</li>
        <li>The object must be triangulated, this means exactly 3 vertices
per face.</li>
        <li>Basic materials and textures are supported.</li>
        </ul>
        E.g. when exporting a model from blender make sure you check
<i>Normals</i> and <i>Triangulate</i>.
        <h2>Attribution</h2>
        <ul>
        <li>This app contains code developed by the Android Open Source
Project, released under the Apache License.</li>
        <li>This app contains models from <a
href="http://resources.blogscopia.com/modelos_en.html">resources.blogscopia.com<
/a> released under the <a
href="http://creativecommons.org/licenses/by/3.0/">Creative Commons 3.0 Unported
license</a>, see also: <a href="http://www.scopia.es">www.scopia.es</a>.</li>
            <li>This product includes software developed by the <a
href="http://mij.oltrelinux.com/devel/simclist/">SimCList  project</a>.</li>
            <li>This project includes code from the <a
href=http://code.google.com/p/andar/AndAR</a> project.</li>
            </ul>
    </body>
</html>
```

Completed App

That's all the files you need that can be displayed in the book! Download this book's source from this book's page on Apress or from the GitHub repo at http://github.com/RaghavSood/ProAndroidAugmentedReality to get the image, .patt and .obj + .mtl files that are required for the project to run smoothly.

Figures 8-3 and 8-4 show the app in action.

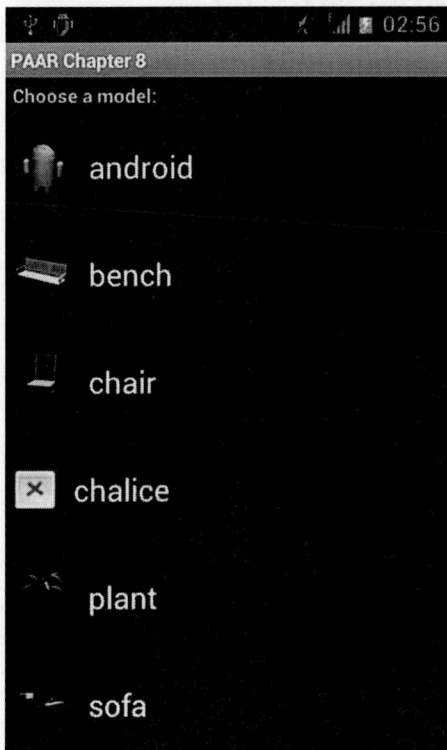

Figure 8-3. *Opening screen of the app.*

Figure 8-4. *Loading the Android model.*

Summary

In this chapter, we created a fully functional 3D AR object viewer using the AndAR framework. Our app has the capability to load both internal and external models; display them in 3D; and allow the user to resize, rotate, and reposition them. In the next chapter, we will build an AR app that explores the social and gaming capabilities of AR.

An Augmented Reality Browser

Welcome to Chapter 9. This is the last chapter in this book, which has covered the different aspects of augmented reality (AR) from making a basic app, using markers, overlaying widgets, and making navigational apps. This final chapter discusses the example app of a real-world AR browser. This browser is something along the lines of the extremely popular Wikitude and Layar apps, but not quite as extensive. Wikitude and Layar are very powerful tools that were developed over a long period of time and provide many, many features. Our AR browser will be relatively humble, but still very, very powerful and useful:

- It will have a live camera preview

- Twitter posts and topics of Wikipedia articles that are located nearby will be displayed over this preview

- There will be a small radar visible that allows the user to see whether any other overlays are available outside their field of view

- Overlays will be moved in and out of the view as the user moves and rotates

- The user can set the radius of data collection from 0m to 100,000m (100 km)

Figure 9-1 shows the app running, with markers from both data sources visible.

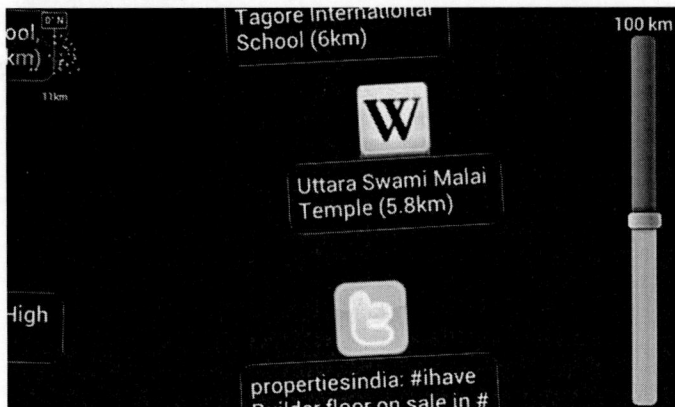

Figure 9-1. *A screenshot of the app when it is running.*

To accomplish all this, we will write our own mini AR engine and use two freely available resources to get the Wikipedia and Twitter data. Compared with Chapter 8, the code isn't very long, but some of it is new, especially the moving overlays part. Without further ado, let's get coding.

The XML

The XML in this app consists of only strings.xml and the menu's XML. We'll quickly type those up and then move onto the Java code.

strings.xml

Listing 9-1. *strings.xml*

```
<?xml version="1.0" encoding="utf-8"?>
<resources>
    <string name="app_name">Pro Android AR Chapter 9</string>
</resources>
```

The string app_name simply stores the name of our app. This name is displayed under the icon in the launcher.

menu.xml

Now let's take a look at menu.xml.

Listing 9-2. *menu.xml*

```xml
<menu xmlns:android="http://schemas.android.com/apk/res/android">
    <item android:id="@+id/showRadar"
          android:title="Hide Radar">
    </item>
    <item android:id="@+id/showZoomBar"
          android:title="Hide Zoom Bar">
    </item>
    <item android:id="@+id/exit"
          android:title="Exit">
    </item>
</menu>
```

The first item is the toggle to show and hide the radar that will be used to display the icons for objects outside the user's field of view. The second item is the toggle to show and hide the SeekBar widget that allows the user to adjust the radius of the tweets and Wikipedia information.

With that little bit of XML out of the way, we can move on to the Java code of our app.

The Java Code

In this app, we'll take a look at the Java code in a format in which different classes are grouped by functions. So we'll look at all the data-parsing classes in sequence and so on.

The Activities and AugmentedView

SensorsActivity

Let's start with the basic parts of our app. We have one SensorsActivity, which extends the standard android Activity. SensorsActivity has no user interface. AugmentedActivity then extends this SensorsActivity, which is extended by MainActivity, which is the Activity that will finally be displayed to the user. So let's start by taking a look at SensorsActivity.

Listing 9-3. *SensorsActivity.java Global Variables*

```java
public class SensorsActivity extends Activity implements SensorEventListener,
LocationListener {
    private static final String TAG = "SensorsActivity";
    private static final AtomicBoolean computing = new AtomicBoolean(false);
```

```
private static final int MIN_TIME = 30*1000;
private static final int MIN_DISTANCE = 10;

private static final float temp[] = new float[9];
private static final float rotation[] = new float[9];
private static final float grav[] = new float[3];
private static final float mag[] = new float[3];

private static final Matrix worldCoord = new Matrix();
private static final Matrix magneticCompensatedCoord = new Matrix();
private static final Matrix xAxisRotation = new Matrix();
private static final Matrix magneticNorthCompensation = new Matrix();

private static GeomagneticField gmf = null;
private static float smooth[] = new float[3];
private static SensorManager sensorMgr = null;
private static List<Sensor> sensors = null;
private static Sensor sensorGrav = null;
private static Sensor sensorMag = null;
private static LocationManager locationMgr = null;
```

The first variable is simply a TAG constant with our class' name in it. The second one, computing, which is like a flag, is used to check if a task is currently in progress. MIN_TIME and MIN_DISTANCE specify the minimum time and distance between location updates. Of the four floats up there, the first is a temporary array used while rotating, the second stores the final rotated matrix, grav stores the gravity numbers, and mag stores the magnetic field numbers. In the four matrices after that, worldCoord stores the location of the device on the world, magneticCompensatedCoord and magneticNorthCompensation are used when compensating for the difference in between the geographical north pole and the magnetic north pole, and xAxisRotation is used to store the matrix after it has been rotated by 90 degrees along the X-axis. After that, gmf is used to store an instance of the GeomagneticField later on in the class. The smooth array is used when using a low-pass Filter on the values from grav and mag. sensorMgr is a SensorManager object; sensors is a list of sensors. sensorGrav and sensorMag will store the default gravitational (accelerometer) and magnetic (compass) sensors on the device, just in case the device has more than one sensor. locationMgr is an instance of the LocationManager.

Now let's take a look at our methods. In this particular Activity, we do not need to do anything in onCreate(), so we just implement a basic version of it so that classes that extend this one can use it. Our main work is done in the onStart() method:

Listing 9-4. *SensorsActivity.java onCreate() and onStart()*

```java
@Override
    public void onCreate(Bundle savedInstanceState) {
        super.onCreate(savedInstanceState);
    }

@Override
    public void onStart() {
        super.onStart();

        double angleX = Math.toRadians(-90);
        double angleY = Math.toRadians(-90);

        xAxisRotation.set( 1f,
                0f,
                0f,
                0f,
                (float) Math.cos(angleX),
                (float) -Math.sin(angleX),
                0f,
                (float) Math.sin(angleX),
                (float) Math.cos(angleX));

        try {
            sensorMgr = (SensorManager) getSystemService(SENSOR_SERVICE);

            sensors = sensorMgr.getSensorList(Sensor.TYPE_ACCELEROMETER);

            if (sensors.size() > 0) sensorGrav = sensors.get(0);

            sensors = sensorMgr.getSensorList(Sensor.TYPE_MAGNETIC_FIELD);

            if (sensors.size() > 0) sensorMag = sensors.get(0);

            sensorMgr.registerListener(this, sensorGrav,
SensorManager.SENSOR_DELAY_NORMAL);
            sensorMgr.registerListener(this, sensorMag,
SensorManager.SENSOR_DELAY_NORMAL);

            locationMgr = (LocationManager)
getSystemService(Context.LOCATION_SERVICE);
            locationMgr.requestLocationUpdates(LocationManager.GPS_PROVIDER,
MIN_TIME, MIN_DISTANCE, this);

            try {

                try {
                    Location
gps=locationMgr.getLastKnownLocation(LocationManager.GPS_PROVIDER);
```

```
                    Location
network=locationMgr.getLastKnownLocation(LocationManager.NETWORK_PROVIDER);
                    if(gps!=null)
                    {
                        onLocationChanged(gps);
                    }
                    else if (network!=null)
                    {
                        onLocationChanged(network);
                    }
                    else
                    {
                        onLocationChanged(ARData.hardFix);
                    }
                } catch (Exception ex2) {
                    onLocationChanged(ARData.hardFix);
                }

                gmf = new GeomagneticField((float)
ARData.getCurrentLocation().getLatitude(),
                                    (float)
ARData.getCurrentLocation().getLongitude(),
                                    (float)
ARData.getCurrentLocation().getAltitude(),
                                    System.currentTimeMillis());
                angleY = Math.toRadians(-gmf.getDeclination());

                synchronized (magneticNorthCompensation) {

                    magneticNorthCompensation.toIdentity();

                    magneticNorthCompensation.set( (float) Math.cos(angleY),
                                        0f,
                                        (float) Math.sin(angleY),
                                        0f,
                                        1f,
                                        0f,
                                        (float) -Math.sin(angleY),
                                        0f,
                                        (float) Math.cos(angleY));

                    magneticNorthCompensation.prod(xAxisRotation);
                }
            } catch (Exception ex) {
                ex.printStackTrace();
            }
        } catch (Exception ex1) {
            try {
                if (sensorMgr != null) {
                    sensorMgr.unregisterListener(this, sensorGrav);
```

```
                sensorMgr.unregisterListener(this, sensorMag);
                sensorMgr = null;
            }
            if (locationMgr != null) {
                locationMgr.removeUpdates(this);
                locationMgr = null;
            }
        } catch (Exception ex2) {
            ex2.printStackTrace();
        }
    }
}
```

As mentioned before the code, the onCreate() method is simply a default implementation. The onStart() method, on the other hand, has a good amount of sensor and location related code in it. We begin by setting the value of the xAxisRotation Matrix. We then set the values for sensorMag and sensorGrav and then register the two sensors. We then assign a value to gmf and reassign the value of angleY to the negative declination , which is the difference between true north (North Pole) and magnetic north (currently located somewhere off the coast of Greenland, moving toward Siberia at roughly 40 miles/year) of gmf in radians. After this reassignment, we have some code in a synchronized block. This code is used to first set the value of magneticNorthCompensation and then multiply it with xAxisRotation. After this, we have a catch block, followed by another catch block with a try block inside it. This try block's code simply attempts to unregister the sensors and location listeners.

Next in this file is our onStop() method, which is the same as the onResume() and onStop() methods used previously in the book. We simply use it to let go of the sensors and GPS to save the user's battery life, and stop collecting data when it is not required.

Listing 9-5. *SensorsActivity.java onStop()*

```
@Override
    protected void onStop() {
        super.onStop();

        try {
            try {
                sensorMgr.unregisterListener(this, sensorGrav);
                sensorMgr.unregisterListener(this, sensorMag);
            } catch (Exception ex) {
                ex.printStackTrace();
            }
            sensorMgr = null;

            try {
```

```
                    locationMgr.removeUpdates(this);
                } catch (Exception ex) {
                    ex.printStackTrace();
                }
                locationMgr = null;
            } catch (Exception ex) {
                ex.printStackTrace();
            }
        }
    }
```

After the onStop() method, we have the methods for getting the data from the three sensors. If you look at the class declaration given previously, you'll notice that this time we implement SensorEventListener and LocationListener for the entire class instead of having small code blocks for them, as we did in our previous apps. We do this so that any class that extends this class can easily override the sensor-related methods.

Listing 9-6. *SensorsActivity.java Listening to the Sensors*

```java
public void onSensorChanged(SensorEvent evt) {
        if (!computing.compareAndSet(false, true)) return;

        if (evt.sensor.getType() == Sensor.TYPE_ACCELEROMETER) {
            smooth = LowPassFilter.filter(0.5f, 1.0f, evt.values, grav);
            grav[0] = smooth[0];
            grav[1] = smooth[1];
            grav[2] = smooth[2];
        } else if (evt.sensor.getType() == Sensor.TYPE_MAGNETIC_FIELD) {
            smooth = LowPassFilter.filter(2.0f, 4.0f, evt.values, mag);
            mag[0] = smooth[0];
            mag[1] = smooth[1];
            mag[2] = smooth[2];
        }

        SensorManager.getRotationMatrix(temp, null, grav, mag);

        SensorManager.remapCoordinateSystem(temp, SensorManager.AXIS_Y,
SensorManager.AXIS_MINUS_X, rotation);

        worldCoord.set(rotation[0], rotation[1], rotation[2], rotation[3],
rotation[4], rotation[5], rotation[6], rotation[7], rotation[8]);

        magneticCompensatedCoord.toIdentity();

        synchronized (magneticNorthCompensation) {
            magneticCompensatedCoord.prod(magneticNorthCompensation);
        }

        magneticCompensatedCoord.prod(worldCoord);
```

```java
        magneticCompensatedCoord.invert();

        ARData.setRotationMatrix(magneticCompensatedCoord);

        computing.set(false);
    }

    public void onProviderDisabled(String provider) {
        //Not Used
    }

    public void onProviderEnabled(String provider) {
        //Not Used
    }

    public void onStatusChanged(String provider, int status, Bundle extras) {
        //Not Used
    }

    public void onLocationChanged(Location location) {
        ARData.setCurrentLocation(location);
        gmf = new GeomagneticField((float)
ARData.getCurrentLocation().getLatitude(),
                (float) ARData.getCurrentLocation().getLongitude(),
                (float) ARData.getCurrentLocation().getAltitude(),
                System.currentTimeMillis());

        double angleY = Math.toRadians(-gmf.getDeclination());

        synchronized (magneticNorthCompensation) {
            magneticNorthCompensation.toIdentity();

            magneticNorthCompensation.set((float) Math.cos(angleY),
                                          0f,
                                          (float) Math.sin(angleY),
                                          0f,
                                          1f,
                                          0f,
                                          (float) -Math.sin(angleY),
                                          0f,
                                          (float) Math.cos(angleY));

            magneticNorthCompensation.prod(xAxisRotation);
        }
    }

    public void onAccuracyChanged(Sensor sensor, int accuracy) {
                if (sensor==null) throw new NullPointerException();
```

```
        if(sensor.getType() == Sensor.TYPE_MAGNETIC_FIELD &&
accuracy==SensorManager.SENSOR_STATUS_UNRELIABLE) {
            Log.e(TAG, "Compass data unreliable");
        }
    }
}
```

Six methods are present in this code. These are onSensorChanged(), onProviderDisabled(), onProviderEnabled(), onStatusChanged, onLocationChanged(), and onAccuracyChanged(). onProviderDisabled(), onProviderEnabled() and onStatusChanged() are not used, but are still there because they must be implemented.

Now let's take a look at the three that are used. In onSensorChanged() we first get the sensor values from the compass and accelerometer and pass them through a low-pass filter before storing them. The low pass filter is discussed and explained in detail later on in this chapter when we write the code for it. After storing the values, we find out the real world coordinates and store them in the temp array. Immediately after that we remap the coordinates to work with the Android device in landscape mode and store it in the rotation array. We then convert the rotation array to a matrix by transferring the data into the worldCoord matrix. We then multiply magneticCompensatedCoord with magneticNorthCompensation and then multiply magneticCompensatedCoord with worldCoord. magneticCompensatedCoord is then inverted, and set as the rotation matrix for ARData. This rotation matrix will be used to convert the latitude and longitude of our tweets and Wikipedia articles to X and Y coordinates for our display.

In onLocationChanged(), we first update the location in ARData, recalculate the gmf with the new data, and then execute the same code as we did in onStart().

In onAccuracyChanged(), we check to see whether the data is null first. If it is, a NullPointerException is thrown. If the data isn't null, and the compass seems to have become unreliable, we add an error message to the LogCat saying so.

AugmentedView

Before we move on to AugmentedActivity, we need to create AugmentedView, which is our own custom extension of the View class found in the Android framework. It is designed to draw the Radar, the zoom bar controlling the radius of the data and the markers that show the data over our camera preview. Let's start with the class and global variable declarations.

Listing 9-7. *Declaring AugmentedView and its Variables*

```
public class AugmentedView extends View {
    private static final AtomicBoolean drawing = new AtomicBoolean(false);
    private static final Radar radar = new Radar();
    private static final float[] locationArray = new float[3];
    private static final List<Marker> cache = new ArrayList<Marker>();
    private static final TreeSet<Marker> updated = new TreeSet<Marker>();
    private static final int COLLISION_ADJUSTMENT = 100;
```

The AtomicBoolean drawing is a flag to check whether the process of drawing is currently going on. radar is an instance of the Radar class, which we will write later in the book after we have finished with all the Activities. locationArray is used to store the locations of the markers we work on later on. cache is used as, well, a temporary cache when drawing. updated is used when we have updated the data we get from our data sources for the Wikipedia articles and tweets. COLLISION_ADJUSTMENT is used to adjust the locations of the markers onscreen, so that they do not overlap each other.

Now let's take a look at its constructor and the onDraw() method.

Listing 9-8. *The onDraw() Method and the Constructor for AugmentedView*

```
public AugmentedView(Context context) {
        super(context);
    }

    @Override
    protected void onDraw(Canvas canvas) {
        if (canvas==null) return;

        if (drawing.compareAndSet(false, true)) {
                List<Marker> collection = ARData.getMarkers();

            cache.clear();
            for (Marker m : collection) {
                m.update(canvas, 0, 0);
                if (m.isOnRadar()) cache.add(m);
                }
            collection = cache;

                if (AugmentedActivity.useCollisionDetection)
adjustForCollisions(canvas,collection);

                        ListIterator<Marker> iter =
collection.listIterator(collection.size());
                        while (iter.hasPrevious()) {
                        Marker marker = iter.previous();
                        marker.draw(canvas);
```

```
        }
        if (AugmentedActivity.showRadar) radar.draw(canvas);
        drawing.set(false);
    }
}
```

The constructor for this class merely ties it to View via super(). In the onDraw() method, we first add all the markers that are on the radar to the cache variable and then duplicate it into collection. Then the markers are adjusted for collision (see the next code listing for details), and finally all the markers are drawn, and the radar is updated.

Now let's take a look at the code for adjusting the markers for collision:

Listing 9-9. *Adjusting for Collisions*

```
private static void adjustForCollisions(Canvas canvas, List<Marker> collection)
{
        updated.clear();
        for (Marker marker1 : collection) {
            if (updated.contains(marker1) || !marker1.isInView()) continue;

            int collisions = 1;
            for (Marker marker2 : collection) {
                if (marker1.equals(marker2) || updated.contains(marker2) ||
!marker2.isInView()) continue;

                if (marker1.isMarkerOnMarker(marker2)) {
                    marker2.getLocation().get(locationArray);
                    float y = locationArray[1];
                    float h = collisions*COLLISION_ADJUSTMENT;
                    locationArray[1] = y+h;
                    marker2.getLocation().set(locationArray);
                    marker2.update(canvas, 0, 0);
                    collisions++;
                    updated.add(marker2);
                }
            }
            updated.add(marker1);
        }
}
}       //Closes class
```

We use this code to check whether one or more markers overlap another marker and then adjust their location data so that when they are drawn, they do not overlap. We use methods from the marker class (written later on in this chapter) to check whether the markers are overlapping and then adjust their location in our locationArray appropriately.

AugmentedActivity

Now that we have written up AugmentedView, we can get to work on AugmentedActivity. We had to extend the view class first because we will be using AugmentedView in AugmentedActivity. Let's start with class and global variables.

Listing 9-10. *Declaring AugmentedActivity and its Global Variables*

```
public class AugmentedActivity extends SensorsActivity implements
OnTouchListener {
    private static final String TAG = "AugmentedActivity";
    private static final DecimalFormat FORMAT = new DecimalFormat("#.##");
    private static final int ZOOMBAR_BACKGROUND_COLOR =
Color.argb(125,55,55,55);
    private static final String END_TEXT =
FORMAT.format(AugmentedActivity.MAX_ZOOM)+" km";
    private static final int END_TEXT_COLOR = Color.WHITE;

    protected static WakeLock wakeLock = null;
    protected static CameraSurface camScreen = null;
    protected static VerticalSeekBar myZoomBar = null;
    protected static TextView endLabel = null;
    protected static LinearLayout zoomLayout = null;
    protected static AugmentedView augmentedView = null;

    public static final float MAX_ZOOM = 100; //in KM
    public static final float ONE_PERCENT = MAX_ZOOM/100f;
    public static final float TEN_PERCENT = 10f*ONE_PERCENT;
    public static final float TWENTY_PERCENT = 2f*TEN_PERCENT;
    public static final float EIGHTY_PERCENTY = 4f*TWENTY_PERCENT;

    public static boolean useCollisionDetection = true;
    public static boolean showRadar = true;
    public static boolean showZoomBar = true;
```

TAG is used as a string constant when outputting to the LogCat. FORMAT is used to format the output when displaying the current radius on the radar. ZOOMBAR_BACKGROUND_COLOR is an ARGB_8888 definition for the background color of the slider we use to allow the user to alter the radius. END_TEXT is the formatted piece of text we need to display on the radar. END_TEXT_COLOR is the color of the END_TEXT. wakeLock, camScreen, myZoomBar, endLabel, zoomLayout, and augmentedView are objects of the classes we need. They are all currently given a null value and will be initialized later on in the chapter. MAX_ZOOM is our radius limit in kilometers. The four floats that follow are various percentages of this maximum radius limit. useCollisionDetection is a flag that allows us to enable or disable collisions detection for the markers. showRadar is a flag the toggles the visibility of the radar. showZoomBar does the same toggle, except it does so for the seekbar that controls the radius.

Now let's take a look at the onCreate() method of this Activity:

Listing 9-11. *AugmentedActivity onCreate()*

```
@Override
    public void onCreate(Bundle savedInstanceState) {
        super.onCreate(savedInstanceState);

        camScreen = new CameraSurface(this);
        setContentView(camScreen);

        augmentedView = new AugmentedView(this);
        augmentedView.setOnTouchListener(this);
        LayoutParams augLayout = new LayoutParams(  LayoutParams.WRAP_CONTENT,
LayoutParams.WRAP_CONTENT);
        addContentView(augmentedView,augLayout);

        zoomLayout = new LinearLayout(this);

zoomLayout.setVisibility((showZoomBar)?LinearLayout.VISIBLE:LinearLayout.GONE);
        zoomLayout.setOrientation(LinearLayout.VERTICAL);
        zoomLayout.setPadding(5, 5, 5, 5);
        zoomLayout.setBackgroundColor(ZOOMBAR_BACKGROUND_COLOR);

        endLabel = new TextView(this);
        endLabel.setText(END_TEXT);
        endLabel.setTextColor(END_TEXT_COLOR);
        LinearLayout.LayoutParams zoomTextParams =  new
LinearLayout.LayoutParams(LayoutParams.WRAP_CONTENT,LayoutParams.WRAP_CONTENT);
        zoomLayout.addView(endLabel, zoomTextParams);

        myZoomBar = new VerticalSeekBar(this);
        myZoomBar.setMax(100);
        myZoomBar.setProgress(50);
        myZoomBar.setOnSeekBarChangeListener(myZoomBarOnSeekBarChangeListener);
        LinearLayout.LayoutParams zoomBarParams =  new
LinearLayout.LayoutParams(LayoutParams.WRAP_CONTENT, LayoutParams.FILL_PARENT);
        zoomBarParams.gravity = Gravity.CENTER_HORIZONTAL;
        zoomLayout.addView(myZoomBar, zoomBarParams);

        FrameLayout.LayoutParams frameLayoutParams = new
FrameLayout.LayoutParams(  LayoutParams.WRAP_CONTENT, LayoutParams.FILL_PARENT,
Gravity.RIGHT);
        addContentView(zoomLayout,frameLayoutParams);

        updateDataOnZoom();
```

```
        PowerManager pm = (PowerManager)
getSystemService(Context.POWER_SERVICE);
wakeLock = pm.newWakeLock(PowerManager.SCREEN_DIM_WAKE_LOCK, "DimScreen");
 }
```

We begin by assigning and instance of CameraSurface to camScreen. We will be writing CameraSurface a little later in the chapter, but basically it deals with the setup of the Camera's surface view, as we have done numerous times in the previous chapters. We then set the basic content view to this CameraSurface. After this, we create an instance of AugmentedView, set its layout parameters to WRAP_CONTENT, and add it to the screen. We then add the base layout for the SeekBar and the END_TEXT to the screen. We then add the SeekBar to the screen and call a method to update the data. Finally, we use the PowerManager to acquire a WakeLock to keep the screen on, but dim it if not in use.

We then have the onPause() and onResume() methods, in which we simply release and reacquire the WakeLock:

Listing 9-12. *onPause() and onResume()*

```
@Override
        public void onResume() {
 super.onResume();

 wakeLock.acquire();
}

@Override
        public void onPause() {
 super.onPause();

 wakeLock.release();
}
```

Now we have our onSensorChanged() method:

Listing 9-13. *onSensorChanged()*

```
@Override
 public void onSensorChanged(SensorEvent evt) {
        super.onSensorChanged(evt);

        if (evt.sensor.getType() == Sensor.TYPE_ACCELEROMETER ||
            evt.sensor.getType() == Sensor.TYPE_MAGNETIC_FIELD)
        {
                augmentedView.postInvalidate();
        }
}
```

We use the method to listen for changes on the compass and accelerometer sensors. If any of those sensors change, we invalidate the augmentedView by calling postInvalidate(). It automatically calls invalidate(), which calls the onDraw() of the view.

We then have the methods that handle the changes for the SeekBar:

Listing 9-14. *Handling the SeekBar*

```
private OnSeekBarChangeListener myZoomBarOnSeekBarChangeListener = new
OnSeekBarChangeListener() {
        public void onProgressChanged(SeekBar seekBar, int progress, boolean
fromUser) {
            updateDataOnZoom();
            camScreen.invalidate();
        }

        public void onStartTrackingTouch(SeekBar seekBar) {
            //Not used
        }

        public void onStopTrackingTouch(SeekBar seekBar) {
            updateDataOnZoom();
            camScreen.invalidate();
        }
    };
```

In the methods that are called while the SeekBar is being altered (onProgressChanged()), and after it has stopped being altered (onStopTrackingTouch()), we update our data by calling updateDataOnZoom() and then invalidate the camera preview.

Now we have a method to calculate the zoom level of our app. We call it *zoom level*, but it is actually the radius in which we are displaying data. It's just that zoom level is easier to remember and say than *radius level*.

Listing 9-15. *Calculating the Zoom Level*

```
private static float calcZoomLevel(){
        int myZoomLevel = myZoomBar.getProgress();
        float out = 0;

        float percent = 0;
        if (myZoomLevel <= 25) {
            percent = myZoomLevel/25f;
            out = ONE_PERCENT*percent;
        } else if (myZoomLevel > 25 && myZoomLevel <= 50) {
            percent = (myZoomLevel-25f)/25f;
            out = ONE_PERCENT+(TEN_PERCENT*percent);
```

```
        } else if (myZoomLevel > 50 && myZoomLevel <= 75) {
            percent = (myZoomLevel-50f)/25f;
            out = TEN_PERCENT+(TWENTY_PERCENT*percent);
        } else {
            percent = (myZoomLevel-75f)/25f;
            out = TWENTY_PERCENT+(EIGHTY_PERCENTY*percent);
        }
        return out;
    }
```

We start by getting the progress on the SeekBar as the zoom level. We then create the float out to store the final result and float percent to store the percentage. We then have some simple math to determine the radius being used. We use these kinds of calculations because it allows the user to set the radius even in meters. The higher up on the bar you go, the less accurate the radius setting becomes. Finally, we return out as the current zoom level.

We now have the methods for dealing with touches and updating the data.

Listing 9-16. *Updating the Data and Handling Touch*

```
protected void updateDataOnZoom() {
        float zoomLevel = calcZoomLevel();
        ARData.setRadius(zoomLevel);
        ARData.setZoomLevel(FORMAT.format(zoomLevel));
        ARData.setZoomProgress(myZoomBar.getProgress());
    }

        public boolean onTouch(View view, MotionEvent me) {
            for (Marker marker : ARData.getMarkers()) {
                if (marker.handleClick(me.getX(), me.getY())) {
                    if (me.getAction() == MotionEvent.ACTION_UP)
markerTouched(marker);
                    return true;
                }
            }
    return                  super.onTouchEvent(me);
    };

        protected void markerTouched(Marker marker) {
                Log.w(TAG, "markerTouched() not implemented.");
    }
}
```

In updateDataOnZoom(), we get the zoom level, set the radius to the new zoom level, and update the text for the zoom level and the seek bar's progress, all in ARData. In onTouch(), we check if a marker has been touched, and the call markerTouched() from there. After that, markerTouched() puts a message out to the LogCat saying that we currently do nothing in markerTouched().

This brings us to the end of AugmentedActivity. Now we need to write our final Activity class: MainActivity.

MainActivity

Once again, let's start with the class and global variable declarations:

Listing 9-17. *Declaring the Class and Global Variables*

```
public class MainActivity extends AugmentedActivity {
    private static final String TAG = "MainActivity";
    private static final String locale = "en";
    private static final BlockingQueue<Runnable> queue = new
ArrayBlockingQueue<Runnable>(1);
    private static final ThreadPoolExecutor exeService = new
ThreadPoolExecutor(1, 1, 20, TimeUnit.SECONDS, queue);
    private static final Map<String,NetworkDataSource> sources = new
ConcurrentHashMap<String,NetworkDataSource>();
```

TAG serves the same purpose as in the previous classes that we wrote. The locale string stores the locale in the two-letter code as English. You can also use Locale.getDefault().getLanguage() to get the locale, but it is best to leave it as "en" because we use it to get the Twitter and Wikipedia data nearby, and our data sources may not support all languages. To simplify our threading, we have the queue variable that is an instance of BlockingQueue. exeService is a ThreadPoolExecutor with queue as its working queue. Finally, we have a Map called sources, which will store data sources.

Now let's take a look at the onCreate() and onStart() methods for this class:

Listing 9-18. *onCreate() and onStart()*

```
@Override
    public void onCreate(Bundle savedInstanceState) {
        super.onCreate(savedInstanceState);
        LocalDataSource localData = new LocalDataSource(this.getResources());
        ARData.addMarkers(localData.getMarkers());

        NetworkDataSource twitter = new TwitterDataSource(this.getResources());
        sources.put("twitter", twitter);
        NetworkDataSource wikipedia = new
WikipediaDataSource(this.getResources());
        sources.put("wiki", wikipedia);
    }

@Override
    public void onStart() {
        super.onStart();
```

```
        Location last = ARData.getCurrentLocation();
        updateData(last.getLatitude(), last.getLongitude(), last.getAltitude());
    }
```

In onCreate(), we begin by creating an instance of the LocalDataSource class and adding its markers to ARData. We then create a NetworkDataSource for both Twitter and Wikipedia, and add them to the sources Map. In onStart(), we get the last location data and update our data with it.

With this, we can now move onto the menu part of the code:

Listing 9-19. *Working with the menu*

```java
@Override
    public boolean onCreateOptionsMenu(Menu menu) {
        MenuInflater inflater = getMenuInflater();
        inflater.inflate(R.menu.menu, menu);
        return true;
    }

    @Override
    public boolean onOptionsItemSelected(MenuItem item) {
        Log.v(TAG, "onOptionsItemSelected() item="+item);
        switch (item.getItemId()) {
            case R.id.showRadar:
                showRadar = !showRadar;
                item.setTitle(((showRadar)? "Hide" : "Show")+" Radar");
                break;
            case R.id.showZoomBar:
                showZoomBar = !showZoomBar;
                item.setTitle(((showZoomBar)? "Hide" : "Show")+" Zoom Bar");

zoomLayout.setVisibility((showZoomBar)?LinearLayout.VISIBLE:LinearLayout.GONE);
                break;
            case R.id.exit:
                finish();
                break;
        }
        return true;
    }
```

This is standard Android code, which we have used numerous times before. We simply create the menu from our XML menu resource, and then listen for clicks on the menus. For the Show Radar/Zoom bar options, we simply toggle their display, and for the exit option we, well, exit.

Now let's take a look at location updates and handling touches.

Listing 9-20. *Location Change and Touch Input*

```
    @Override
     public void onLocationChanged(Location location) {
          super.onLocationChanged(location);

          updateData(location.getLatitude(), location.getLongitude(),
location.getAltitude());
      }

 @Override
        protected void markerTouched(Marker marker) {
        Toast t = Toast.makeText(getApplicationContext(), marker.getName(),
Toast.LENGTH_SHORT);
        t.setGravity(Gravity.CENTER, 0, 0);
        t.show();
  }
```

When we get a new location object, we use it to update the data. We override
the markerTouched() method to display a toast with the details of the marker
that was touched.

Now let's take a look at this class's implementation of updateDataOnZoom():

Listing 9-21. *updateDataOnZoom()*

```
@Override
      protected void updateDataOnZoom() {
            super.updateDataOnZoom();
          Location last = ARData.getCurrentLocation();
          updateData(last.getLatitude(),last.getLongitude(),last.getAltitude());
 }
```

In this implementation of updateDataOnZoom(), we get the location and then call
updateData() and pass it the new location information.

Now let's take a look at the updateData() method:

Listing 9-22. *updateData()*

```
private void updateData(final double lat, final double lon, final double alt) {
      try {
          exeService.execute(
              new Runnable() {

                  public void run() {
                      for (NetworkDataSource source : sources.values())
                          download(source, lat, lon, alt);
                  }
              }
```

```
        );
    } catch (RejectedExecutionException rej) {
        Log.w(TAG, "Not running new download Runnable, queue is full.");
    } catch (Exception e) {
        Log.e(TAG, "Exception running download Runnable.",e);
    }
}
```

In this method, we attempt to use a Runnable to download the data we need to show the Twitter posts and Wikipedia articles. If a RejectedExecutionException is encountered, a message to the LogCat is sent saying that the queue is full and cannot download the data right now. If any other exception is encountered, another message saying so is displayed in the Logcat.

Finally, we have the download() method:

Listing 9-23. *download()*

```
private static boolean download(NetworkDataSource source, double lat, double
lon, double alt) {
            if (source==null) return false;

            String url = null;
  try            {
                    url = source.createRequestURL(lat, lon, alt,
ARData.getRadius(), locale);
            } catch (NullPointerException e) {
  return                      false;
            }

            List<Marker> markers = null;
  try            {
  markers                       = source.parse(url);
            } catch (NullPointerException e) {
  return                      false;
            }

    ARData.addMarkers(markers);
    return true;
    }
}
```

In the download method, we first check to see whether the source is null. If it is, we return false. If it isn't null, we construct a URL to get the data. After this, we parse the result from the URL and store the data we get in the List markers. This data is then added to ARData via ARData.addMarkers.

This brings us to the end of all the Activities. We will now write the code for obtaining the data for the Twitter posts and the Wikipedia articles.

Getting the Data

To get the data, we will be creating five classes: the basic DataSource class, which will be extended by LocalDataSource and NetworkDataSource; TwitterDataSource and WikipediaDataSource will further extend NetworkDataSource.

Let's start with DataSource.

DataSource

DataSource is an exceptionally small abstract class:

Listing 9-24. *DataSource*

```
public abstract class DataSource {
    public abstract List<Marker> getMarkers();
}
```

There is simply only one member of this class: the List getMarkers(). This class is the base for all our other data classes.

Now let's take a look at the LocalDataSource.

LocalDataSource

LocalDataSource is used by MainActivity to add markers to ARData. The class is quite small.

Listing 9-25. *LocalDataSource*

```
public class LocalDataSource extends DataSource{
    private List<Marker> cachedMarkers = new ArrayList<Marker>();
    private static Bitmap icon = null;

    public LocalDataSource(Resources res) {
        if (res==null) throw new NullPointerException();

        createIcon(res);
    }

    protected void createIcon(Resources res) {
        if (res==null) throw new NullPointerException();

        icon=BitmapFactory.decodeResource(res, R.drawable.ic_launcher);
    }
```

```java
    public List<Marker> getMarkers() {
        Marker atl = new IconMarker("ATL", 39.931269, -75.051261, 0,
Color.DKGRAY, icon);
        cachedMarkers.add(atl);

        Marker home = new Marker("Mt Laurel", 39.95, -74.9, 0, Color.YELLOW);
        cachedMarkers.add(home);

        return cachedMarkers;
    }
}
```

The constructor for this class takes a `Resource` object as an argument. It then calls `createIcon()`, which then assigns our app's default icon to the `icon` Bitmap. `getMarkers()`, well, gets the markers.

With this class done, let's take a look at `NetworkDataSource`.

NetworkDataSource

`NetworkDataSource` contains the basic setup for getting the data from our Twitter and Wikipedia sources.

Let's start with the class and global variable declarations:

Listing 9-26. *NetworkDataSource*

```java
public abstract class NetworkDataSource extends DataSource {
    protected static final int MAX = 1000;
    protected static final int READ_TIMEOUT = 10000;
    protected static final int CONNECT_TIMEOUT = 10000;

    protected List<Marker> markersCache = null;

    public abstract String createRequestURL(double lat, double lon, double alt,
                                            float radius, String locale);

    public abstract List<Marker> parse(JSONObject root);
```

`MAX` specifies the maximum number of results to be displayed to the user. `READ_TIMEOUT` and `CONNECT_TIMEOUT` are the timeout values for the connection in milliseconds. `markersCache` is a List<markers> object that we will be using later on in this class. `createRequestURL` and `parse` are stubs that we will override in the extensions of this class.

Now let's take a look at the `getMarkers()` and `getHttpGETInputStream()` methods:

Listing 9-27. *getMarkers() and getHttpGETInputStream()*

```
public List<Marker> getMarkers() {
      return markersCache;
   }

   protected static InputStream getHttpGETInputStream(String urlStr) {
      if (urlStr == null)
         throw new NullPointerException();

      InputStream is = null;
      URLConnection conn = null;

      try {
         if (urlStr.startsWith("file://"))
            return new FileInputStream(urlStr.replace("file://", ""));

         URL url = new URL(urlStr);
         conn = url.openConnection();
         conn.setReadTimeout(READ_TIMEOUT);
         conn.setConnectTimeout(CONNECT_TIMEOUT);

         is = conn.getInputStream();

         return is;
      } catch (Exception ex) {
         try {
            is.close();
         } catch (Exception e) {
            // Ignore
         }
         try {
            if (conn instanceof HttpURLConnection)
               ((HttpURLConnection) conn).disconnect();
         } catch (Exception e) {
            // Ignore
         }
         ex.printStackTrace();
      }
      return null;
   }
```

The getMarkers() method simply returns the markersCache.
getHttpGETInputStream() is used to get an InputStream for the specified URL,
which is passed to it as a String.

Now let's take a look at the getHttpInputString() and parse() methods:

Listing 9-28. *getHttpInputString() and parse()*

```
protected String getHttpInputString(InputStream is) {
        if (is == null)
            throw new NullPointerException();

        BufferedReader reader = new BufferedReader(new InputStreamReader(is),
                8 * 1024);
        StringBuilder sb = new StringBuilder();

        try {
            String line;
            while ((line = reader.readLine()) != null) {
                sb.append(line + "\n");
            }
        } catch (IOException e) {
            e.printStackTrace();
        } finally {
            try {
                is.close();
            } catch (IOException e) {
                e.printStackTrace();
            }
        }
        return sb.toString();
    }

    public List<Marker> parse(String url) {
        if (url == null)
            throw new NullPointerException();

        InputStream stream = null;
        stream = getHttpGETInputStream(url);
        if (stream == null)
            throw new NullPointerException();

        String string = null;
        string = getHttpInputString(stream);
        if (string == null)
            throw new NullPointerException();

        JSONObject json = null;
        try {
            json = new JSONObject(string);
        } catch (JSONException e) {
            e.printStackTrace();
        }
        if (json == null)
            throw new NullPointerException();
```

```
        return parse(json);
    }
}
```

In `getHttpInputString()`, we get the contents of the `InputStream` and put them in a `String`. In `parse()`, we get the JSON object from our data source and then call the other `parse()` method on it. In this class, the second `parse()` method is a stub, but it is overridden and implemented in the other classes.

Let's write up the two classes that extend `NetworkDataSource`: `TwitterDataSource` and `WikipediaDataSource`.

TwitterDataSource

`TwitterDataSource` extends `NetworkDataSource`. It is responsible for pulling the data about nearby tweets from Twitter's servers. `TwitterDataSource` has only two global variables to it.

Listing 9-29. *Declaring TwitterDataSource and its Global Variables*

```
public class TwitterDataSource extends NetworkDataSource {
        private static final String URL =
"http://search.twitter.com/search.json";
        private static Bitmap icon = null;
```

The string URL stores the base of the Twitter search URL. We will construct the parameters dynamically in `createRequestURL()`. The icon Bitmap, currently `null`, will store the Twitter logo in it. We will display this logo as the icon for each of our markers when showing Tweets.

Now let's take a look at the constructor, `createIcon()`, and `createRequestURL()` methods:

Listing 9-30. *The constructor, createIcon(), and createRequestURL()*

```
public TwitterDataSource(Resources res) {
        if (res==null) throw new NullPointerException();

 createIcon(res);
}

protected void createIcon(Resources res) {
        if (res==null) throw new NullPointerException();

 icon=BitmapFactory.decodeResource(res,        R.drawable.twitter);
}

@Override
```

```
public String createRequestURL(double lat, double lon, double alt, float radius,
String locale) {
        return URL+"?geocode=" + lat + "%2C" + lon + "%2C" + Math.max(radius,
1.0) + "km";
}
```

In the constructor, we take a Resource object as a parameter and then pass it to createIcon(). This is the exact same behavior as in NetworkDataSource. In createIcon(), we once again do the same thing we did in NetworkDataSource, except we use a different icon. Here we assign the Twitter drawable to the icon Bitmap, instead of the ic_launcher one. In createRequestURL(), we formulate a complete request URL for the Twitter JSON search application programming interface (API). The Twitter search API allows us to search tweets easily and anonymously. We supply the user's location in the geocode parameter and choose the bigger radius limit from the one that has been set by the user, and one kilometer.

Now we have two parse() methods and one processJSONObject().

Listing 9-31. *The two parse() Methods and the processJSONObject() Method*

```
@Override
    public List<Marker> parse(String url) {
            if (url==null) throw new NullPointerException();

            InputStream stream = null;
    stream = getHttpGETInputStream(url);
    if (stream==null) throw new NullPointerException();

    String string = null;
    string = getHttpInputString(stream);
    if (string==null) throw new NullPointerException();

    JSONObject json = null;
    try {
            json = new JSONObject(string);
    } catch (JSONException e) {
        e.printStackTrace();
    }
    if (json==null) throw new NullPointerException();

    return parse(json);
}

@Override
    public List<Marker> parse(JSONObject root) {
            if (root==null) throw new NullPointerException();

            JSONObject jo = null;
```

```java
            JSONArray dataArray = null;
        List<Marker> markers=new ArrayList<Marker>();

  try              {
    if(root.has("results"))                         dataArray =
root.getJSONArray("results");
                        if (dataArray == null) return markers;
                        int top = Math.min(MAX, dataArray.length());
                        for (int i = 0; i < top; i++) {

    jo                             = dataArray.getJSONObject(i);
    Marker                         ma = processJSONObject(jo);
    if(ma!=null)                         markers.add(ma);
                    }
                } catch (JSONException e) {
                    e.printStackTrace();
                }
  return              markers;
 }


        private Marker processJSONObject(JSONObject jo) {
            if (jo==null) throw new NullPointerException();

            if (!jo.has("geo")) throw new NullPointerException();

            Marker ma = null;
  try              {
    Double                      lat=null, lon=null;

    if(!jo.isNull("geo"))                       {
    JSONObject                          geo = jo.getJSONObject("geo");
    JSONArray                        coordinates =
geo.getJSONArray("coordinates");

 lat=Double.parseDouble(coordinates.getString(0));

 lon=Double.parseDouble(coordinates.getString(1));
    }                    else if(jo.has("location")) {
    Pattern                          pattern = Pattern.compile("\\D*([0-
9.]+),\\s?([0-9.]+)");
    Matcher                        matcher =
pattern.matcher(jo.getString("location"));

    if(matcher.find()){

 lat=Double.parseDouble(matcher.group(1));

 lon=Double.parseDouble(matcher.group(2));
                        }
                }
```

```
    if(lat!=null)                        {
       String                               user=jo.getString("from_user");

      ma                            = new IconMarker(
        user+":                                   "+jo.getString("text"),
        lat,
        lon,
                                       0,

        Color.RED,
        icon);
                    }
              } catch (Exception e) {
      e.printStackTrace();
                    }
      return             ma;
     }
}
```

The first parse() method takes a URL in the form of a string parameter. The URL is then put through the getHttpGETInputStream() method, and the resulting Input Stream is passed to the getHttpInputString() method. Finally, a new JSONObject is created from the resulting String, and it is passed to the second parse() method.

In the second parse() method, we receive the JSONObject from the previous method as a parameter. We then first make sure that the object we received is not null. We then transfer the data from the object into a JSONArray, if it has any results in it. After this we need to loop through the array to create a marker for each of the results. To make sure we don't go outside of the array index, we find the smaller value between our maximum markers and the number of results. We then loop through the array, calling processJSONObject() to create each marker.

Finally, let's go through processJSONObject(). We once again start the method by checking if the JSONObject passed is null. After that, we check if the data in the object contains the geo data. If it doesn't, we don't use it because the geo data is important for placing it on the screen and radar. We then go through the JSONObject to get the coordinates of the tweet, the user, and the contents. All this data is then compiled into a marker, which is then returned to the second parse() method. The second parse method adds it to its markers List. Once all such markers have been created, the entire list is returned to the first parse() method, which further returns it to its caller in MainActivity.

Now let's take a look at the final Data Source class, WikipediaDataSource.

WikipediaDataSource

WikipediaDataSource is very similar to TwitterDataSource in structure and logic. The only major difference is in the parsing of the JSONObject.

Listing 9-32. *WikipediaDataSource*

```
public class WikipediaDataSource extends NetworkDataSource {
        private static final String BASE_URL =
"http://ws.geonames.org/findNearbyWikipediaJSON";

        private static Bitmap icon = null;

        public WikipediaDataSource(Resources res) {
            if (res==null) throw new NullPointerException();

        createIcon(res);
    }

    protected void createIcon(Resources res) {
        if (res==null) throw new NullPointerException();

        icon=BitmapFactory.decodeResource(res, R.drawable.wikipedia);
    }

 @Override
        public String createRequestURL(double lat, double lon, double alt, float
radius, String locale) {
   return                BASE_URL+
        "?lat=" + lat +
        "&lng=" + lon +
        "&radius="+ radius +
        "&maxRows=40" +
        "&lang=" + locale;

    }

 @Override
        public List<Marker> parse(JSONObject root) {
                if (root==null) return null;

                JSONObject jo = null;
                JSONArray dataArray = null;
        List<Marker> markers=new ArrayList<Marker>();

  try               {
   if(root.has("geonames"))                         dataArray =
root.getJSONArray("geonames");
                        if (dataArray == null) return markers;
```

```
    int                        top = Math.min(MAX, dataArray.length());
                           for (int i = 0; i < top; i++) {

    jo                              = dataArray.getJSONObject(i);
    Marker                          ma = processJSONObject(jo);
    if(ma!=null)                            markers.add(ma);
                       }
               } catch (JSONException e) {
  e.printStackTrace();
               }
 return                 markers;
}


      private Marker processJSONObject(JSONObject jo) {
            if (jo==null) return null;

      Marker ma = null;
      if (    jo.has("title") &&
                  jo.has("lat") &&
                  jo.has("lng") &&
                  jo.has("elevation")
      ) {
            try {
                  ma = new IconMarker(
                              jo.getString("title"),
                              jo.getDouble("lat"),
                              jo.getDouble("lng"),
                              jo.getDouble("elevation"),
                              Color.WHITE,
                              icon);
            } catch (JSONException e) {
                  e.printStackTrace();
            }
      }
      return ma;
  }
}
```

Unlike Twitter, Wikipedia does not provide an official search facility. However, geonames.org provides a JSON-based search for Wikipedia, and we will be using it. The next difference from the TwitterDataSource is the icon. We just use a different drawable when creating the icon. The basic code for getting and parsing the JSONObject is the same; only the values are different.

We will now write to classes that help us with positioning the markers on the screen and in real life.

Positioning Classes

We need a set of classes that handle the position related work for our app. These classes handle the user's physical location, and the positiong of objects on the screen.

PhysicalLocationUtility

This class is used to represent the user's location in the real world in three dimensions.

Listing 9-33. *PhysicalLocationUtility.java*

```java
public class PhysicalLocationUtility {
        private double latitude = 0.0;
        private double longitude = 0.0;
        private double altitude = 0.0;

        private static float[] x = new float[1];
        private static double y = 0.0d;
        private static float[] z = new float[1];

        public PhysicalLocationUtility() { }

        public PhysicalLocationUtility(PhysicalLocationUtility pl) {
                if (pl==null) throw new NullPointerException();

  set(pl.latitude,               pl.longitude, pl.altitude);
 }

        public void set(double latitude, double longitude, double altitude) {
        this.latitude = latitude;
        this.longitude = longitude;
        this.altitude = altitude;
 }

        public void setLatitude(double latitude) {
  this.latitude               = latitude;
 }

        public double getLatitude() {
  return               latitude;
 }

        public void setLongitude(double longitude) {
  this.longitude               = longitude;
 }
```

```java
        public double getLongitude() {
  return             longitude;
  }

        public void setAltitude(double altitude) {
  this.altitude          = altitude;
  }

        public double getAltitude() {
  return             altitude;
  }

        public static synchronized void convLocationToVector(Location org,
PhysicalLocationUtility gp, Vector v) {
                if (org==null || gp==null || v==null)
                    throw new NullPointerException("Location,
PhysicalLocationUtility, and Vector cannot be NULL.");

  Location.distanceBetween(                            org.getLatitude(),
org.getLongitude(),

        gp.getLatitude(), org.getLongitude(),
         z);

  Location.distanceBetween(                            org.getLatitude(),
org.getLongitude(),

        org.getLatitude(), gp.getLongitude(),
         x);
                y = gp.getAltitude() - org.getAltitude();
                if (org.getLatitude() < gp.getLatitude())
  z[0]                     *= -1;
                if (org.getLongitude() > gp.getLongitude())
  x[0]                     *= -1;

                v.set(x[0], (float) y, z[0]);
  }

  @Override
        public String toString() {
                return "(lat=" + latitude + ", lng=" + longitude + ", alt=" +
altitude + ")";
  }
}
```

The first three doubles are used to store the latitude, longitude and altitude
respectively, as their names suggest. The x, y, and z store the final three-
dimensional position data. The setLatitude(), setLongitude(), and
setAltitude() methods set the latitude, longitude, and altitude, respectively.

Their get() counterparts simply return the current value. The convLocationToVector() methods convert the location to a Vector. We will write a Vector class later on in this chapter. The toString() method simply compiles the latitude, longitude, and altitude into a String and returns it to the calling method.

Now let's take a look at ScreenPositionUtility.

ScreenPositionUtility

ScreenPositionUtility is used when displaying the lines for the radar.

Listing 9-34. *ScreenPositionUtility.java*

```java
public class ScreenPositionUtility {
    private float x = 0f;
    private float y = 0f;

    public ScreenPositionUtility() {
        set(0, 0);
    }

    public void set(float x, float y) {
        this.x = x;
        this.y = y;
    }

    public float getX() {
        return          x;
    }

    public void setX(float x) {
        this.x          = x;
    }

    public float getY() {
        return          y;
    }

    public void setY(float y) {
        this.y          = y;
    }

    public void rotate(double t) {
        float xp = (float) Math.cos(t) * x - (float) Math.sin(t) * y;
        float yp = (float) Math.sin(t) * x + (float) Math.cos(t) * y;

        x = xp;
```

```
        y = yp;
    }

    public void add(float x, float y) {
        this.x += x;
        this.y += y;
    }

    @Override
    public String toString() {
        return "x="+x+" y="+y;
    }
}
```

The setX() and setY() methods set the values for the x and y variable floats, respectively. The set() method sets the values for both x and y together. The getX() and getY() methods simply return the values of x and y. The rotate() method rotates the x and y values around the angle t. The add() method adds the passed values to x and y, respectively. Finally, the toString() method returns a string with the value of both x and y in it.

Now let's take a look at the UI code.

The UI Works

PaintableObject

PaintableObject is the base class for all our custom bits of the user interface. Some of its methods are just stubs that we override in its subclasses. This class contains a lot of methods for drawing certain objects such as lines, bitmaps, points, etc. on a given canvas.

Listing 9-35. *PaintableObject.java*

```
public abstract class PaintableObject {
    private Paint paint = new Paint(Paint.ANTI_ALIAS_FLAG);

    public PaintableObject() {
        if (paint==null) {
            paint = new Paint();
            paint.setTextSize(16);
            paint.setAntiAlias(true);
            paint.setColor(Color.BLUE);
            paint.setStyle(Paint.Style.STROKE);
        }
    }
```

```java
    public abstract float getWidth();

    public abstract float getHeight();

    public abstract void paint(Canvas canvas);

    public void setFill(boolean fill) {
        if (fill)
            paint.setStyle(Paint.Style.FILL);
        else
            paint.setStyle(Paint.Style.STROKE);
    }

    public void setColor(int c) {
        paint.setColor(c);
    }

    public void setStrokeWidth(float w) {
        paint.setStrokeWidth(w);
    }

    public float getTextWidth(String txt) {
        if (txt==null) throw new NullPointerException();
        return paint.measureText(txt);
    }

    public float getTextAsc() {
        return -paint.ascent();
    }

    public float getTextDesc() {
        return paint.descent();
    }

    public void setFontSize(float size) {
        paint.setTextSize(size);
    }

    public void paintLine(Canvas canvas, float x1, float y1, float x2, float y2)
{
        if (canvas==null) throw new NullPointerException();

        canvas.drawLine(x1, y1, x2, y2, paint);
    }

    public void paintRect(Canvas canvas, float x, float y, float width, float
height) {
        if (canvas==null) throw new NullPointerException();
```

```
        canvas.drawRect(x, y, x + width, y + height, paint);
    }

    public void paintRoundedRect(Canvas canvas, float x, float y, float width,
float height) {
        if (canvas==null) throw new NullPointerException();

        RectF rect = new RectF(x, y, x + width, y + height);
        canvas.drawRoundRect(rect, 15F, 15F, paint);
    }

    public void paintBitmap(Canvas canvas, Bitmap bitmap, Rect src, Rect dst) {
        if (canvas==null || bitmap==null) throw new NullPointerException();

        canvas.drawBitmap(bitmap, src, dst, paint);
    }

    public void paintBitmap(Canvas canvas, Bitmap bitmap, float left, float top)
{
        if (canvas==null || bitmap==null) throw new NullPointerException();

        canvas.drawBitmap(bitmap, left, top, paint);
    }

    public void paintCircle(Canvas canvas, float x, float y, float radius) {
        if (canvas==null) throw new NullPointerException();

        canvas.drawCircle(x, y, radius, paint);
    }

    public void paintText(Canvas canvas, float x, float y, String text) {
        if (canvas==null || text==null) throw new NullPointerException();

        canvas.drawText(text, x, y, paint);
    }

    public void paintObj(        Canvas canvas, PaintableObject obj,
                                        float x, float y,
                                        float rotation, float scale)
    {
        if (canvas==null || obj==null) throw new NullPointerException();

        canvas.save();
        canvas.translate(x+obj.getWidth()/2, y+obj.getHeight()/2);
        canvas.rotate(rotation);
        canvas.scale(scale,scale);
        canvas.translate(-(obj.getWidth()/2), -(obj.getHeight()/2));
        obj.paint(canvas);
        canvas.restore();
    }
```

```
    public void paintPath(       Canvas canvas, Path path,
                                             float x, float y, float width,
                                             float height, float rotation,
float scale)
    {
        if (canvas==null || path==null) throw new NullPointerException();

        canvas.save();
        canvas.translate(x + width / 2, y + height / 2);
        canvas.rotate(rotation);
        canvas.scale(scale, scale);
        canvas.translate(-(width / 2), -(height / 2));
        canvas.drawPath(path, paint);
        canvas.restore();
    }
}
```

The entire class has only one global variable: a `paint` object with anti-aliasing enabled. Anti-aliasing smoothes out the lines of the object being drawn. The constructor initializes the `paint` object by setting the text size to 16, enabling anti-aliasing, setting the paint color to blue, and setting the paint style to `Paint.Style.STROKE`.

The following three methods—`getWidth()`, `getHeight()`, and `paint()`—are left as method stubs to be overridden if required.

The `setFill()` method allows us to change the paint style to `Paint.Style.FILL` or `Paint.Style.STROKE`. The `setColor()` method sets the color of the paint to the color corresponding to the integer it takes as an argument. The `setStrokeWidth()` allows us to set the width of the paint's stroke. `getTextWidth()` returns the width of the text it takes as an argument. `getTextAsc()` and `getTextDesc()` return the ascent and descent of the text, respectively. `setFontSize()` allows us to set the font size of the paint. All the remaining methods with paint prefixed to their names draw the object that is written after the paint on the supplied `canvas`. For example, `paintLine()` draws a line with the supplied coordinates on the supplied `canvas`.

Now let's take a look at the set of classes that extends `PaintableObject`.

PaintableBox

The `PaintableBox` class allows us to draw a box outline. It's a simple class and not very big.

Listing 9-36. *PaintableBox.java*

```java
public class PaintableBox extends PaintableObject {
    private float width=0, height=0;
        private int borderColor = Color.rgb(255, 255, 255);
        private int backgroundColor = Color.argb(128, 0, 0, 0);

        public PaintableBox(float width, float height) {
                this(width, height, Color.rgb(255, 255, 255), Color.argb(128, 0,
0, 0));
 }

        public PaintableBox(float width, float height, int borderColor, int
bgColor) {
                set(width, height, borderColor, bgColor);
 }

    public void set(float width, float height) {
        set(width, height, borderColor, backgroundColor);
    }

        public void set(float width, float height, int borderColor, int bgColor)
{
            this.width = width;
            this.height = height;
            this.borderColor = borderColor;
  this.backgroundColor             = bgColor;
 }

@Override
        public void paint(Canvas canvas) {
                if (canvas==null) throw new NullPointerException();

  setFill(true);
  setColor(backgroundColor);
                paintRect(canvas, 0, 0, width, height);

  setFill(false);
  setColor(borderColor);
                paintRect(canvas, 0, 0, width, height);
 }

@Override
        public float getWidth() {
  return              width;
 }

@Override
        public float getHeight() {
  return              height;
```

```
  }
}
```

This class has two constructors, one of which calls the other. The reason is that one of the constructors allows you to set only the width and height of the box, while the second one allows you to set its colors as well. When calling the first one, it uses the supplied width and height to call the second one with the default colors. The second constructor then calls the second `set()` method to set those values. The `paint()` method simply draws the box on the specified `canvas`. `getWidth()` and `getHeight()` just return the width and height of the box.

Now let's take a look at the `PaintableBoxedText`.

PaintableBoxedText

PaintableBoxedText draws text on the canvas with a box around it.

Listing 9-37. *PaintableBox.java*

```
public class PaintableBoxedText extends PaintableObject {
    private float width=0, height=0;
        private float areaWidth=0, areaHeight=0;
        private ArrayList<String> lineList = null;
        private String[] lines = null;
        private float[] lineWidths = null;
        private float lineHeight = 0;
        private float maxLineWidth = 0;
        private float pad = 0;

        private String txt = null;
    private float fontSize = 12;
        private int borderColor = Color.rgb(255, 255, 255);
        private int backgroundColor = Color.argb(160, 0, 0, 0);
        private int textColor = Color.rgb(255, 255, 255);

        public PaintableBoxedText(String txtInit, float fontSizeInit, float
maxWidth) {
                this(txtInit, fontSizeInit, maxWidth, Color.rgb(255, 255, 255),
Color.argb(128, 0, 0, 0), Color.rgb(255, 255, 255));
    }

        public PaintableBoxedText(String txtInit, float fontSizeInit, float
maxWidth, int borderColor, int bgColor, int textColor) {
                set(txtInit, fontSizeInit, maxWidth, borderColor, bgColor,
textColor);
    }
```

```java
        public void set(String txtInit, float fontSizeInit, float maxWidth, int
borderColor, int bgColor, int textColor) {
                if (txtInit==null) throw new NullPointerException();

  this.borderColor              = borderColor;
  this.backgroundColor            = bgColor;
  this.textColor              = textColor;
  this.pad            = getTextAsc();

  set(txtInit,            fontSizeInit, maxWidth);
  }

        public void set(String txtInit, float fontSizeInit, float maxWidth) {
                if (txtInit==null) throw new NullPointerException();

  try            {
    prepTxt(txtInit,                        fontSizeInit, maxWidth);
                } catch (Exception ex) {
    ex.printStackTrace();
                    prepTxt("TEXT PARSE ERROR", 12, 200);
                }
  }

        private void prepTxt(String txtInit, float fontSizeInit, float maxWidth)
{
                if (txtInit==null) throw new NullPointerException();

  setFontSize(fontSizeInit);

  txt              = txtInit;
  fontSize                = fontSizeInit;
                areaWidth = maxWidth - pad;
                lineHeight = getTextAsc() + getTextDesc();

                if (lineList==null) lineList = new ArrayList<String>();
  else              lineList.clear();

                BreakIterator boundary = BreakIterator.getWordInstance();
  boundary.setText(txt);

                int start = boundary.first();
                int end = boundary.next();
                int prevEnd = start;
                while (end != BreakIterator.DONE) {
                        String line = txt.substring(start, end);
                        String prevLine = txt.substring(start, prevEnd);
  float                  lineWidth = getTextWidth(line);

                        if (lineWidth > areaWidth) {
    if(prevLine.length()>0)                        lineList.add(prevLine);
```

```
    start                           = prevEnd;
                        }

  prevEnd                   = end;
  end                   = boundary.next();
            }
            String line = txt.substring(start, prevEnd);
  lineList.add(line);

            if (lines==null || lines.length!=lineList.size()) lines = new
String[lineList.size()];
            if (lineWidths==null || lineWidths.length!=lineList.size())
lineWidths = new float[lineList.size()];
  lineList.toArray(lines);

  maxLineWidth              = 0;
            for (int i = 0; i < lines.length; i++) {
  lineWidths[i]                   = getTextWidth(lines[i]);
  if              (maxLineWidth < lineWidths[i])
    maxLineWidth                      = lineWidths[i];
            }
  areaWidth               = maxLineWidth;
            areaHeight = lineHeight * lines.length;

            width = areaWidth + pad * 2;
            height = areaHeight + pad * 2;
}

@Override
      public void paint(Canvas canvas) {
            if (canvas==null) throw new NullPointerException();

        setFontSize(fontSize);

  setFill(true);
  setColor(backgroundColor);
            paintRoundedRect(canvas, 0, 0, width, height);

  setFill(false);
  setColor(borderColor);
            paintRoundedRect(canvas, 0, 0, width, height);

            for (int i = 0; i < lines.length; i++) {
  String              line = lines[i];
  setFill(true);
  setStrokeWidth(0);
  setColor(textColor);
                  paintText(canvas, pad, pad + lineHeight * i +
getTextAsc(), line);
```

```
                    }
        }

        @Override
              public float getWidth() {
         return                 width;
        }

        @Override
              public float getHeight() {
         return                 height;
        }
}
```

Once again, there are two constructors that do the same thing as those in
PaintableBox. The first major difference from PaintableBox is that of the new
method prepTxt(). prepTxt() prepares text by cutting it into different lines sized
to fit into the box, instead of having one long string that happily leaves the box
and overflows outside. The paint() method then draws the basic box first and
then uses a for loop to add each of the lines to it.

Now let's take a look at PaintableCircle.

PaintableCircle

PaintableCircle allows us to, well, paint a circle onto the supplied Canvas. It's a
simple class, with simple code:

Listing 9-38. *PaintableCircle.java*

```
public class PaintableCircle extends PaintableObject {
    private int color = 0;
    private float radius = 0;
    private boolean fill = false;

    public PaintableCircle(int color, float radius, boolean fill) {
        set(color, radius, fill);
    }

    public void set(int color, float radius, boolean fill) {
        this.color = color;
        this.radius = radius;
        this.fill = fill;
    }

    @Override
    public void paint(Canvas canvas) {
        if (canvas==null) throw new NullPointerException();
```

```
            setFill(fill);
            setColor(color);
            paintCircle(canvas, 0, 0, radius);
        }

        @Override
        public float getWidth() {
            return radius*2;
        }

        @Override
        public float getHeight() {
            return radius*2;
        }
    }
```

This time, there is only one constructor that allows us to set the radius and the colors of the circle. There is also only one set() method, which is called by the constructor. The paint() method draws a circle with the specified properties on the given canvas. The getWidth() and getHeight() methods return the diameter because this is a circle.

Now let's take a look at PaintableGps.

PaintableGps

PaintableGps is a lot like PaintableCircle, except that it also allows us to set the stroke width of the circle being drawn.

Listing 9-39. *PaintableGps.java*

```
public class PaintableGps extends PaintableObject {
    private float radius = 0;
    private float strokeWidth = 0;
    private boolean fill = false;
    private int color = 0;

    public PaintableGps(float radius, float strokeWidth, boolean fill, int
color) {
        set(radius, strokeWidth, fill, color);
    }

    public void set(float radius, float strokeWidth, boolean fill, int color) {
        this.radius = radius;
        this.strokeWidth = strokeWidth;
        this.fill = fill;
        this.color = color;
```

```
    }

@Override
    public void paint(Canvas canvas) {
        if (canvas==null) throw new NullPointerException();

        setStrokeWidth(strokeWidth);
        setFill(fill);
        setColor(color);
        paintCircle(canvas, 0, 0, radius);
    }

@Override
    public float getWidth() {
        return radius*2;
    }

@Override
    public float getHeight() {
            return radius*2;
    }
}
```

Once more, there is only one constructor, which calls the set() method to set the colors, size of the circle being drawn and the width of the stroke. The paint() method draws the circle with the specified properties on the supplied Canvas as usual. Once again, getWidth() and getHeight() return the circle's diameter.

Now let's take a look at PaintableIcon.

PaintableIcon

We use PaintableIcon to draw the icons for Twitter and Wikipedia.

Listing 9-40. *PaintableIcon.java*

```
public Class PaintableIcon Extends PaintableObject {
private Bitmap bitmap=null;

public PaintableIcon(Bitmap bitmap, int width, int height) {
    set(bitmap,width,height);
}

public void set(Bitmap bitmap, int width, int height) {
    if (bitmap==null) throw new NullPointerException();

    this.bitmap = Bitmap.createScaledBitmap(bitmap, width, height, true);
```

```
        }

    @Override
        public void paint(Canvas canvas) {
            if (canvas==null || bitmap==null) throw new NullPointerException();

            paintBitmap(canvas, bitmap, -(bitmap.getWidth()/2), -
(bitmap.getHeight()/2));
        }

    @Override
        public float getWidth() {
            return bitmap.getWidth();
        }

    @Override
        public float getHeight() {
            return bitmap.getHeight();
        }
}
```

The constructor takes the bitmap to be drawn, along with the width and height according to which it is to be drawn and then calls the set() method to set them. In the set() method, the Bitmap is scaled to the size specified. The paint() method then draws it onto the supplied canvas. The getWidth() and getHeight() methods return the width and height of the bitmap we drew in the end, not the bitmap that was passed in the constructor.

Now we'll take a look at creating a class that paints lines.

PaintableLine

PaintableLine allows us to paint a line in a specified color onto a supplied Canvas.

Listing 9-41. *PaintableLine.java*

```
public class PaintableLine extends PaintableObject {
    private int color = 0;
    private float x = 0;
    private float y = 0;

    public PaintableLine(int color, float x, float y) {
        set(color, x, y);
    }

    public void set(int color, float x, float y) {
        this.color = color;
```

```
        this.x = x;
        this.y = y;
    }

@Override
    public void paint(Canvas canvas) {
        if (canvas==null) throw new NullPointerException();

        setFill(false);
        setColor(color);
        paintLine(canvas, 0, 0, x, y);
    }

@Override
    public float getWidth() {
        return x;
    }

@Override
    public float getHeight() {
        return y;
    }
}
```

The constructor takes the color and X and Y points of the line and passes them to set() to set them. The paint() method draws it on the Canvas using PaintableObject. getWidth() and getHeight() return x and y, respectively.

Now we'll take a look at PaintablePoint.

PaintablePoint

PaintablePoint is used to draw a single point on a single canvas. It is used when making our radar.

Listing 9-42. *PaintablePoint*

```
public class PaintablePoint extends PaintableObject {
    private static int width=2;
    private static int height=2;
    private int color = 0;
    private boolean fill = false;

    public PaintablePoint(int color, boolean fill) {
        set(color, fill);
    }

    public void set(int color, boolean fill) {
```

```
            this.color = color;
            this.fill = fill;
        }

    @Override
        public void paint(Canvas canvas) {
            if (canvas==null) throw new NullPointerException();

            setFill(fill);
            setColor(color);
            paintRect(canvas, -1, -1, width, height);
        }

    @Override
        public float getWidth() {
            return width;
        }

    @Override
        public float getHeight() {
            return height;
        }
    }
```

The point being drawn is not actually a point; it is just a really small rectangle. The constructor accepts the colors and sets them via the set() method, and then paint() draws a really small rectangle. getWidth() and getHeight() simply return the width and height of the rectangle being drawn.

Now let's take a look at PaintablePosition.

PaintablePosition

PaintablePosition extends PaintableObject and adds the ability to rotate and scale the thing being painted.

Listing 9-43. *PaintablePosition*

```
public class PaintablePosition extends PaintableObject {
    private float width=0, height=0;
    private float objX=0, objY=0, objRotation=0, objScale=0;
    private PaintableObject obj = null;

    public PaintablePosition(PaintableObject drawObj, float x, float y, float
rotation, float scale) {
        set(drawObj, x, y, rotation, scale);
    }
```

```java
    public void set(PaintableObject drawObj, float x, float y, float rotation,
float scale) {
        if (drawObj==null) throw new NullPointerException();

        this.obj = drawObj;
        this.objX = x;
        this.objY = y;
        this.objRotation = rotation;
        this.objScale = scale;
        this.width = obj.getWidth();
        this.height = obj.getHeight();
    }

    public void move(float x, float y) {
        objX = x;
        objY = y;
    }

    public float getObjectsX() {
        return objX;
    }

    public float getObjectsY() {
        return objY;
    }

@Override
    public void paint(Canvas canvas) {
        if (canvas==null || obj==null) throw new NullPointerException();

        paintObj(canvas, obj, objX, objY, objRotation, objScale);
    }

@Override
    public float getWidth() {
        return width;
    }

@Override
    public float getHeight() {
        return height;
    }

    @Override
        public String toString() {
            return "objX="+objX+" objY="+objY+" width="+width+" height="+height;
    }
}
```

The constructor takes an instance of the PaintableObject class, the X and Y coordinates of the position, the rotation angle, and the scale amount. The constructor then passes all this data to the set() method, which sets the values. We now have three new methods more than the others that have been there in the classes that have extended PaintableObject so far: move(), getObjectsX(), and getObjectsY(). getObjectsX() and getObjectsY() return the x and y values that were passed to the constructor, respectively. move() allows us to move the object to new X and Y coordinates. The paint() method once again draws the object on the supplied canvas. getWidth() and getHeight() return the width and the height of the object. toString() returns X coordinate, Y coordinate, width, and height of the object in a single string.

Now let's take a look at PaintableRadarPoints.

PaintableRadarPoints

PaintableRadarPoints is used to draw all the markers' relative positions on the radar.

Listing 9-44. *PaintableRadarPoints*

```
public class PaintableRadarPoints extends PaintableObject {
    private final float[] locationArray = new float[3];
        private PaintablePoint paintablePoint = null;
        private PaintablePosition pointContainer = null;

 @Override
    public void paint(Canvas canvas) {
                if (canvas==null) throw new NullPointerException();

                float range = ARData.getRadius() * 1000;
                float scale = range / Radar.RADIUS;
                for (Marker pm : ARData.getMarkers()) {
                    pm.getLocation().get(locationArray);
                    float x = locationArray[0] / scale;
                    float y = locationArray[2] / scale;
                    if ((x*x+y*y)<(Radar.RADIUS*Radar.RADIUS)) {
                        if (paintablePoint==null) paintablePoint = new
PaintablePoint(pm.getColor(),true);
                        else paintablePoint.set(pm.getColor(),true);

                        if (pointContainer==null) pointContainer = new
PaintablePosition(      paintablePoint,
                                (x+Radar.RADIUS-1),
                                (y+Radar.RADIUS-1),
                                0,
```

```
                              1);
                  else pointContainer.set(paintablePoint,
                      (x+Radar.RADIUS-1),
                      (y+Radar.RADIUS-1),
                      0,
                      1);

              pointContainer.paint(canvas);
          }
      }
  }

@Override
    public float getWidth() {
        return Radar.RADIUS * 2;
    }

@Override
    public float getHeight() {
        return Radar.RADIUS * 2;
    }
}
```

In this class, there is no constructor. Instead, only the paint(), getWidth(), and getHeight() methods are present. getWidth() and getHeight() return the diameter of the point we draw to represent a marker. In the paint() method, we use a for loop to draw a dot on the radar for every marker.

Now let's take a look at PaintableText.

PaintableText

PaintableText is an extension of PaintableObject that draws text. We use it to display the text on the radar:

Listing 9-45. *PaintableText*

```
public class PaintableText extends PaintableObject {
    private static final float WIDTH_PAD = 4;
    private static final float HEIGHT_PAD = 2;

    private String text = null;
    private int color = 0;
    private int size = 0;
    private float width = 0;
    private float height = 0;
    private boolean bg = false;
```

```java
    public PaintableText(String text, int color, int size, boolean
paintBackground) {
        set(text, color, size, paintBackground);
    }

    public void set(String text, int color, int size, boolean paintBackground) {
        if (text==null) throw new NullPointerException();

        this.text = text;
        this.bg = paintBackground;
        this.color = color;
        this.size = size;
        this.width = getTextWidth(text) + WIDTH_PAD * 2;
        this.height = getTextAsc() + getTextDesc() + HEIGHT_PAD * 2;
    }

@Override
    public void paint(Canvas canvas) {
        if (canvas==null || text==null) throw new NullPointerException();

        setColor(color);
        setFontSize(size);
        if (bg) {
            setColor(Color.rgb(0, 0, 0));
            setFill(true);
            paintRect(canvas, -(width/2), -(height/2), width, height);
            setColor(Color.rgb(255, 255, 255));
            setFill(false);
            paintRect(canvas, -(width/2), -(height/2), width, height);
        }
        paintText(canvas, (WIDTH_PAD - width/2), (HEIGHT_PAD + getTextAsc() -
height/2), text);
    }

@Override
    public float getWidth() {
        return width;
    }

@Override
    public float getHeight() {
        return height;
    }
}
```

This class's constructor takes the text, its color, its size, and its background color as arguments and then passes all that to the set() method to be set. The paint() method draws the text, along with its background color. The getWidth() and getHeight() once again return the width and height.

Now before we get to the main UI components such as the `Radar` class, `Marker` class, and `IconMarker` class, we need to create some utility classes.

Utility Classes

In our app, we have some Utility classes. These classes handle the Vector and Matrix functions, implement the LowPassFilter and also handle the calculation of values like the pitch.

Vector

The first of our utility classes is the `Vector` class. This class handles the maths behind `Vectors`. We had a similar class called `Vector3D` in the previous chapter, but this one is far more comprehensive. All of it is pure Java, with nothing Android-specific in it. The code is adapted from the `Vector` class of the free and open source Mixare framework (http://www.mixare.org/). We'll look at the methods grouped by type, such as mathematical functions, setting values, and so on.

First, let's take a look at the global variables and the constructors.

Listing 9-46. *Vector's Constructors and Global Variables*

```
public class Vector {
    private final float[] matrixArray = new float[9];

        private volatile float x = 0f;
    private volatile float y = 0f;
        private volatile float z = 0f;

        public Vector() {
  this(0,           0, 0);
}

        public Vector(float x, float y, float z) {
            set(x, y, z);
    }
}
```

`matrixArray` is an array that we use in the `prod()` method later on in this class. The floats x, y, and z are the three values of any given `Vector`. The first constructor creates a `Vector` with x, y, and z, all set to zero. The second constructor sets x, y, and z to the supplied values.

Now let's take a look at the getter and setter methods for this class:

Listing 9-47. *get() and set()*

```java
    public synchronized float getX() {
    return x;
}
public synchronized void setX(float x) {
    this.x = x;
}

public synchronized float getY() {
    return y;
}

public synchronized void setY(float y) {
    this.y = y;
}

public synchronized float getZ() {
    return z;
}

public synchronized void setZ(float z) {
    this.z = z;
}

public synchronized void get(float[] array) {
    if (array==null || array.length!=3)
        throw new IllegalArgumentException("get() array must be non-NULL and
size of 3");

    array[0] = this.x;
    array[1] = this.y;
    array[2] = this.z;
}

public void set(Vector v) {
    if (v==null) return;

    set(v.x, v.y, v.z);
}

public void set(float[] array) {
    if (array==null || array.length!=3)
        throw new IllegalArgumentException("get() array must be non-NULL and
size of 3");

    set(array[0], array[1], array[2]);
}

    public synchronized void set(float x, float y, float z) {
```

```
    this.x              = x;
    this.y              = y;
    this.z              = z;
}
```

getX(), getY(), and getZ() return the values of x, y, and z to the calling method, respectively, while their set() counterparts update said value. The get() method that takes a float array as an argument will give you the values of x, y, and z in one go. Out of the remaining three set() methods, two of them end up calling set(float x, float y, float z), which sets the values for x, y, and z. The other two set() methods that call this one simply exist to allow us to set the values using an array or pre-existing Vector, instead of always having to pass individual values for x, y, and z.

Now we'll move onto the maths part of this class:

Listing 9-48. *The maths Part of the Vector Class*

```
@Override
        public synchronized boolean equals(Object obj) {
                if (obj==null) return false;

                Vector v = (Vector) obj;
                return (v.x == this.x && v.y == this.y && v.z == this.z);
}

        public synchronized void add(float x, float y, float z) {
    this.x              += x;
    this.y              += y;
    this.z              += z;
}

        public void add(Vector v) {
    if              (v==null) return;

    add(v.x,                v.y, v.z);
}

        public void sub(Vector v) {
    if              (v==null) return;

    add(-v.x,                -v.y, -v.z);
}

        public synchronized void mult(float s) {
            this.x *= s;
            this.y *= s;
            this.z *= s;
}
```

```java
        public synchronized void divide(float s) {
            this.x /= s;
            this.y /= s;
            this.z /= s;
    }

        public synchronized float length() {
                return (float) Math.sqrt(this.x * this.x + this.y * this.y +
this.z * this.z);
    }

        public void norm() {
  divide(length());
}

        public synchronized void cross(Vector u, Vector v) {
                if (v==null || u==null) return;

                float x = u.y * v.z - u.z * v.y;
                float y = u.z * v.x - u.x * v.z;
                float z = u.x * v.y - u.y * v.x;
    this.x          = x;
    this.y          = y;
    this.z          = z;
    }

        public synchronized void prod(Matrix m) {
    if              (m==null) return;

  m.get(matrixArray);
        float xTemp = matrixArray[0] * this.x + matrixArray[1] * this.y +
matrixArray[2] * this.z;
        float yTemp = matrixArray[3] * this.x + matrixArray[4] * this.y +
matrixArray[5] * this.z;
        float zTemp = matrixArray[6] * this.x + matrixArray[7] * this.y +
matrixArray[8] * this.z;

    this.x             = xTemp;
    this.y             = yTemp;
    this.z             = zTemp;
    }

  @Override
        public synchronized String toString() {
                return "x = " + this.x + ", y =  " + this.y + ", z = " + this.z;
    }
}
```

The equals() method compares the vector to a given object to see whether they are equal. The add() and sub() methods add and subtract the arguments to and from the vector, respectively. The mult() method multiplies all the values by the passed float. The divide() method divides all the values by the passed float. The length() method returns the length of the Vector. The norm() method divides the Vector by its length. The cross() method cross multiplies two Vectors. The prod() method multiplies the Vector with the supplied Matrix. toString() returns the values of x, y, and z in a human readable format.

Next we have the Utilities class.

Utilities

The Utilities class contains a single getAngle() method that we use to get the angle when calculating stuff like the pitch in PitchAzimuthCalculator. The math in it is simple trigonometry.

Listing 9-49. *Utilities*

```
public abstract class Utilities {

    private Utilities() { }

    public static final float getAngle(float center_x, float center_y, float
post_x, float post_y) {
        float tmpv_x = post_x - center_x;
        float tmpv_y = post_y - center_y;
        float d = (float) Math.sqrt(tmpv_x * tmpv_x + tmpv_y * tmpv_y);
        float cos = tmpv_x / d;
        float angle = (float) Math.toDegrees(Math.acos(cos));

        angle = (tmpv_y < 0) ? angle * -1 : angle;

        return angle;
    }
}
```

Now let's take a look at that PitchAzimuthCalculator.

PitchAzimuthCalculator

PitchAzimuthCalculator is a class that is used to calculate the pitch and azimuth when given a matrix:

Listing 9-50. *PitchAzimuthCalculator*

```
public class PitchAzimuthCalculator {
    private static final Vector looking = new Vector();
    private static final float[] lookingArray = new float[3];

    private static volatile float azimuth = 0;

    private static volatile float pitch = 0;

    private PitchAzimuthCalculator() {};

    public static synchronized float getAzimuth() {
        return PitchAzimuthCalculator.azimuth;
    }
    public static synchronized float getPitch() {
        return PitchAzimuthCalculator.pitch;
    }

    public static synchronized void calcPitchBearing(Matrix rotationM) {
        if (rotationM==null) return;

        looking.set(0, 0, 0);
        rotationM.transpose();
        looking.set(1, 0, 0);
        looking.prod(rotationM);
        looking.get(lookingArray);
        PitchAzimuthCalculator.azimuth = ((Utilities.getAngle(0, 0,
lookingArray[0], lookingArray[2])  + 360 ) % 360);

        rotationM.transpose();
        looking.set(0, 1, 0);
        looking.prod(rotationM);
        looking.get(lookingArray);
        PitchAzimuthCalculator.pitch = -Utilities.getAngle(0, 0,
lookingArray[1], lookingArray[2]);
    }
}
```

Now let's take a look at the LowPassFilter.

LowPassFilter

A low-pass filter is an electronic filter that passes low-frequency signals, but attenuates (reduces the amplitude of) signals with frequencies higher than the cutoff frequency. The actual amount of attenuation for each frequency varies from filter to filter. It is sometimes called a *high-cut filter* or *treble cut filter* when used in audio applications.

Listing 9-51. *LowPassFilter*

```java
public class LowPassFilter {

    private static final float ALPHA_DEFAULT = 0.333f;
    private static final float ALPHA_STEADY        = 0.001f;
    private static final float ALPHA_START_MOVING = 0.6f;
    private static final float ALPHA_MOVING        = 0.9f;

    private LowPassFilter() { }

    public static float[] filter(float low, float high, float[] current, float[]
previous) {
        if (current==null || previous==null)
            throw new NullPointerException("Input and prev float arrays must be
non-NULL");
        if (current.length!=previous.length)
            throw new IllegalArgumentException("Input and prev must be the same
length");

        float alpha = computeAlpha(low,high,current,previous);

        for ( int i=0; i<current.length; i++ ) {
            previous[i] = previous[i] + alpha * (current[i] - previous[i]);
        }
        return previous;
    }

    private static final float computeAlpha(float low, float high, float[]
current, float[] previous) {
        if(previous.length != 3 || current.length != 3) return ALPHA_DEFAULT;

        float x1 = current[0],
              y1 = current[1],
              z1 = current[2];

        float x2 = previous[0],
              y2 = previous[1],
              z2 = previous[2];

        float distance = (float)(Math.sqrt( Math.pow((double)(x2 - x1), 2d) +
                                             Math.pow((double)(y2 - y1), 2d) +
                                             Math.pow((double)(z2 - z1), 2d))
        );

        if(distance < low) {
            return ALPHA_STEADY;
        } else if(distance >= low || distance < high) {
            return ALPHA_START_MOVING;
        }
```

```
        return ALPHA_MOVING;
    }
}
```

Now we'll take a look at the Matrix class.

Matrix

The Matrix class handles the functions related to Matrices like the Vector class does for Vectors. Once again, this class has been adapted from the Mixare framework.

We'll break it down as we did with the Vector class:

Listing 9-52. *Matrix's getters and setters, and the constructor*

```java
public class Matrix {
    private static final Matrix tmp = new Matrix();

    private volatile float a1=0f, a2=0f, a3=0f;
    private volatile float b1=0f, b2=0f, b3=0f;
    private volatile float c1=0f, c2=0f, c3=0f;

    public Matrix() { }

    public synchronized float getA1() {
        return a1;
    }
    public synchronized void setA1(float a1) {
        this.a1 = a1;
    }

    public synchronized float getA2() {
        return a2;
    }
    public synchronized void setA2(float a2) {
        this.a2 = a2;
    }

    public synchronized float getA3() {
        return a3;
    }
    public synchronized void setA3(float a3) {
        this.a3 = a3;
    }

    public synchronized float getB1() {
        return b1;
    }
```

```
public synchronized void setB1(float b1) {
    this.b1 = b1;
}

public synchronized float getB2() {
    return b2;
}
public synchronized void setB2(float b2) {
    this.b2 = b2;
}

public synchronized float getB3() {
    return b3;
}
public synchronized void setB3(float b3) {
    this.b3 = b3;
}

public synchronized float getC1() {
    return c1;
}
public synchronized void setC1(float c1) {
    this.c1 = c1;
}

public synchronized float getC2() {
    return c2;
}
public synchronized void setC2(float c2) {
    this.c2 = c2;
}

public synchronized float getC3() {
    return c3;
}
public synchronized void setC3(float c3) {
    this.c3 = c3;
}

public synchronized void get(float[] array) {
    if (array==null || array.length!=9)
        throw new IllegalArgumentException("get() array must be non-NULL and
size of 9");

    array[0] = this.a1;
    array[1] = this.a2;
    array[2] = this.a3;

    array[3] = this.b1;
    array[4] = this.b2;
```

```
        array[5] = this.b3;

        array[6] = this.c1;
        array[7] = this.c2;
        array[8] = this.c3;
    }

    public void set(Matrix m) {
        if (m==null) throw new NullPointerException();

        set(m.a1,m. a2, m.a3, m.b1, m.b2, m.b3, m.c1, m.c2, m.c3);
    }

    public synchronized void set(float a1, float a2, float a3, float b1, float
b2, float b3, float c1, float c2, float c3) {
        this.a1 = a1;
        this.a2 = a2;
        this.a3 = a3;

        this.b1 = b1;
        this.b2 = b2;
        this.b3 = b3;

        this.c1 = c1;
        this.c2 = c2;
        this.c3 = c3;
    }
```

The methods like getA1(), getA2(), etc. return the values of the specific part of the Matrix, while their set() counterparts update it. The other get() method populates the passed array with all nine values from the Matrix. The remaining set() methods set the values of the matrix to those of the supplied Matrix or to the supplied floats.

Now let's take a look at the math functions of this class:

Listing 9-53. *Matrix's Math Functions*

```
public void toIdentity() {
        set(1, 0, 0, 0, 1, 0, 0, 0, 1);
    }

public synchronized void adj() {
        float a11 = this.a1;
        float a12 = this.a2;
        float a13 = this.a3;

        float a21 = this.b1;
        float a22 = this.b2;
        float a23 = this.b3;
```

```
        float a31 = this.c1;
        float a32 = this.c2;
        float a33 = this.c3;

        this.a1 = det2x2(a22, a23, a32, a33);
        this.a2 = det2x2(a13, a12, a33, a32);
        this.a3 = det2x2(a12, a13, a22, a23);

        this.b1 = det2x2(a23, a21, a33, a31);
        this.b2 = det2x2(a11, a13, a31, a33);
        this.b3 = det2x2(a13, a11, a23, a21);

        this.c1 = det2x2(a21, a22, a31, a32);
        this.c2 = det2x2(a12, a11, a32, a31);
        this.c3 = det2x2(a11, a12, a21, a22);
    }

    public void invert() {
        float det = this.det();

        adj();
        mult(1 / det);
    }

    public synchronized void transpose() {
        float a11 = this.a1;
        float a12 = this.a2;
        float a13 = this.a3;

        float a21 = this.b1;
        float a22 = this.b2;
        float a23 = this.b3;

        float a31 = this.c1;
        float a32 = this.c2;
        float a33 = this.c3;

        this.b1 = a12;
        this.a2 = a21;
        this.b3 = a32;
        this.c2 = a23;
        this.c1 = a13;
        this.a3 = a31;

        this.a1 = a11;
        this.b2 = a22;
        this.c3 = a33;
    }
```

```java
    private float det2x2(float a, float b, float c, float d) {
        return (a * d) - (b * c);
    }

    public synchronized float det() {
        return (this.a1 * this.b2 * this.c3) - (this.a1 * this.b3 * this.c2) -
(this.a2 * this.b1 * this.c3) +
        (this.a2 * this.b3 * this.c1) + (this.a3 * this.b1 * this.c2) - (this.a3
* this.b2 * this.c1);
    }

    public synchronized void mult(float c) {
        this.a1 = this.a1 * c;
        this.a2 = this.a2 * c;
        this.a3 = this.a3 * c;

        this.b1 = this.b1 * c;
        this.b2 = this.b2 * c;
        this.b3 = this.b3 * c;

        this.c1 = this.c1 * c;
        this.c2 = this.c2 * c;
        this.c3 = this.c3 * c;
    }

    public synchronized void prod(Matrix n) {
        if (n==null) throw new NullPointerException();

        tmp.set(this);
        this.a1 = (tmp.a1 * n.a1) + (tmp.a2 * n.b1) + (tmp.a3 * n.c1);
        this.a2 = (tmp.a1 * n.a2) + (tmp.a2 * n.b2) + (tmp.a3 * n.c2);
        this.a3 = (tmp.a1 * n.a3) + (tmp.a2 * n.b3) + (tmp.a3 * n.c3);

        this.b1 = (tmp.b1 * n.a1) + (tmp.b2 * n.b1) + (tmp.b3 * n.c1);
        this.b2 = (tmp.b1 * n.a2) + (tmp.b2 * n.b2) + (tmp.b3 * n.c2);
        this.b3 = (tmp.b1 * n.a3) + (tmp.b2 * n.b3) + (tmp.b3 * n.c3);

        this.c1 = (tmp.c1 * n.a1) + (tmp.c2 * n.b1) + (tmp.c3 * n.c1);
        this.c2 = (tmp.c1 * n.a2) + (tmp.c2 * n.b2) + (tmp.c3 * n.c2);
        this.c3 = (tmp.c1 * n.a3) + (tmp.c2 * n.b3) + (tmp.c3 * n.c3);
    }

    @Override
    public synchronized String toString() {
        return "(" + this.a1 + "," + this.a2 + "," + this.a3 + ")"+
                " (" + this.b1 + "," + this.b2 + "," + this.b3 + ")"+
                " (" + this.c1 + "," + this.c2 + "," + this.c3 + ")";
    }
}
```

toIdentity() sets the value of the matrix to 1, 0, 0, 0, 1, 0, 0, 0, 1. adj() finds the adjoint of the Matrix. invert() inverts the matrix by calling adj() and then dividing it by the determinant found by calling the det() method. The transpose() method transposes the matrix. The det2x2() method finds the determinant for the supplied values, while the det() method does it for the entire matrix. mult() multiplies every value in the matrix with the supplied float, while prod() multiplies the matrix with the supplied Matrix. toString() returns all the values in a human readable string format.

Now let's write the classes for the main components, namely the Radar, Marker, and IconMarker classes.

Components

These classes are the ones responsible for the major compononents of our app, like the Radar and the Marker. The Marker component is divided into two classes, IconMarker and Marker.

Radar

The Radar class is used to draw our Radar, along with all its elements like the lines and points representing the Markers.

We'll start by looking at the Global variables and the constructor:

Listing 9-54. *The Variables and Constructor of the Radar class*

```
public class Radar {
    public static final float RADIUS = 48;
    private static final int LINE_COLOR = Color.argb(150,0,0,220);
    private static final float PAD_X = 10;
    private static final float PAD_Y = 20;
    private static final int RADAR_COLOR = Color.argb(100, 0, 0, 200);
    private static final int TEXT_COLOR = Color.rgb(255,255,255);
    private static final int TEXT_SIZE = 12;

    private static ScreenPositionUtility leftRadarLine = null;
    private static ScreenPositionUtility rightRadarLine = null;
    private static PaintablePosition leftLineContainer = null;
    private static PaintablePosition rightLineContainer = null;
    private static PaintablePosition circleContainer = null;

    private static PaintableRadarPoints radarPoints = null;
    private static PaintablePosition pointsContainer = null;
```

```
        private static PaintableText paintableText = null;
        private static PaintablePosition paintedContainer = null;

    public Radar() {
        if (leftRadarLine==null) leftRadarLine = new ScreenPositionUtility();
        if (rightRadarLine==null) rightRadarLine = new ScreenPositionUtility();
    }
```

The first seven constants set the values for the colors of the Radar, its Radius, the text color, and the padding. The remaining variables are created to be null objects of various classes that will be initialized later. In the constructor, we check to see whether we have already created the radar lines showing the area currently being viewed. If they haven't been created, they are created to be new instances of the ScreenPositionUtility.

Now let's add the actual methods of the class:

Listing 9-55. *Radar's Methods*

```
public void draw(Canvas canvas) {
        if (canvas==null) throw new NullPointerException();

        PitchAzimuthCalculator.calcPitchBearing(ARData.getRotationMatrix());
        ARData.setAzimuth(PitchAzimuthCalculator.getAzimuth());
        ARData.setPitch(PitchAzimuthCalculator.getPitch());

        drawRadarCircle(canvas);
        drawRadarPoints(canvas);
        drawRadarLines(canvas);
        drawRadarText(canvas);
    }

    private void drawRadarCircle(Canvas canvas) {
        if (canvas==null) throw new NullPointerException();

        if (circleContainer==null) {
            PaintableCircle paintableCircle = new
PaintableCircle(RADAR_COLOR,RADIUS,true);
            circleContainer = new
PaintablePosition(paintableCircle,PAD_X+RADIUS,PAD_Y+RADIUS,0,1);
        }
        circleContainer.paint(canvas);
    }

    private void drawRadarPoints(Canvas canvas) {
        if (canvas==null) throw new NullPointerException();

        if (radarPoints==null) radarPoints = new PaintableRadarPoints();

        if (pointsContainer==null)
```

```
                pointsContainer = new PaintablePosition( radarPoints,
                                                PAD_X,
                                                PAD_Y,
                                                -ARData.getAzimuth(),
                                                1);
        else
                pointsContainer.set(radarPoints,
                                PAD_X,
                                PAD_Y,
                                -ARData.getAzimuth(),
                                1);

        pointsContainer.paint(canvas);
    }

    private void drawRadarLines(Canvas canvas) {
        if (canvas==null) throw new NullPointerException();

        if (leftLineContainer==null) {
            leftRadarLine.set(0, -RADIUS);
            leftRadarLine.rotate(-CameraModel.DEFAULT_VIEW_ANGLE / 2);
            leftRadarLine.add(PAD_X+RADIUS, PAD_Y+RADIUS);

            float leftX = leftRadarLine.getX()-(PAD_X+RADIUS);
            float leftY = leftRadarLine.getY()-(PAD_Y+RADIUS);
            PaintableLine leftLine = new PaintableLine(LINE_COLOR, leftX,
leftY);
            leftLineContainer = new PaintablePosition( leftLine,
                                                PAD_X+RADIUS,
                                                PAD_Y+RADIUS,
                                                0,
                                                1);
        }
        leftLineContainer.paint(canvas);

        if (rightLineContainer==null) {
            rightRadarLine.set(0, -RADIUS);
            rightRadarLine.rotate(CameraModel.DEFAULT_VIEW_ANGLE / 2);
            rightRadarLine.add(PAD_X+RADIUS, PAD_Y+RADIUS);

            float rightX = rightRadarLine.getX()-(PAD_X+RADIUS);
            float rightY = rightRadarLine.getY()-(PAD_Y+RADIUS);
            PaintableLine rightLine = new PaintableLine(LINE_COLOR, rightX,
rightY);
            rightLineContainer = new PaintablePosition( rightLine,
                                                PAD_X+RADIUS,
                                                PAD_Y+RADIUS,
                                                0,
                                                1);
        }
```

```java
                rightLineContainer.paint(canvas);
        }

        private void drawRadarText(Canvas canvas) {
            if (canvas==null) throw new NullPointerException();
            int range = (int) (ARData.getAzimuth() / (360f / 16f));
            String  dirTxt = "";
            if (range == 15 || range == 0) dirTxt = "N";
            else if (range == 1 || range == 2) dirTxt = "NE";
            else if (range == 3 || range == 4) dirTxt = "E";
            else if (range == 5 || range == 6) dirTxt = "SE";
            else if (range == 7 || range == 8) dirTxt= "S";
            else if (range == 9 || range == 10) dirTxt = "SW";
            else if (range == 11 || range == 12) dirTxt = "W";
            else if (range == 13 || range == 14) dirTxt = "NW";
            int bearing = (int) ARData.getAzimuth();
            radarText(   canvas,
                        ""+bearing+((char)176)+" "+dirTxt,
                        (PAD_X + RADIUS),
                        (PAD_Y - 5),
                        true
                    );

            radarText(   canvas,
                        formatDist(ARData.getRadius() * 1000),
                        (PAD_X + RADIUS),
                        (PAD_Y + RADIUS*2 -10),
                        false
                    );
        }

        private void radarText(Canvas canvas, String txt, float x, float y, boolean
bg) {
            if (canvas==null || txt==null) throw new NullPointerException();

            if (paintableText==null) paintableText = new
PaintableText(txt,TEXT_COLOR,TEXT_SIZE,bg);
            else paintableText.set(txt,TEXT_COLOR,TEXT_SIZE,bg);

            if (paintedContainer==null) paintedContainer = new
PaintablePosition(paintableText,x,y,0,1);
            else paintedContainer.set(paintableText,x,y,0,1);

            paintedContainer.paint(canvas);
        }

        private static String formatDist(float meters) {
            if (meters < 1000) {
                return ((int) meters) + "m";
            } else if (meters < 10000) {
```

```
            return formatDec(meters / 1000f, 1) + "km";
        } else {
            return ((int) (meters / 1000f)) + "km";
        }
    }

    private static String formatDec(float val, int dec) {
        int factor = (int) Math.pow(10, dec);

        int front = (int) (val);
        int back = (int) Math.abs(val * (factor) ) % factor;

        return front + "." + back;
    }
}
```

The draw() method starts the process by getting the pitch and azimuth and then calling the other drawing methods in the required order. drawRadarCircle() simply draws the base circle for the Radar. drawRadarPoints() draws all the points denoting Markers on the Radar circle. drawRadarLines() draws the two lines that show which of the markers are currently within the camera's viewing area. drawRadarText() calls radarText() format the text, before drawing it onto the Radar.

This brings us to the end of the Radar class. Now let's take a look at the Marker class.

Marker

The Marker class handles the majority of the coding related to the Markers we display. It calculates whether the marker should be visible on our screen and draws the image and text accordingly.

Global variables

We'll start as usual with the global variables:

Listing 9-56. *Global Variables*

```
public class Marker implements Comparable<Marker> {
    private static final DecimalFormat DECIMAL_FORMAT = new DecimalFormat("@#");

    private static final Vector symbolVector = new Vector(0, 0, 0);
    private static final Vector textVector = new Vector(0, 1, 0);

    private final Vector screenPositionVector = new Vector();
```

```
    private final Vector tmpSymbolVector = new Vector();
    private final Vector tmpVector = new Vector();
    private final Vector tmpTextVector = new Vector();
    private final float[] distanceArray = new float[1];
    private final float[] locationArray = new float[3];
    private final float[] screenPositionArray = new float[3];

    private float initialY = 0.0f;

    private volatile static CameraModel cam = null;

    private volatile PaintableBoxedText textBox = null;
    private volatile PaintablePosition textContainer = null;

    protected final float[] symbolArray = new float[3];
    protected final float[] textArray = new float[3];

    protected volatile PaintableObject gpsSymbol = null;
    protected volatile PaintablePosition symbolContainer = null;
    protected String name = null;
    protected volatile PhysicalLocationUtility physicalLocation = new
PhysicalLocationUtility();
    protected volatile double distance = 0.0;
    protected volatile boolean isOnRadar = false;
    protected volatile boolean isInView = false;
    protected final Vector symbolXyzRelativeToCameraView = new Vector();
    protected final Vector textXyzRelativeToCameraView = new Vector();
    protected final Vector locationXyzRelativeToPhysicalLocation = new Vector();
    protected int color = Color.WHITE;

    private static boolean debugTouchZone = false;
    private static PaintableBox touchBox = null;
    private static PaintablePosition touchPosition = null;

    private static boolean debugCollisionZone = false;
    private static PaintableBox collisionBox = null;
    private static PaintablePosition collisionPosition = null;
```

DECIMAL_FORMAT is used to format the distance we show on the Radar.

symbolVector and textVector are used to find the location of the text and the marker symbol. symbolVector and textVector are used when finding the location of the text and its accompanying symbol using the rotation matrix.

The next four vectors and three float arrays are used in positioning and drawing the marker symbol and its accompanying text.

initialY is the initial Y-axis position for each marker. It is set to 0 to begin with, but its value is different for each marker.

textBox, textContainer, and cam are instances of the PaintableBoxedText, PaintablePostion, and CameraModel respectively. We have not yet written CameraModel; we will do so after we finish all the UI pieces of the app.

symbolArray and textArray are used when drawing the symbol and text later on in this class.

gpsSymbol is, well, the GPS symbol. symbolContainer is the container for the GPS symbol. name is a unique identifier for each marker, set using the article title for Wikipedia articles and the username for Tweets. physicalLocation is the physical location of the marker (the real-world position). distance stores the distance from the user to the physicalLocation in meters. isOnRadar and isInView are used as flags to keep track of the marker's visibility. symbolXyzRelativeToCameraView, textXyzRelativeToCameraView, and locationXyzRelativeToPhysicalLocation are used to determine the location of the marker symbol and text relative to the camera view, and the location of the user relative to the physical location, respectively. x is up/down; y is left/right; and z is not used, but is there to complete the Vector. The color int is the default color of the marker, and is set to white.

debugTouchZone and debugCollisionZone are two flags we use to enable and disable debugging for both of the zones. touchBox, touchPosition, collisionBox, and collisionPosition are used to draw opaque boxes to help us debug the app.

Figure 9-1 shows the app running without debugTouchZone and debugCollisionZone set to false; in Figure 9.2 they are set to true.

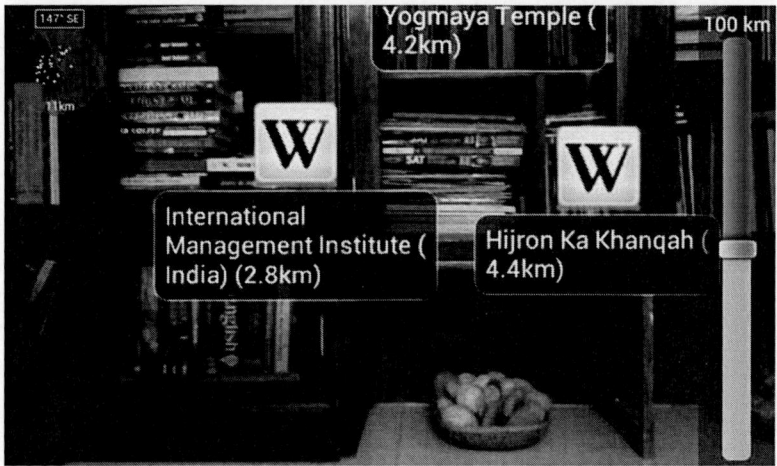

Figure 9-2. *The app running with touch and collision debugging disabled*

Figure 9-3. *The app running with touch and collision debugging enabled*

The Constructor and set() method

Now let's take a look at the constructor and set() method:

Listing 9-57. *The constructor and set() method*

```
        public Marker(String name, double latitude, double longitude, double
altitude, int color) {
                set(name, latitude, longitude, altitude, color);
    }
        public synchronized void set(String name, double latitude, double
longitude, double altitude, int color) {
                if (name==null) throw new NullPointerException();

    this.name                  = name;
    this.physicalLocation.set(latitude,longitude,altitude);
    this.color                 = color;
    this.isOnRadar                 = false;
    this.isInView                  = false;
    this.symbolXyzRelativeToCameraView.set(0,              0, 0);
    this.textXyzRelativeToCameraView.set(0,           0, 0);
    this.locationXyzRelativeToPhysicalLocation.set(0,             0, 0);
    this.initialY              = 0.0f;
    }
```

The constructor takes the Marker's name; its latitude, longitude, and altitude for the PhysicalLocation; and its color as parameters and then passes them to the set() method. The set() method sets these values to our variables described and given in Listing 9-56. It also handles some basic initialization for the camera and the marker's position on screen.

The get() methods

Now let's take a look at the various get() methods for the Marker class:

Listing 9-58. *The get() methods*

```
public synchronized String getName(){
  return                 this.name;
}

    public synchronized int getColor() {
        return this.color;
    }

    public synchronized double getDistance() {
        return this.distance;
    }

    public synchronized float getInitialY() {
        return this.initialY;
    }

    public synchronized boolean isOnRadar() {
        return this.isOnRadar;
    }

    public synchronized boolean isInView() {
        return this.isInView;
    }

    public synchronized Vector getScreenPosition() {
        symbolXyzRelativeToCameraView.get(symbolArray);
        textXyzRelativeToCameraView.get(textArray);
        float x = (symbolArray[0] + textArray[0])/2;
        float y = (symbolArray[1] + textArray[1])/2;
        float z = (symbolArray[2] + textArray[2])/2;

        if (textBox!=null) y += (textBox.getHeight()/2);

        screenPositionVector.set(x, y, z);
        return screenPositionVector;
    }

    public synchronized Vector getLocation() {
        return this.locationXyzRelativeToPhysicalLocation;
    }
```

```
public synchronized float getHeight() {
    if (symbolContainer==null || textContainer==null) return 0f;
    return symbolContainer.getHeight()+textContainer.getHeight();
}

public synchronized float getWidth() {
    if (symbolContainer==null || textContainer==null) return 0f;
    float w1 = textContainer.getWidth();
    float w2 = symbolContainer.getWidth();
    return (w1>w2)?w1:w2;
}
```

getName(), getColor(), getDistance(), getLocation(), isInView(), isOnRadar(), and getInitialY() simply return the values indicated by the name. getHeight() adds up the height of the text and the symbol image and returns it. getWidth() checks and returns the greater width between the text and the symbol image. getScreenPosition() calculates the marker's position on the screen by using the positions of the text and symbol, relative to the camera view.

The update() and populateMatrices() methods

Now let's take a look at the update() and populateMatrices() methods:

Listing 9-59. *update() and populateMatrices()*

```
public synchronized void update(Canvas canvas, float addX, float addY) {
        if (canvas==null) throw new NullPointerException();

        if (cam==null) cam = new CameraModel(canvas.getWidth(),
canvas.getHeight(), true);
        cam.set(canvas.getWidth(), canvas.getHeight(), false);
        cam.setViewAngle(CameraModel.DEFAULT_VIEW_ANGLE);
        populateMatrices(cam, addX, addY);
        updateRadar();
        updateView();
    }

        private synchronized void populateMatrices(CameraModel cam, float addX,
float addY) {
                if (cam==null) throw new NullPointerException();

    tmpSymbolVector.set(symbolVector);
                tmpSymbolVector.add(locationXyzRelativeToPhysicalLocation);
        tmpSymbolVector.prod(ARData.getRotationMatrix());

    tmpTextVector.set(textVector);
```

```
tmpTextVector.add(locationXyzRelativeToPhysicalLocation);
tmpTextVector.prod(ARData.getRotationMatrix());

            cam.projectPoint(tmpSymbolVector, tmpVector, addX, addY);
symbolXyzRelativeToCameraView.set(tmpVector);
            cam.projectPoint(tmpTextVector, tmpVector, addX, addY);
textXyzRelativeToCameraView.set(tmpVector);
}
```

The update() method is used to update the views and populate the matrices. We first ensure that the canvas is not a null value, and initialize cam if it hasn't already been initialized. We then update the properties of cam to go with the canvas being used, and set its viewing angle. The viewing angle is defined in CameraModel, a class that we will be writing later on in this chapter. It then calls the populateMatrices() method, passing the cam object, and the values to be added to the X and Y position of the marker as parameters. After that, update() further calls updateRadar() and updateView(). In populateMatrices(), we find the position of the text and symbol of the marker given the rotation matrix we get from ARData, a class that we will be writing later on in this chapter. We then use that data to project the text and symbol onto the camera view.

The updateView() and updateRadar() Methods

Now let's take a look at the updateView() and updateRadar() methods called by update().

Listing 9-60. *updateRadar() and updateView()*

```
    private synchronized void updateRadar() {
 isOnRadar                = false;

            float range = ARData.getRadius() * 1000;
            float scale = range / Radar.RADIUS;
 locationXyzRelativeToPhysicalLocation.get(locationArray);
    float x = locationArray[0] / scale;
    float y = locationArray[2] / scale; // z==y Switched on purpose
    symbolXyzRelativeToCameraView.get(symbolArray);
            if ((symbolArray[2] < -1f) &&
((x*x+y*y)<(Radar.RADIUS*Radar.RADIUS))) {
 isOnRadar                    = true;
            }
}

  private synchronized void updateView() {
      isInView = false;

      symbolXyzRelativeToCameraView.get(symbolArray);
```

```
float x1 = symbolArray[0] + (getWidth()/2);
float y1 = symbolArray[1] + (getHeight()/2);
float x2 = symbolArray[0] - (getWidth()/2);
float y2 = symbolArray[1] - (getHeight()/2);
if (x1>=-1 && x2<=(cam.getWidth())
    &&
    y1>=-1 && y2<=(cam.getHeight())
) {
    isInView = true;
}
}
```

updateRadar() is used to update the position of the marker on the radar. If the marker's location is found to be such that it should show on the radar, its OnRadar is updated to true. updateView() does the same thing as updateRadar(), except it checks to see whether the marker is currently visible.

The calcRelativePosition() and updateDistance() methods

Now let's take a look at the calcRelativePosition() and updateDistance() methods:

Listing 9-61. *calcRelativePosition() and updateDistance()*

```
public synchronized void calcRelativePosition(Location location) {
            if (location==null) throw new NullPointerException();

        updateDistance(location);

  if            (physicalLocation.getAltitude()==0.0)
physicalLocation.setAltitude(location.getAltitude());

    PhysicalLocationUtility.convLocationToVector(location,
physicalLocation, locationXyzRelativeToPhysicalLocation);
    this.initialY              = locationXyzRelativeToPhysicalLocation.getY();
    updateRadar();
    }

    private synchronized void updateDistance(Location location) {
        if (location==null) throw new NullPointerException();

        Location.distanceBetween(physicalLocation.getLatitude(),
physicalLocation.getLongitude(), location.getLatitude(),
location.getLongitude(), distanceArray);
        distance = distanceArray[0];
    }
```

In calcRelativePosition(), we calculate the new relative position using the location received as a parameter. We check to see whether we have a valid altitude for the marker in the physicalLocation; if we don't, we set it to the user's current altitude. We then use the data to create a vector, use the vector to update the initialY variable, and finally we call updateRadar() to update the radar with the new relative location. updateDistance() simply calculates the new distance between the physical location of the marker, and the user's location.

The handleClick(), isMarkerOnMarker(), and isPointOnMarker() Methods

Now let's take a look at how we handle clicks and see whether the marker is overlapping with another marker:

Listing 9-62. *Checking for clicks and overlaps*

```
public synchronized boolean handleClick(float x, float y) {
        if (!isOnRadar || !isInView) return false;
        return isPointOnMarker(x,y,this);
    }

    public synchronized boolean isMarkerOnMarker(Marker marker) {
        return isMarkerOnMarker(marker,true);
    }

    private synchronized boolean isMarkerOnMarker(Marker marker, boolean
reflect) {
        marker.getScreenPosition().get(screenPositionArray);
        float x = screenPositionArray[0];
        float y = screenPositionArray[1];
        boolean middleOfMarker = isPointOnMarker(x,y,this);
        if (middleOfMarker) return true;

        float halfWidth = marker.getWidth()/2;
        float halfHeight = marker.getHeight()/2;

        float x1 = x - halfWidth;
        float y1 = y - halfHeight;
        boolean upperLeftOfMarker = isPointOnMarker(x1,y1,this);
        if (upperLeftOfMarker) return true;

        float x2 = x + halfWidth;
        float y2 = y1;
        boolean upperRightOfMarker = isPointOnMarker(x2,y2,this);
        if (upperRightOfMarker) return true;

        float x3 = x1;
```

```
        float y3 = y + halfHeight;
        boolean lowerLeftOfMarker = isPointOnMarker(x3,y3,this);
        if (lowerLeftOfMarker) return true;

        float x4 = x2;
        float y4 = y3;
        boolean lowerRightOfMarker = isPointOnMarker(x4,y4,this);
        if (lowerRightOfMarker) return true;

        return (reflect)?marker.isMarkerOnMarker(this,false):false;
    }

        private synchronized boolean isPointOnMarker(float x, float y, Marker
marker) {
        marker.getScreenPosition().get(screenPositionArray);
        float myX = screenPositionArray[0];
        float myY = screenPositionArray[1];
        float adjWidth = marker.getWidth()/2;
        float adjHeight = marker.getHeight()/2;

        float x1 = myX-adjWidth;
        float y1 = myY-adjHeight;
        float x2 = myX+adjWidth;
        float y2 = myY+adjHeight;

        if (x>=x1 && x<=x2 && y>=y1 && y<=y2) return true;

        return false;
    }
```

handleClick() takes the X and Y points of the click as arguments. If the marker isn't on the radar and isn't in view, it returns false. Otherwise, it returns whatever is found by calling isPointOnMarker().

The first isMarkerOnMarker() simply returns whatever the second isMarkerOnMarker() method finds out. The second isMarkerOnMarker() method contains all the code we use to determine whether the marker received as the parameter is overlapping with the current marker. We check for overlaps on all four corners and the center of the marker. If any of them is true, we can safely say that the markers are overlapping.

isPointOnMarker() checks to see whether the passed X and Y coordinates are located on the marker.

The draw() method

Now let's take a look at the draw() method:

Listing 9-63. *draw()*

```
public synchronized void draw(Canvas canvas) {
        if (canvas==null) throw new NullPointerException();

        if (!isOnRadar || !isInView) return;

        if (debugTouchZone) drawTouchZone(canvas);
        if (debugCollisionZone) drawCollisionZone(canvas);
        drawIcon(canvas);
        drawText(canvas);
    }
```

The draw() method is very simple. It determines whether the marker should be shown. If it is to be shown, it draws it and draws the debug boxes if required. That's all it does.

The drawTouchZone(), drawCollisionZone(), drawIcon(), and drawText() Methods

The main work for drawing is done in the drawTouchZone(), drawCollisionZone(), drawIcon(), and drawText() methods, which we will take a look at now:

Listing 9-64. *drawTouchZone(), drawCollisionZone(), drawIcon(), and drawText()*

```
protected synchronized void drawCollisionZone(Canvas canvas) {
        if (canvas==null) throw new NullPointerException();

        getScreenPosition().get(screenPositionArray);
        float x = screenPositionArray[0];
        float y = screenPositionArray[1];

        float width = getWidth();
        float height = getHeight();
        float halfWidth = width/2;
        float halfHeight = height/2;

        float x1 = x - halfWidth;
        float y1 = y - halfHeight;

        float x2 = x + halfWidth;
        float y2 = y1;

        float x3 = x1;
        float y3 = y + halfHeight;
```

```
        float x4 = x2;
        float y4 = y3;

        Log.w("collisionBox", "ul (x="+x1+" y="+y1+")");
        Log.w("collisionBox", "ur (x="+x2+" y="+y2+")");
        Log.w("collisionBox", "ll (x="+x3+" y="+y3+")");
        Log.w("collisionBox", "lr (x="+x4+" y="+y4+")");

        if (collisionBox==null) collisionBox = new
PaintableBox(width,height,Color.WHITE,Color.RED);
        else collisionBox.set(width,height);

        float currentAngle = Utilities.getAngle(symbolArray[0], symbolArray[1],
textArray[0], textArray[1])+90;

        if (collisionPosition==null) collisionPosition = new
PaintablePosition(collisionBox, x1, y1, currentAngle, 1);
        else collisionPosition.set(collisionBox, x1, y1, currentAngle, 1);
        collisionPosition.paint(canvas);
    }

    protected synchronized void drawTouchZone(Canvas canvas) {
        if (canvas==null) throw new NullPointerException();

        if (gpsSymbol==null) return;

        symbolXyzRelativeToCameraView.get(symbolArray);
        textXyzRelativeToCameraView.get(textArray);
        float x1 = symbolArray[0];
        float y1 = symbolArray[1];
        float x2 = textArray[0];
        float y2 = textArray[1];
        float width = getWidth();
        float height = getHeight();
        float adjX = (x1 + x2)/2;
        float adjY = (y1 + y2)/2;
        float currentAngle = Utilities.getAngle(symbolArray[0], symbolArray[1],
textArray[0], textArray[1])+90;
        adjX -= (width/2);
        adjY -= (gpsSymbol.getHeight()/2);

        Log.w("touchBox", "ul (x="+(adjX)+" y="+(adjY)+")");
        Log.w("touchBox", "ur (x="+(adjX+width)+" y="+(adjY)+")");
        Log.w("touchBox", "ll (x="+(adjX)+" y="+(adjY+height)+")");
        Log.w("touchBox", "lr (x="+(adjX+width)+" y="+(adjY+height)+")");

        if (touchBox==null) touchBox = new
PaintableBox(width,height,Color.WHITE,Color.GREEN);
        else touchBox.set(width,height);
```

```
        if (touchPosition==null) touchPosition = new PaintablePosition(touchBox,
adjX, adjY, currentAngle, 1);
        else touchPosition.set(touchBox, adjX, adjY, currentAngle, 1);
        touchPosition.paint(canvas);
    }

    protected synchronized void drawIcon(Canvas canvas) {
        if (canvas==null) throw new NullPointerException();

        if (gpsSymbol==null) gpsSymbol = new PaintableGps(36, 36, true,
getColor());

        textXyzRelativeToCameraView.get(textArray);
        symbolXyzRelativeToCameraView.get(symbolArray);

        float currentAngle = Utilities.getAngle(symbolArray[0], symbolArray[1],
textArray[0], textArray[1]);
        float angle = currentAngle + 90;

        if (symbolContainer==null) symbolContainer = new
PaintablePosition(gpsSymbol, symbolArray[0], symbolArray[1], angle, 1);
        else symbolContainer.set(gpsSymbol, symbolArray[0], symbolArray[1],
angle, 1);

        symbolContainer.paint(canvas);
    }

    protected synchronized void drawText(Canvas canvas) {
            if (canvas==null) throw new NullPointerException();

        String textStr = null;
        if (distance<1000.0) {
            textStr = name + " ("+ DECIMAL_FORMAT.format(distance) + "m)";
        } else {
            double d=distance/1000.0;
            textStr = name + " (" + DECIMAL_FORMAT.format(d) + "km)";
        }

        textXyzRelativeToCameraView.get(textArray);
        symbolXyzRelativeToCameraView.get(symbolArray);

        float maxHeight = Math.round(canvas.getHeight() / 10f) + 1;
        if (textBox==null) textBox = new PaintableBoxedText(textStr,
Math.round(maxHeight / 2f) + 1, 300);
        else textBox.set(textStr, Math.round(maxHeight / 2f) + 1, 300);

        float currentAngle = Utilities.getAngle(symbolArray[0],
symbolArray[1], textArray[0], textArray[1]);
        float angle = currentAngle + 90;
```

```
            float x = textArray[0] - (textBox.getWidth() / 2);
            float y = textArray[1] + maxHeight;

            if (textContainer==null) textContainer = new
PaintablePosition(textBox, x, y, angle, 1);
            else textContainer.set(textBox, x, y, angle, 1);
            textContainer.paint(canvas);
 }
```

The drawCollisionZone() method draws the collision zone between two markers if there is one to be drawn. The drawTouchZone() draws a red rectangle over the area we listen to for touches on the marker. The drawIcon() method draws the icon, and the drawText() method draws the related text.

The compareTo() and equals() Methods

Now let's take a look at the final two methods, compareTo() and equals():

Listing 9-65. *compareTo() and equals()*

```
public synchronized int compareTo(Marker another) {
        if (another==null) throw new NullPointerException();

        return name.compareTo(another.getName());
    }

    @Override
    public synchronized boolean equals(Object marker) {
        if(marker==null || name==null) throw new NullPointerException();

        return name.equals(((Marker)marker).getName());
    }
}
```

compareTo() compares the names of the two markers using the standard Java String functions. equals() uses the standard Java String functions to check the name of one marker against another.

This brings us to the end of the Marker.java file. Now let's take a look at its only subclass, IconMarker.java.

IconMarker.java

IconMarker draws a bitmap as an icon for a marker, instead of leaving it at the default. It is an extension of Marker.java.

Listing 9-66. *IconMarker*

```java
public class IconMarker extends Marker {
    private Bitmap bitmap = null;

    public IconMarker(String name, double latitude, double longitude, double
altitude, int color, Bitmap bitmap) {
        super(name, latitude, longitude, altitude, color);
        this.bitmap = bitmap;
    }

    @Override
    public void drawIcon(Canvas canvas) {
        if (canvas==null || bitmap==null) throw new NullPointerException();

        if (gpsSymbol==null) gpsSymbol = new PaintableIcon(bitmap,96,96);

        textXyzRelativeToCameraView.get(textArray);
        symbolXyzRelativeToCameraView.get(symbolArray);

        float currentAngle = Utilities.getAngle(symbolArray[0], symbolArray[1],
textArray[0], textArray[1]);
        float angle = currentAngle + 90;

        if (symbolContainer==null) symbolContainer = new
PaintablePosition(gpsSymbol, symbolArray[0], symbolArray[1], angle, 1);
        else symbolContainer.set(gpsSymbol, symbolArray[0], symbolArray[1],
angle, 1);

        symbolContainer.paint(canvas);
    }
}
```

The constructor takes all the parameters required for a super() call to
Marker.java, along with an extra parameter that is the bitmap for the marker.
drawIcon() then uses data from Marker.java to draw the bitmap we received in
the constructor as the icon for this marker.

This brings us to the end of the UI components. Now let's take a look at
VerticalSeekBar.java, our custom extension of the Android SeekBar.

Customized Widget

We have one customization of the standard Android widgets in our app. We
have extended SeekBar to create VerticalSeekBar.

VerticalSeekBar.java

VerticalSeekBar is an extension of Android's SeekBar implementation. Our additional code allows it to work vertically instead of horizontally. The zoomBar used in the app is an instance of this class.

Listing 9-67. VerticalSeekBar.java

```java
public class VerticalSeekBar extends SeekBar {

    public VerticalSeekBar(Context context) {
        super(context);
    }

    public VerticalSeekBar(Context context, AttributeSet attrs, int defStyle) {
        super(context, attrs, defStyle);
    }

    public VerticalSeekBar(Context context, AttributeSet attrs) {
        super(context, attrs);
    }

    @Override
    protected void onSizeChanged(int w, int h, int oldw, int oldh) {
        super.onSizeChanged(h, w, oldh, oldw);
    }

    @Override
    protected synchronized void onMeasure(int widthMeasureSpec, int
heightMeasureSpec) {
        super.onMeasure(heightMeasureSpec, widthMeasureSpec);
        setMeasuredDimension(getMeasuredHeight(), getMeasuredWidth());
    }

    @Override
    protected void onDraw(Canvas c) {
        c.rotate(-90);
        c.translate(-getHeight(), 0);

        super.onDraw(c);
    }

    @Override
    public boolean onTouchEvent(MotionEvent event) {
        if (!isEnabled()) {
            return false;
        }

        switch (event.getAction()) {
```

```
        case MotionEvent.ACTION_DOWN:
        case MotionEvent.ACTION_MOVE:
        case MotionEvent.ACTION_UP:
            setProgress(getMax() - (int) (getMax() * event.getY() /
getHeight()));
            onSizeChanged(getWidth(), getHeight(), 0, 0);
            break;

        case MotionEvent.ACTION_CANCEL:
            break;
        }
        return true;
    }
}
```

Our three constructors are used to tie it to the parent SeekBar class. onSizeChanged() also ties back to the SeekBar class. onMeasure() does a super() call, and also sets the measured height and width using the methods provided by Android's View class. The actual modification is done in onDraw(), when we rotate the canvas by 90 degrees before passing it to SeekBar, so that the drawing is done vertically, not horizontally. In onTouchEvent(), we call setProgress() and onSizeChanged()to allow for our rotation of the SeekBar to work properly.

Now let's take a look at the three classes required to control the camera.

Controlling the Camera

As with any AR app, we must use the camera in this one as well. Due to the nature of this app, the camera control has been put in three classes, which we will go through now.

CameraSurface.java

The first class we will look at is CameraSurface. This class handles all the Camera's SurfaceView–related code:

Listing 9-68. *Variables and Constructor*

```java
public class CameraSurface extends SurfaceView implements SurfaceHolder.Callback
{
    private static SurfaceHolder holder = null;
    private static Camera camera = null;

    public CameraSurface(Context context) {
```

```
        super(context);

        try {
            holder = getHolder();
            holder.addCallback(this);
            holder.setType(SurfaceHolder.SURFACE_TYPE_PUSH_BUFFERS);
        } catch (Exception ex) {
                ex.printStackTrace();
        }
    }
```

We declare the SurfaceHolder and camera right at the beginning. We then use the constructor to initialize the SurfaceHolder and set its type to SURFACE_TYPE_PUSH_BUFFERS, which allows it to receive data from the camera.

Now let's take a look at the surfaceCreated() method:

Listing 9-69. *surfaceCreated()*

```
public void surfaceCreated(SurfaceHolder holder) {
        try {
            if (camera != null) {
                try {
                    camera.stopPreview();
                } catch (Exception ex) {
                        ex.printStackTrace();
                }
                try {
                    camera.release();
                } catch (Exception ex) {
                        ex.printStackTrace();
                }
                camera = null;
            }

            camera = Camera.open();
            camera.setPreviewDisplay(holder);
        } catch (Exception ex) {
            try {
                if (camera != null) {
                    try {
                        camera.stopPreview();
                    } catch (Exception ex1) {
                        ex.printStackTrace();
                    }
                    try {
                        camera.release();
                    } catch (Exception ex2) {
                        ex.printStackTrace();
                    }
                }
```

```
                camera = null;
            }
        } catch (Exception ex3) {
            ex.printStackTrace();
        }
    }
}
```

We use surfaceCreated() to create the camera object and to release it as well if it already exists or if we encounter a problem.

Now let's move on to surfaceDestroyed().

Listing 9-70. *surfaceDestroyed()*

```
public void surfaceDestroyed(SurfaceHolder holder) {
    try {
        if (camera != null) {
            try {
                camera.stopPreview();
            } catch (Exception ex) {
                ex.printStackTrace();
            }
            try {
                camera.release();
            } catch (Exception ex) {
                ex.printStackTrace();
            }
            camera = null;
        }
    } catch (Exception ex) {
        ex.printStackTrace();
    }
}
```

This is simple code, pretty much the same as our other example apps. We stop using the camera and release it so that our own or another third-party or system app can access it.

Without further ado, let's take a look at the last method of this class, surfaceChanged():

Listing 9-71. *surfaceChanged()*

```
public void surfaceChanged(SurfaceHolder holder, int format, int w, int h) {
    try {
        Camera.Parameters parameters = camera.getParameters();
        try {
            List<Camera.Size> supportedSizes = null;
```

```
            supportedSizes =
CameraCompatibility.getSupportedPreviewSizes(parameters);

            float ff = (float)w/h;

            float bff = 0;
            int bestw = 0;
            int besth = 0;
            Iterator<Camera.Size> itr = supportedSizes.iterator();

            while(itr.hasNext()) {
                Camera.Size element = itr.next();
                float cff = (float)element.width/element.height;

                if ((ff-cff <= ff-bff) && (element.width <= w) &&
(element.width >= bestw)) {
                        bff=cff;
                    bestw = element.width;
                    besth = element.height;
                }
            }

            if ((bestw == 0) || (besth == 0)){
                bestw = 480;
                besth = 320;
            }
            parameters.setPreviewSize(bestw, besth);
        } catch (Exception ex) {
            parameters.setPreviewSize(480 , 320);
        }

        camera.setParameters(parameters);
        camera.startPreview();
    } catch (Exception ex) {
            ex.printStackTrace();
    }
  }
}
```

We use surfaceChanged() to calculate the preview size that gives us an aspect ratio (form factor, stored in bff) that is closest to the device's screen's aspect ratio (ff). We also make sure that the preview size is not greater than that of the screen, as some phones like the HTC Hero report sizes that are bigger and crash when an app uses them. We also have an if statement at the end to guard against a 0 value for the width and the height, as might occur on some Samsung phones.

Now let's move on to the remaining two classes: CameraCompatibility and CameraModel.

CameraCompatibility

CameraCompatibility allows our app to maintain compatibility with all versions of Android and get around limitations of the older versions' APIs. It is adapted from the Mixare project, like the Vector class.

Listing 9-72. *CameraCompatibility*

```
public class CameraCompatibility {
        private static Method getSupportedPreviewSizes = null;
        private static Method mDefaultDisplay_getRotation = null;

 static         {
  initCompatibility();
 };

        private static void initCompatibility() {
  try             {
   getSupportedPreviewSizes                 =
Camera.Parameters.class.getMethod("getSupportedPreviewSizes", new Class[] { } );
   mDefaultDisplay_getRotation              =
Display.class.getMethod("getRotation", new Class[] { } );
                } catch (NoSuchMethodException nsme) {
                }
 }

        public static int getRotation(Activity activity) {
            int result = 1;
            try {
            Display display = ((WindowManager)
activity.getSystemService(Context.WINDOW_SERVICE)).getDefaultDisplay();
            Object retObj = mDefaultDisplay_getRotation.invoke(display);
            if(retObj != null) result = (Integer) retObj;
            } catch (Exception ex) {
                ex.printStackTrace();
            }
            return result;
 }

        public static List<Camera.Size>
getSupportedPreviewSizes(Camera.Parameters params) {
                List<Camera.Size> retList = null;

  try                {
   Object                       retObj = getSupportedPreviewSizes.invoke(params);
                        if (retObj != null) {
    retList                        = (List<Camera.Size>)retObj;
                        }
                } catch (InvocationTargetException ite) {
```

```
    Throwable                          cause = ite.getCause();
                         if (cause instanceof RuntimeException) {
    throw                              (RuntimeException) cause;
                         } else if (cause instanceof Error) {
    throw                              (Error) cause;
    }                        else {
    throw                              new RuntimeException(ite);
                         }
                 } catch (IllegalAccessException ie) {
      ie.printStackTrace();
                 }
    return               retList;
    }
}
```

initCompatibility() fails on devices lower than Android 2.0, and this allows us to gracefully set the camera to the default preview size of 480 by 320. getRotation() allows us to retrieve the rotation of the device. getSupportedPreviewSizes() returns a list of the preview sizes available on the device.

Now let's take a look at CameraModel, the last of the camera classes, and second-to-last class of this app.

CameraModel

CameraModel represents the camera and its view, and also allows us to project points. It is another class that has been adapted from Mixare.

Listing 9-73. *CameraModel*

```java
public class CameraModel {
    private static final float[] tmp1 = new float[3];
    private static final float[] tmp2 = new float[3];

        private int width = 0;
        private int height = 0;
        private float distance = 0F;

        public static final float DEFAULT_VIEW_ANGLE = (float)
Math.toRadians(45);

        public CameraModel(int width, int height, boolean init) {
      set(width,               height, init);
    }

        public void set(int width, int height, boolean init) {
      this.width               = width;
```

```
 this.height              = height;
}

        public int getWidth() {
            return width;
}

    public int getHeight() {
        return height;
    }

        public void setViewAngle(float viewAngle) {
                this.distance = (this.width / 2) / (float) Math.tan(viewAngle /
2);
 }

        public void projectPoint(Vector orgPoint, Vector prjPoint, float addX,
float addY) {
            orgPoint.get(tmp1);
            tmp2[0]=(distance * tmp1[0] / -tmp1[2]);
            tmp2[1]=(distance * tmp1[1] / -tmp1[2]);
            tmp2[2]=(tmp1[2]);
            tmp2[0]=(tmp2[0] + addX + width / 2);
            tmp2[1]=(-tmp2[1] + addY + height / 2);
            prjPoint.set(tmp2);
 }
}
```

The constructor sets up the width and height for the class. getWidth() and
getHeight() return the width and height, respectively. setViewAngle() updates
the distance with a new viewing angle. projectPoint() projects a point using
the origin vector, the project vector, and the additions to the X and
Ycoordinates.

The Global Class

Now let's take a look at our last class, ARData.

ARData.java

ARData serves as a global control and storage class; it stores the data that is
used throughout the app and is essential for its running. It makes it simpler for
us to store all this data in one place, instead of having bits and pieces of it
scattered all over.

Listing 9-74. *ARData's Global Variables*

```
public abstract class ARData {
    private static final String TAG = "ARData";
        private static final Map<String,Marker> markerList = new
ConcurrentHashMap<String,Marker>();
    private static final List<Marker> cache = new
CopyOnWriteArrayList<Marker>();
    private static final AtomicBoolean dirty = new AtomicBoolean(false);
    private static final float[] locationArray = new float[3];

    public static final Location hardFix = new Location("ATL");
    static {
        hardFix.setLatitude(0);
        hardFix.setLongitude(0);
        hardFix.setAltitude(1);
    }

    private static final Object radiusLock = new Object();
    private static float radius = new Float(20);
    private static String zoomLevel = new String();
    private static final Object zoomProgressLock = new Object();
    private static int zoomProgress = 0;
    private static Location currentLocation = hardFix;
    private static Matrix rotationMatrix = new Matrix();
    private static final Object azimuthLock = new Object();
    private static float azimuth = 0;
    private static final Object pitchLock = new Object();
    private static float pitch = 0;
    private static final Object rollLock = new Object();
    private static float roll = 0;
```

TAG is a string used when showing messages in the LogCat. markerList is a Hashmap of the markers and their names. cache is, well, a cache. dirty is used to tell whether the state is dirty or not. locationArray is an array of the location data. hardFix is a default location, the same as the ATL marker we have. radius is that radius of the radar; zoomProgress is the progress of the zoom in our app. pitch, azimuth, and roll hold the pitch, azimuth, and roll values, respectively. The previous variables with Lock added to the name are the lock objects for the synchronized blocks for those variables. zoomLevel is the level of zoom currently there. currentLocation stores the current location, set by default to hardFix. Finally, rotationMatrix stores the rotation matrix.

Now let's take a look at the various getter and setter methods of this class:

Listing 9-75. *The getters and setters for ARData*

```
public static void setZoomLevel(String zoomLevel) {
```

```java
        if (zoomLevel==null) throw new NullPointerException();

        synchronized (ARData.zoomLevel) {
            ARData.zoomLevel = zoomLevel;
        }
    }

    public static void setZoomProgress(int zoomProgress) {
        synchronized (ARData.zoomProgressLock) {
            if (ARData.zoomProgress != zoomProgress) {
                ARData.zoomProgress = zoomProgress;
                if (dirty.compareAndSet(false, true)) {
                    Log.v(TAG, "Setting DIRTY flag!");
                    cache.clear();
                }
            }
        }
    }

    public static void setRadius(float radius) {
        synchronized (ARData.radiusLock) {
            ARData.radius = radius;
        }
    }

    public static float getRadius() {
        synchronized (ARData.radiusLock) {
            return ARData.radius;
        }
    }

    public static void setCurrentLocation(Location currentLocation) {
        if (currentLocation==null) throw new NullPointerException();

        Log.d(TAG, "current location. location="+currentLocation.toString());
        synchronized (currentLocation) {
            ARData.currentLocation = currentLocation;
        }
        onLocationChanged(currentLocation);
    }

    public static Location getCurrentLocation() {
        synchronized (ARData.currentLocation) {
            return ARData.currentLocation;
        }
    }

    public static void setRotationMatrix(Matrix rotationMatrix) {
        synchronized (ARData.rotationMatrix) {
            ARData.rotationMatrix = rotationMatrix;
```

```
            }
        }

        public static Matrix getRotationMatrix() {
            synchronized (ARData.rotationMatrix) {
                return rotationMatrix;
            }
        }

        public static List<Marker> getMarkers() {
            if (dirty.compareAndSet(true, false)) {
                Log.v(TAG, "DIRTY flag found, resetting all marker heights to
zero.");
                for(Marker ma : markerList.values()) {
                    ma.getLocation().get(locationArray);
                    locationArray[1]=ma.getInitialY();
                    ma.getLocation().set(locationArray);
                }

                Log.v(TAG, "Populating the cache.");
                List<Marker> copy = new ArrayList<Marker>();
                copy.addAll(markerList.values());
                Collections.sort(copy,comparator);
                cache.clear();
                cache.addAll(copy);
            }
            return Collections.unmodifiableList(cache);
        }

        public static void setAzimuth(float azimuth) {
            synchronized (azimuthLock) {
                ARData.azimuth = azimuth;
            }
        }

        public static float getAzimuth() {
            synchronized (azimuthLock) {
                return ARData.azimuth;
            }
        }

        public static void setPitch(float pitch) {
            synchronized (pitchLock) {
                ARData.pitch = pitch;
            }
        }

        public static float getPitch() {
            synchronized (pitchLock) {
                return ARData.pitch;
```

```
        }
    }

    public static void setRoll(float roll) {
        synchronized (rollLock) {
            ARData.roll = roll;
        }
    }

    public static float getRoll() {
        synchronized (rollLock) {
            return ARData.roll;
        }
    }
```

All the methods simply set or get the variable mentioned in their name, using a synchronized block to ensure that the data isn't modified by two different parts of the app at once. In the getMarkers() methods, we iterate over the markers to return all them. Now let's take a look at the last few methods of this class.

Listing 9-76. *addMarkers(), comparator, and onLocationChanged()*

```
private static final Comparator<Marker> comparator = new Comparator<Marker>() {
        public int compare(Marker arg0, Marker arg1) {
            return Double.compare(arg0.getDistance(),arg1.getDistance());
        }
    };

    public static void addMarkers(Collection<Marker> markers) {
        if (markers==null) throw new NullPointerException();

        if (markers.size()<=0) return;

        Log.d(TAG, "New markers, updating markers. new
markers="+markers.toString());
        for(Marker marker : markers) {
            if (!markerList.containsKey(marker.getName())) {
                marker.calcRelativePosition(ARData.getCurrentLocation());
                markerList.put(marker.getName(),marker);
            }
        }

        if (dirty.compareAndSet(false, true)) {
            Log.v(TAG, "Setting DIRTY flag!");
            cache.clear();
        }
    }

    private static void onLocationChanged(Location location) {
```

```
        Log.d(TAG, "New location, updating markers.
location="+location.toString());
        for(Marker ma: markerList.values()) {
            ma.calcRelativePosition(location);
        }

        if (dirty.compareAndSet(false, true)) {
            Log.v(TAG, "Setting DIRTY flag!");
            cache.clear();
        }
    }
}
```

comparator is used to compare the distance of one marker to another.
addMarkers() is used to add new markers from the passed collection.
onLocationChanged() is used to update the relative positions of the markers with
respect to the new location.

AndroidManifest.xml

Finally, we must create the Android Manifest as follows:

Listing 9-77. *AndroidManifest.xml*

```
<?xml version="1.0" encoding="utf-8"?>
<manifest xmlns:android="http://schemas.android.com/apk/res/android"
    package="com.paar.ch9"
    android:versionCode="1"
    android:versionName="1.0" >

    <uses-sdk android:minSdkVersion="7" />
 <uses-permission        android:name="android.permission.CAMERA"/>
 <uses-permission        android:name="android.permission.INTERNET"/>
 <uses-permission
android:name="android.permission.ACCESS_FINE_LOCATION"/>
 <uses-permission
android:name="android.permission.ACCESS_CORSE_LOCATION"/>
 <uses-permission        android:name="android.permission.WAKE_LOCK"/>

    <application
        android:icon="@drawable/ic_launcher"
                    android:label="@string/app_name"

android:theme="@android:style/Theme.NoTitleBar.Fullscreen">

        <activity android:name=".MainActivity"
                android:label="@string/app_name"
                android:screenOrientation="landscape">
```

```
        <intent-filter >
            <action android:name="android.intent.action.MAIN" />

            <category android:name="android.intent.category.LAUNCHER" />
        </intent-filter>
    </activity>
 </application>

</manifest>
```

Running the App

There are a few things you should keep in mind when running the app.

If there is no Internet connection, no data will turn up, and hence no markers will be shown.

There are some places where no data will be found for tweets and Wikipedia articles. This is more likely for tweets. Also, at certain times of the night, tweets might be few in number.

Some of the marker may be higher than others. This is due to the collisions avoidance and because of the altitude property in the locations.

Figures 9.4 and 9.5 show the app in action. Debugging has been disabled.

Figure 9-4. *App showing a marker*

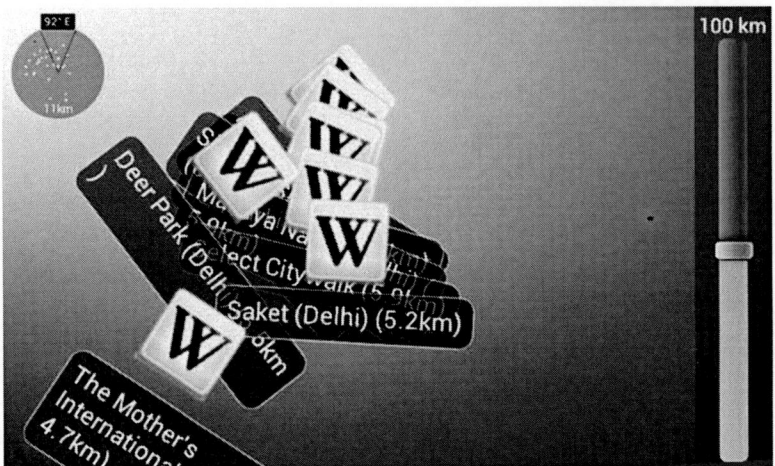

Figure 9-5. *Several markers converge due to the compass going haywire next to a metallic object.*

Summary

This chapter covered the process and provided code for the creation of an AR browser, one of the most popular kind of AR apps. And with Google Goggles coming up, it will get even more popular among people who want to use something like the goggles without actually owing a set. Be sure to download the source code for this chapter from this book's page on Apress or from the GitHub repository. You can reach me directly at raghavsood@appaholics.in or via Twitter at @Appaholics16.

Index

◼ A, B

Accelerometer
  axes, 25
  definition, 24
  onCreate() method, 26
  onResume(), 27
  sensorEventListener(), 26–27
  variables, 26
AndroidManifest errors
  common permissions in AR apps, 100
  security exceptions, 100
  <uses-feature> element, 101–102
  <uses-library> element, 101
AndroidManifest.xml
  AR browser, 316–317
  artificial horizons, 77–78
  3D AR model viewer, 162–163
  full listing, 36–37
  GPS access, 83
  navigational AR application, 155
  widget overlay, 52, 62–63
  XML editing, 109–111
API keys, 117
  debug key, 118
  signing key, 118
Application testing, 53
AR demo application
  application testing, 92–93
  Java file updation

altitude calculation,
  updateAltitude() method, 91–92
altitude display,
  AHActivity.java, 88–90
GPS access, AHActivity.java, 88–90
transparent compass,
  HorizonView.java, 86–88
project creation, 81–82
XML updation
  altitude display, strings.xml, 83
  GPS access, AndroidManifest.xml, 83
  RelativeLayout, main.xml, 84–85
  two-color display, colours.xml, 84
Architectural applications, 6
Art applications, 8
Artificial horizons
  AHActivity.java, 75–77
  AndroidManifest, 77–78
  application testing, 78–80
  AR demo application, 80–81
    application testing, 92–93
    Java file updation, 86–92
    project creation, 81–82
    XML updation, 82–85
  definition, 65
  HorizonView.java file, 67–68

Artificial horizons, HorizonView.java file (*cont.*)
 Bearing, Pitch, and Roll methods, 68
 initCompassView(), 68–70
 onDraw() method, 71–75
 onMeasure() and Measure() methods, 70–71
 XML, 66–67
Assembly lines, 7
Astronomical applications, 9
Augmented reality (AR) applications
 AndroidManifest errors
  common permissions in AR apps, 100
  security exceptions, 100
  <uses-feature> element, 101–102
  <uses-library> element, 101
 architecture, 6
 art, 8
 assembly lines, 7
 astronomy, 9
 camera errors
  camera service connection failure, 97–98
  Camera.setParameters() failure, 98–99
  setPreviewDisplay() exception, 99–100
 cinema, 7
 cubical simulations, 10
 debugging
  black and white squares, camera usage, 104
  LogCat, 103–104
 3D model *See* 3D model viewer
 education, 8
 entertainment, 7–8
 gesture control, 12
 holograms, 11
 layout errors
  ClassCastException, 96–97
  user interface alignment issues, 95–96
 map-related errors
  Google Maps API keys, 102
  MapActivity, 103
  normal activity, 103
 medicine, 5
 military and law enforcement agencies, 4
 miscellaneous errors
  compass failure, 105
  GPS fix failure, 105
 movies, 11
 SpecTrek, 2–3
 television, 9
 text translation, 8
 tourism, 6
 vehicles, 4
 video conferencing, 11
 virtual experiences, 10
 vs. virtual reality, 1
 virtual trial room, 6
 weather forecasting, 9
Augmented reality (AR) browser
 application execution, 222
 camera control
  CameraCompatibility class, 309–310
  CameraModel class, 310–311
  CameraSurface.java, 305–308
 DataSource, 242
 global class
  AndroidManifest.xml, 316
  application execution, 317–318
  ARData.java, 311–316
 IconMarker.java, 302–303
 Java code
  AugmentedActivity, 233–238
  AugmentedView, 230–232
  MainActivity, 238–241
  SensorsActivity.java, 223–230
 Layar, 221

LocalDataSource, 242–243
Marker class
    application execution,
        disabled touch and collision
        debugging, 291
    application execution, enabled
        touch and collision
        debugging, 292
    calcRelativePosition() method,
        296–297
    compareTo() method, 302
    constructor, 292
    drawCollisionZone() method,
        299–302
    drawIcon() method, 299–302
    draw() method, 298
    drawTouchZone() method,
        299–302
    equals() method, 302
    get() method, 293–294
    global variables, 289–291
    handleClick() method, 297–
        298
    isMarkerOnMarker() method,
        297–298
    isPointOnMarker() method,
        297–298
    populateMatrices() method,
        294–295
    set() method, 292
    updateDistance() method,
        296–297
    update() method, 294–295
    updateRadar() method, 295–
        96
    updateView() method, 295–
        296
NetworkDataSource, 243–246
positioning classes
    PhysicalLocationUtility, 252–
        254
    ScreenPositionUtility, 254–255
Radar class, 285–289

TwitterDataSource, 246–249
user interface
    PaintableBoxedText.java, 260–
        263
    PaintableBox.java, 258–260
    PaintableCircle.java, 263
    PaintableGps.java, 264–265
    PaintableIcon.java, 265–266
    PaintableLine.java, 266–267
    PaintableObject.java, 255–258
    PaintablePoint.java, 267–268
    PaintablePosition.java, 268–
        270
    PaintableRadarPoints.java,
        270–271
    PaintableText.java, 271–273
utility classes
    getAngle() method, 277
    LowPassFilter, 278–280
    Matrix class, 280–285
    PitchAzimuthCalculator, 277–
        278
    vector, 273–277
widget customization, 303
    VerticalSeekBar.java, 304–305
WikipediaDataSource, 250–251
Wikitude, 221
XML
    menu.xml, 222
    strings.xml, 222
Augmented reality on Android
        platform
    accelerometer, 24–27
    AndroidManifest.xml, 36–37
    application creation, 13
    camera, 14–21
    global positioning system, 28
    lattitude and longitude, 29–32,
        32–36
    LogCat output, 37–38
    main.xml, 37
    orientation sensor, 21–24

C

CalcRelativePosition() method, 296–297

Camera, 14–21

CameraCompatibility class, 309–310

Camera control
  CameraCompatibility class, 309–310
  CameraModel class, 310–311
  CameraSurface.java, 305
    surfaceChanged() method, 307-3-8
    surfaceCreated() method, 306–307
    surfaceDestroyed() method, 307
    variables and constructor, 305

Camera errors, AR application
  camera service connection failure, 97–98
  Camera.setParameters() failure, 98–99
  setPreviewDisplay() exception, 99–100

CameraModel class, 310–311

Camera preview layout file, 112–116

Camera service connection failure, 97–98

Camera.setParameters() failure, 98–99

CameraSurface.java
  surfaceChanged() method, 307–308
  surfaceCreated() method, 306–307
  variables and constructor, 305

Cinema applications, 7

CompareTo() method, 302

Custom object overlays, 56–60

CustomRenderer, 60–62

D

Data overlaying, 41

DataSource, 242

Debugging, AR application
  black and white squares, camera usage, 104
  LogCat, 103–104

DrawCollisionZone() method, 299–302

DrawIcon() method, 299–302

Draw() method, 298

DrawTouchZone() method, 299–302

E

Educational applications, 8

Entertainment applications, 7–8

Equals() method, 302

F

FixLocation.java, 132–135

FlatBack.java
  imports, variable declarations and onCreate() method, 119–120
  isRouteDisplayed() method, 132
  launchCameraView() method, 131
  onCreateOptionsMenu() method, 129–130
  onOptionsItemSelected() method, 129–130
  onPause() method, 125–126
  onResume() method, 125–126
  SensorEventListener, 130–131
  zoomToMyLocation() method, 132

Frame layout, 44

G

Gesture control, 12

GetAngle() method, 277

Get() method, 293–294

GetTextAsc(), 258

GetTextDesc(), 258
GetTextWidth(), 258
Global class
    AndroidManifest.xml, 316
    application execution, 317–318
    ARData.java, 311–316
Global positioning system (GPS), 28

▨ H

HandleClick() method, 297–298
Help dialog box layout file, 116
High-cut filter. *See* LowPassFilter
Holograms, 11
HTML help file, 217–218

▨ I

IconMarker.java, 302–303
InitCompassView() method, 68–70
IsMarkerOnMarker() method, 297–298
IsPointOnMarker() method, 297–298
IsRouteDisplayed() method, 132

▨ J, K

Java code
    AugmentedActivity
        global variable declaration, 233
        markerTouched(), 237–238
        onCreate() method, 238–239
        onPause() method, 238–239
        onResume() method, 235
        onSensorChanged() method, 235
        onTouch(), 237–238
        SeekBar, 236, 237
        updateDataOnZoom(), 237–238
        zoom level calculation, 236–237
    AugmentedView, 230
        collision adjustment, 232

constructor, 231–232
        onDraw() method, 231–232
        variable declaration, 231
    FixLocation.java, 132–135
    FlatBack.java, 128–132
        imports, variable declarations and onCreate() method, 119–120
        isRouteDisplayed() method, 132
        launchCameraView() method, 131
        onCreateOptionsMenu() method, 129–130
        onOptionsItemSelected() method, 129–130
        onPause() method, 125–126
        onResume() method, 125–126
        SensorEventListener, 130–131
        zoomToMyLocation() method, 132
    imports and variable declarations, 119–120
    launchFlatBack() method, 122
    LocationListener, 121–122
    MainActivity
        class and global variable declaration, 238
        download() method, 241
        location change and touch input, 240
        menu creation, 239
        onCreate() method, 238–239
        onStart() method, 238–239
        updateData() method, 240–241
        updateDataOnZoom() method, 240
    onCreate() method, 120–121
    onDestroy() method, 125–126
    onPause() method, 125–126
    onResume() method, 125–126
    Options menu, 123

Java code (*cont.*)
  SensorEventListener, 124
  SensorsActivity.java
    global variables, 223
    listening to sensors, 228–230
    onCreate() method, 224–227
    onStart() method, 224–227
    onStop() method, 227–228
  showHelp() method, 123
  SurfaceView and camera
    management, 126–128
Java files
  AssetsFileUtility.java, 168–169
  BaseFileUtil.java, 169–170
  CheckFileManagerActivity.java
    declarations, 170
    installPickFileIntent() method,
      173
    isPickFileIntentAvailable()
      method, 173
    onActivityResult() method,
      171–173
    onCreateDialog() method, 174
    onCreate() method, 171
    onResume() method, 171
    selectFile() method, 173
  Config.java, 175
  FixedPointUtilities.java, 175–178
  Group.java, 178–180
  Instructions.java, 180–181
  LightingRenderer.java, 181–183
  Material.java, 183–186
  MemUtil.java, 186–187
  ModelChooser.java, 163
    list adapter, 165–168
    onCreate() method, 192–193
    onListItemClick() method, 165
  Model3D.java, 189–191
  Model.java, 187–189
  ModelViewer.java, 191
    constructor, 192
    global variable declarations,
      192

    ModelLoader inner class, 195–
      198
    onCreate() method, 192–193
    surfaceCreated() method, 194
    TakeAsynScreenshot inner
      class, 198–199
    TouchEventHandler inner
      class, 194–195
    uncaughtException() method,
      193–194
  MtlParser.java, 199–203
  ObjParser.java, 203–207
  ParseException.java, 207
  Renderer.java, 207–209
  SDCardFileUtil.java, 209–210
  SimpleTokenizer.java, 210–211
  Util.java, 211–212
  Vector3D.java, 213

■ L

LaunchCameraView() method, 131
LaunchFlatBack() method, 122
Layout errors, AR application
  ClassCastException, 96–97
  user interface alignment issues,
    95–96
Layout files
  camera preview, 112–116
  help dialog box, 116
  map layout, 117
Layout options
  frame, 44
  linear, 44
  relative, 44
  table, 44
Linear layout, 44
LocalDataSource, 242–243
Location-based AR application
  API keys, 117
    debug key, 118
    signing key, 118
  basic features, 107–108

common errors, 138–139
execution, 135–138
Java code, 118
    FixLocation.java, 132–135
    FlatBack.java, 128–132
    imports and variable
      declarations, 119–120
    launchFlatBack() method, 122
    LocationListener, 121–122
    onCreate() method, 120–121
    onDestroy() method, 125–126
    onPause() method, 125–126
    onResume() method, 125–126
    Options menu, 123
    SensorEventListener, 124
    showHelp() method, 123
    SurfaceView and camera
      management, 126–128
new project creation, 108–109
XML editing, 109–111
    layout files, 112–117
    menu resource creation, 111–
      112
LocationListener, 121–122
LowPassFilter, 278–280

M

Map layout file, 117
Map-related errors, AR application
    Google Maps API keys, 102
    MapActivity, 103
    normal activity, 103
Marker class
    application execution, disabled
      touch and collision
      debugging, 291
    application execution, enabled
      touch and collision
      debugging, 292
    calcRelativePosition() method,
      296–297
    compareTo() method, 302

constructor, 292
drawCollisionZone() method, 299–
    302
drawIcon() method, 299–302
draw() method, 298
drawTouchZone() method, 299–
    302
equals() method, 302
get() method, 293–294
global variables, 289–291
handleClick() method, 297–298
isMarkerOnMarker() method,
    297–298
isPointOnMarker() method, 297–
    298
populateMatrices() method, 294–
    295
set() method, 292
updateDistance() method, 296–
    297
update() method, 294–295
updateRadar() method, 295–296
updateView() method, 295–296
Markers, Augmented reality
    Activity.java class, 54–56
    AndroidManifest.xml, 62
    custom object overlays, 56–60
    CustomRenderer, 60–62
Matrix class, 280–285
Measure() method, 70–71
Medical applications, 5
Military and law enforcement
    agencies, 4
Miscellaneous errors, AR application
    compass failure, 105
    GPS fix failure, 105
Movies, 11

N

Navigational AR application
    AndroidManifest.xml updation,
      155

Navigational AR application (*cont.*)
- Help dialog box, 156
- Java file updation
    - FlatBack.java, 145–151
    - LocationListener() method, 153–154
    - onCreate() method, 152–153
    - onResume() method, 154–155
    - package declaration, imports and variables, 151
- location setting, 158
- map view, options menu, 157
- new application, 141–142
- startup mode, 156
- user's current location, 157
- XML file updation, 142
    - map_toggle.xml, 143, 144–145
    - strings.xml, 142

NetworkDataSource
- class and global variable declarations, 243
- getHttpGETInputStream() method, 244
- getHttpInputString() method, 244–246
- getMarkers() method, 244
- parse() method, 244–246

■ O

OnCreate() method, 49, 120–121
OnCreateOptionsMenu() method, 129–130
OnDestroy() method, 125–126
OnDraw() method, 71–75
OnMeasure() method, 70–71
OnOptionsItemSelected() method, 129–130
OnPause() method, 125–126, 125–126
OnResume() method, 125–126, 125–126

Orientation sensor, 21–24
Overlays, Android platform
- markers
    - Activity.java class, 54–56
    - AndroidManifest.xml, 62
    - custom object overlays, 56–60
    - CustomRenderer, 60–62
- widget, 41–43
    - AndroidManifest.xml, 52
    - application testing, 53
    - layout options, 43–45
    - main.xml updation using relative layout, 45–48
    - onCreate() method, 49
    - sensor data display, 49–52
    - TextView variable declarations, 49

■ P, Q

PaintableBox.java, 258–260
PaintableBoxedText.java, 260–263
PaintableCircle.java, 263
PaintableGps.java, 264–265
PaintableIcon.java, 265–266
PaintableLine.java, 266–267
PaintableObject.java, 255–258
PaintablePoint.java, 267–268
PaintablePosition.java, 268–270
PaintableRadarPoints.java, 270–271
PaintableText.java, 271–273
PaintLine(), 258
PhysicalLocationUtility, 252–254
PitchAzimuthCalculator, 277–278
PopulateMatrices() method, 294–295
Positioning classes
- PhysicalLocationUtility, 252–254
- ScreenPositionUtility, 254–255

■ R

Radar class, 285–289
Relative layout, 44
Renderering, 207–209

■ S

ScreenPositionUtility, 254–255
SensorEventListener, 124, 130–131
SetColor() method, 258
SetFill() method, 258
SetFontSize(), 258
Set() method, 292
SetPreviewDisplay() exception, 99–100
SetStrokeWidth(), 258
ShowHelp() method, 123
SpecTrek, 2–3
SurfaceDestroyed() method, 307

■ T

Table layout, 44
Television applications, 9
Text translation, 8
TextView variable declarations, 49
3D model viewer
    Android application info, 160–161
    AndroidManifest.xml, 162–163
    Android model, 160
    application front screen, 219
    AssetsFileUtility.java, 168–169
    BaseFileUtil.java, 169–170
    CheckFileManagerActivity.java
        declarations, 170
        installPickFileIntent() method, 173
        isPickFileIntentAvailable() method, 173
        onActivityResult() method, 171–173
        onCreateDialog() method, 174
        onCreate() method, 171
        onResume() method, 171
        selectFile() method, 173
    Config.java, 175
    FixedPointUtilities.java, 175–178
    Group.java, 178–180
    HTML help file, 217–218
    Instructions.java, 180–181
    LightingRenderer.java, 181–183
    loading Android model, 220
    Material.java, 183–186
    MemUtil.java, 186–187
    ModelChooser.java
        description, 163
        list adapter, 165–168
        onCreate() method, 192–193
        onListItemClick() method, 165
    Model3D.java, 189–191
    Model.java, 187–189
    ModelViewer.java
        constructor, 192
        description, 191
        global variable declarations, 192
        ModelLoader inner class, 195–198
        onCreate() method, 192–193
        surfaceCreated() method, 194
        TakeAsynScreenshot inner class, 198–199
        TouchEventHandler inner class, 194–195
        uncaughtException() method, 193–194
    MtlParser.java, 199–203
    ObjParser.java, 203–207
    ParseException.java, 207
    Renderer.java, 207–209
    SDCardFileUtil.java, 209–210
    SimpleTokenizer.java, 210–211
    Util.java, 211–212
    Vector3D.java, 213
    XML files
        choose_model_row.xml, 215
        instructions_layout.xml, 215–216
        list_header.xml, 216
        main.xml, 216
        Strings.xml, 214
Tourism applications, 6

Treble cut filter. *See* LowPassFilter

TwitterDataSource
constructor, 246–247
createIcon() method, 246–247
createRequestURL() method, 246–247
global variable declaration, 246
parse() methods, 247–249
processJSONObject() method, 247–249

U

UpdateAltitude() method, 91–92
UpdateDistance() method, 296–297
Update() method, 294–295
UpdateRadar() method, 295–296
UpdateView() method, 295–296
User interface
PaintableBoxedText.java, 260–263
PaintableBox.java, 258–260
PaintableCircle.java, 263
PaintableGps.java, 264–265
PaintableIcon.java, 265–266
PaintableLine.java, 266–267
PaintableObject.java, 255–258
PaintablePoint.java, 267–268
PaintablePosition.java, 268–270
PaintableRadarPoints.java, 270–271
PaintableText.java, 271–273
Utility classes
getAngle() method, 277
LowPassFilter, 278–280
Matrix class, 280–285
PitchAzimuthCalculator, 277–278
vector
add() method, 277
constructors, 273
cross() method, 277
divide() method, 277
equals() method, 277

get() method, 274–275
global variables, 273
mathematics of, 275–276
mult() method, 277
norm() method, 277
prod() method, 277
set() method, 274–275
sub() method, 277
toString() method, 277

V

Vector class
add() method, 277
constructors, 273
cross() method, 277
divide() method, 277
equals() method, 277
get() method, 274–275
global variables, 273
mathematics of, 275–276
mult() method, 277
norm() method, 277
prod() method, 277
set() method, 274–275
sub() method, 277
toString() method, 277
VerticalSeekBar.java, 304–305
Video conferencing, 11
Virtual experiences, 10
Virtual reality *vs.* augmented reality, 1
Virtual trial room, 6

W

Weather forecasting applications, 9
Widget customization, 303
VerticalSeekBar.java, 304–305
Widget overlays, Android platform, 41–43
AndroidManifest.xml, 52
application testing, 53
layout options, 43

frame, 44
linear, 44
relative, 44
table, 44
main.xml updation using relative layout, 45–48
onCreate() method, 49
sensor data display, 49–52
TextView variable declarations, 49
WikipediaDataSource, 250–251

▓ X, Y

XML
menu.xml, 222
strings.xml, 222

XML editing
layout files
camera preview, 112–116
help dialog box, 116
map layout, 117
menu resource creation, 111–112
XML files
choose_model_row.xml, 215
instructions_layout.xml, 215–216
list_header.xml, 216
main.xml, 216
Strings.xml, 214

▓ Z

ZoomToMyLocation() method, 132